Moreton Morrell Site

CRITICAL CASES IN
ORGANISATIONAL
BEHAVIOUR

MANAGEMENT, WORK AND ORGANISATIONS

Gibson Burrell, Warwick Business School
Mick Marchington, Manchester School of Management,
UMIST
Paul Thompson, Department of Human Resource Managment,
University of Edinburgh

This series of new textbooks covers the areas of human resource management, employee relations, organisational behaviour and related business and man-agement fields. Each text has been specially commissioned to be written by leading experts in a clear and accessible way. An important feature of the series is the international orientation. The titles will contain serious and challenging material, be analytical rather than prescriptive and be particularly suitable for use by students with no prior specialist knowledge.

The series is relevant for many business and management courses, including MBA and post-experience courses, specialist masters and postgraduate diplomas, professional courses and final-year undergraduate and related courses. The books will become essential reading at business and management schools worldwide.

Published

Paul Blyton and Peter Turnbull **The Dynamics of Employee Relations** (2nd edn)
J. Martin Corbett **Critical Cases in Organisational Behaviour**
Sue Ledwith and Fiona Colgan (eds) **Women in Organisations**
Karen Legge **Human Resource Management**
Stephen Procter and Frank Mueller (eds) **Teamworking**
Michael Rowlinson **Organisations and Institutions**
Harry Scarbrough (ed.) **The Management of Expertise**
Adrian Wilkinson, Mick Marchington, Tom Redman and Ed Snape
 Managing with Total Quality Management
Diana Winstanley and Jean Woodall (eds) **Ethical Issues in Contemporary Human Resource Management**

Forthcoming

Pippa Carter and Norman Jackson **Critical Issues in Organisational Behaviour**
Irena Grugulis **Training and Development**
Marek Korczynski **Human Resource Management in the Service Sector**
John Purcell and Peter Boxall **Managing People for Business Performance**
Helen Rainbird (ed.) **Training in the Workplace**
Jill Rubery and Damian Grimshaw **Employment Policy and Practice**
Hugh Scullion and Len Holden **International Human Resource Mangement**

Series Standing Order

If you would like to receive future titles in this series as they are published, you can make use of our standing order facility. To place a standing order please contact your bookseller or, in case of difficulty, write to us at the address below with your name and address and the name of the series. Please state with which title you wish to begin your standing order. (If you live outside the United Kingdom we may not have the rights for your area, in which case we will forward your order to the publisher concerned.)

Customer Services Department, Macmillan Distribution Ltd
Houndmills, Basingstoke, Hampshire RG21 6XS, England

CRITICAL CASES IN ORGANISATIONAL BEHAVIOUR

J. Martin Corbett

palgrave

Published by
PALGRAVE
Houndmills, Basingstoke, Hampshire RG21 6XS and
175 Fifth Avenue, New York, N. Y. 10010
Companies and representatives throughout the world

PALGRAVE is the new global academic imprint of
St. Martin's Press LLC Scholarly and Reference Division and
Palgrave Publishers Ltd (formerly Macmillan Press Ltd).

ISBN 0–333–57750–7 hardcover
ISBN 0–333–57751–5 paperback

This book is printed on paper suitable for recycling and
made from fully managed and sustained forest sources.

A catalogue record for this book is available
from the British Library.

12   11   10   9   8   7
06   05   04   03   02

Printed and bound in Great Britain by
Antony Rowe Ltd, Chippenham, Wiltshire

To Angie, my wife
and best friend

Contents

Characteristics of the cases

I would not wish to give readers the impression that I attribute little or no educational value to problem-solving case studies. On the contrary, they provide an excellent means of bringing together the generalising, theory-building efforts of social science and concrete organisational experience in a fairly realistic way. They also have the advantage of transforming readers from the role of passive absorber of information into active partners in a learning process.

Approximately one-third of the cases presented in this volume may be termed *problem-solving* cases. These describe a situation which falls short of some decision to be made or some action to be taken. They do, however, contain the facts and circumstances confronting the main characters. In some cases it is clear which character(s) need to make the decisions, in others it is incumbent on the user not only to determine what decisions need to be taken to tackle the problems at hand, but also which character or characters are best placed to tackle them.

Analytical cases predominate in the book. The purpose of these is to aid the user to answer the questions: 'what is going on?' and 'what are the issues involved here?'. Very few of these cases contain a decision-making character. This is because they often contain information from a variety of sources (e.g. private conversations and sub-group meetings) which no single decision-making character could realistically be expected to have access to.

Unless otherwise stated, all the cases presented in ensuing chapters describe real events as they occurred in real organisations. However, where indicated, the true identities of the organisation and its employees have been disguised through the use of pseudonyms and, occasionally, by judicial alterations to company information (e.g. size, location or age). It is worth stressing that any resemblance of these pseudonyms to 'real' organisations or people is entirely coincidental.

About 25 per cent of the cases are based on generalised experience, but essentially describe fictitious situations and organisations. As such, they contain invented names for both organisations and characters.

Views on the use of fictitious case material vary among teachers of organisational behaviour. For his part, John Reynolds (1980) cautions against the use of fictitious ('armchair') case studies:

> Most case study writers turn to writing 'armchair' cases either because they desperately need a case for which they have been unable to find a real-world field source or because they are too lazy to do the field research. Neither of these excuses is usually a good one. If you cannot find a real-world source for a case, there should be at least a suspicion in your mind that the topic is not one best covered by a case (p. 103).

For my part, I find such a view unconvincing. Some issues (e.g. drug use, unethical behaviour, the secret workings of organisational cabals, and violent behaviour) are very difficult to research simply because most organisations are understandably reticent to grant access to (let alone give permission to publish details on) such sensitive areas of corporate activity. My own endeavours to carry out research on the comparatively innocuous subject of failed job redesign programmes bear this out.

Indeed, one of the reasons for focusing on the 'dark side' of organisational behaviour came from my exasperation with the way that mainstream OB journals and textbooks disproportionately favour the dissemination of organisational success stories over failures, and the promotion of issues of managerial concern over those of more general interest. Some recent US texts (Moorhead and Griffiths, 1992 providing an excellent example) contain an increasingly large number of case examples eulogising the supposedly enlightened management practices of many large US and multinational corporations. Maybe it won't be long before the publishers of best-selling OB texts start selling advertising space in such texts to corporations eager to bolster their public image!

An additional danger resides in the logic of Reynolds' argument against fictitious case materials. If all cases were based solely on results of 'real' field research, is there not a very real danger that case study users will become adept analysts of yesterday's organisational problems?

The structure of the book

Although there is an impressive array of textbooks on organisational behaviour currently available, there is surprisingly little variation in the way they are structured. The structure of this book reflects the popularity of the micro- to macro-levels of analysis of behaviour utilised by a majority of textbook authors.

The book is divided into four parts. Part 1 comprises 14 case studies of individual behaviour in organisations. The study of individual behaviour is traditionally labelled 'micro-level OB analysis', and evokes a consideration of issues which lie at the heart of work and organisational psychology (e.g. personality, attitudes, motivation and commitment).

The 14 cases in Part 2 (a meso-level of analysis) focus on interpersonal and group dynamics – the traditional domain of social psychology – whilst Part 3 contains 21 case studies centred around more macro-level issues of inter-group relations, organisational technology, and organisation structure and change. The 7 cases in Part 4 focus on broader issues pertaining to the relationship between organisations and their environment.

To be sure, this four-fold analytical division is nothing more than a literary device. In reality, each of the four levels – individual, group, organisational, environmental – overlap and inter-relate. For example, while theories of individual motivation are primarily psychological in origin, the concept of motivation itself may be examined from any or all of the levels of analysis. Indeed, Case 1 in the book (as well as the very last, Case 56) shows how individual motivation can be affected by macro socio–cultural factors as well as by factors at the psychological micro-level. Hence, the location of motivation case studies in Part 1 simply reflects OB textbook convention, and is not in any way indicative of the appropriate or recommended level of analysis the user should employ. This holds true for all 56 cases in the book.

How to use the book

In the first instance, the cases here are intended for use on advanced undergraduate, postgraduate and post-experience courses with a significant OB component. The book is best studied in conjunction with a good OB textbook (e.g. Thompson and McHugh, 1990; Morgan, 1985), a well-stocked library, and a course tutor. I leave it to course tutors to choose the combination of cases most relevant to their own needs and objectives.

It is not my intention here to recommend how best to undertake case analysis, as this has been skilfully undertaken elsewhere (e.g. Easton, 1982; Schnelle, 1967). However, associated with each case is a guide to a fairly extensive list of readings pertinent to the issues and problems raised by the material. These are only a guide and serve to indicate the range of literatures which may usefully be consulted during analysis. I don't expect anyone to follow up all of these references; indeed, I would urge you to develop your own analytical perspectives and to undertake independent literature searches. Learning can be much more fun and rewarding that way.

Ultimately, I hope that the book will be used in a spirit of critical enquiry. Most of all, I hope it manages in equal measure to challenge, stimulate and entertain.

PART 1

ANALYSING INDIVIDUAL BEHAVIOUR IN ORGANISATIONS

CHAPTER 2

The meaning of work, motivation and commitment

Introduction

A majority of mainstream OB textbooks begin with an outline of the basic 'building blocks' of behaviour. In other words, readers are introduced to some aspects of human psychology. Historically, organisational psychologists have restricted their attention to two key areas of organisational behaviour: namely, fitting the person to the job (through appropriate selection and recruitment techniques) and fitting the job to the person (through appropriate job design techniques).

This two-pronged approach to understanding and coordinating organisational behaviour reflects a long-standing debate within organisational psychology as to whether personality or situational factors are key determinants of behaviour in organisations. Current thinking has it that it is not possible to separate out the situation from the person; rather, they interact in complex ways.

In other words, work organisations can be understood not only as environments in which people produce work, but also as places where work produces people. Hence, any discussion of what people want or need out of work (particularly paid employment) cannot be isolated from the context of that work environment. The experience of working in a particular organisation can itself produce wants and needs in the worker.

Unfortunately, the personality and motivation theories described repeatedly in textbook after OB textbook are based on much simpler models of human behaviour. These tend to view the person as possessing a certain set of stable psychological characteristics which are brought into work each day. The idea that these may change through interaction with others in the organisation is rarely touched on.

Another aspect of the two-pronged approach to the analysis of individual behaviour by organisational psychologists is a tendency to restrict the subject matter to more or less quantifiable elements of behaviour and to those aspects of behaviour which are predictible and controllable from a managerial point of view (Baritz, 1960; Hollway, 1991). Indeed, Thompson and McHugh (1990) argue that:

> The true paradigm of the organisational psychologist is that of ensuring 'effective resource use': supplying advice, resources and training which are aimed at assisting organisations in efficiently managing the conflict and resistance which is a predictable consequence of hierarchically organised production (p. 304).

Hence, one tension within the micro-level of analysis in OB is the extent to which organisational problems (however defined) are to be solved. For the critical psychologist, the call may be: 'Do not change your behaviour, the organisation is at fault.' On the other hand, the call emanating from the vast majority of OB textbooks is: 'Do not change your organisation, the employee is at fault.'

The seven case studies in this chapter explore the dynamics of interaction between person and organisational context from a variety of angles. As such they encourage the analyst to reflect on the irreducibility of this interaction to either personal or organisational characteristics.

Case 1 focuses on the situational influences on the way people view their work. Contrary to most psychological debate about motivation and the meaning of work, this case does not examine individual perceptions, but encourages an examination of the socio–cultural factors which may shape or determine an individual's motivation and work identity.

Case 2 retains this focus on the situational variables affecting organisational behaviour and examines the motivation of torturers employed by the Greek government between 1967 and 1974. This disturbing case reveals how ordinary people can be socialised into extreme and violent behaviour by fairly straightforward psychological techniques. In doing so, the case raises profound questions about the nature of work identity and commitment in quite different (and comparatively innocuous) types of employment.

Case 3 outlines a job enrichment experiment which produced inconsistent results relating to psychological outcomes. Again, the importance of situational factors seems paramount. A modicum of statistical knowledge may prove beneficial in analysing this case. Case 4 outlines a scenario in which a valued employee is known to partake of one of the so-called 'smart drugs' now freely available in the wealthier countries of the world. The issue raised here is the extent to which voluntary use of such drugs represents strong commitment to a job requiring a certain amount of creativity and mind-expansion, as opposed to a desire to gain unfair advantage over one's peers.

Case 5 details the story of Kermit Vandiver, a man who found himself caught up in a web of deception whilst working for a large US manufacturing company. This powerful story reveals how different people can perceive the same situation quite differently. The case also raises questions about the desirability of strong employee commitment and the nature and extent of managerial power. Case 6 is a brief look at the issue of work commitment located within the broader framework of intra-organisational power and conflict.

Case 7 revisits the concept of work identity and reveals the importance of the informal side of organisational behaviour. It offers the clearest example so far of how organisation behaviour, even one's self-identity, may be viewed as an on-going interaction through which the psychological contract between employer and employee is continually being renegotiated and redefined.

Case 1   The lottery question

In considering issues of work motivation and commitment, a distinction may be made between instrumental and non-instrumental reasons for working and being involved with the job. Instrumental reasons for working are essentially economic, whereas non-instrumental reasons are expressive in nature.

A useful indicator of non-instrumental (non-financial) commitment to work is the so-called 'lottery question' which asks people whether or not they would continue working if they won a very large sum of money in a national lottery.[1] Note that, in this context, 'work' refers to paid employment.

The aim of the lottery question is to see whether people would continue to work even when they have no financial reason for doing so. The lottery question states:

> Imagine you have won a lottery or inherited a large sum of money and could live comfortably for the rest of your life without working; what would you do about work?

A choice of responses was offered:

(1) 'I would stop working';
(2) 'I would continue to work (either in the same or a different job)'.

In 1987, the Meaning of Work International Research Team asked the lottery question of 8763 employees in seven different countries.[2] The respondents comprised a random sample of the labour force and were interviewed individually and in a similar fashion by professional interviewers. All respondents were asked the lottery question as quoted above.

The response distributions of the wish to stop or continue working are outlined in Table 2.1.[3]

TABLE 2.1   The lottery question

Country	N	Total Cont.	Total Stop	Male Cont.	Male Stop	Female Cont.	Female Stop
Belgium	450	84.2	15.8	86.9	13.1	78.5	21.5
UK	840	68.8	31.2	65.8	34.2	71.4	28.6
Germany	1278	70.1	29.9	74.5	25.5	61.8	38.2*
Israel	973	87.4	12.6	88.9	11.1	85.5	14.5
Japan	3226	93.4	6.6	94.7	5.3	90.8	9.2*
Netherlands	996	86.3	13.7	86.6	13.4	85.7	14.3
USA	1000	88.1	11.9	89.5	10.5	86.4	13.6

Notes: * Difference between male and female response distribution statistically significant at $p < 0.001$ level (T test)
All scores in percentages

Source: Harpaz (1989).

Issue to consider

- What, if anything, does the data in Table 2.1 tell us about employee motivation and the meaning of work?[4]

Notes

1. The first study to use the 'lottery question' was conducted in the US by Morse and Weiss (1955). 80 per cent of respondents stated they would continue working if they inherited enough money to live comfortably without working. See O'Brien (1992) for details of all subsequent studies.
2. Full details and analysis can be found in the report prepared by the Meaning of Work International Research Team (1987).
3. Table 2.1 is from Harpaz (1989) and is reprinted with the kind permission of the author and the British Psychological Society.
4. See Brief and Nord (1988), de Keyser *et al.* (1988), Fox (1980), and O'Brien (1992). See also *The European Work and Organisational Psychologist*, 1(2) and 1(3) (1991), pp. 81–224. This is a special double issue focusing on work centrality and related work meanings. Numerous authors critically evaluate the data generated by the Meaning of Work International Research Team's 1987 survey. The discussant section (pp. 161–82) is of particular interest. Finally, see Bhagat *et al.* (1990) for a

useful analysis and appraisal of these survey findings in the context of broader cross-cultural research.

Case 2   Employee commitment: on becoming a torturer

Introduction

What kind of person becomes a torturer? For many people it would seem obvious that only psychopaths and cranks would wish to pursue such a career. Yet, torture is currently practised by one government in three and these governments experience little or no difficulty in recruiting torturers.[1] Are there really sufficient numbers of sadists ready, able and willing to take on such a job, or are there other factors which contribute to the creation of a torturer?

There is no hard evidence that torturers are psychopaths or sadists. On the contrary, there is evidence that such people are usually screened out during the selection and recruitment process.[2] Thus, to some extent at least, torturers are selected and recruited from ordinary people:

> A deranged person who receives gratification primarily from feelings of power or from personally inflicting pain on others is usually too unreliable to be counted on by authorities to follow orders.[3]

Whilst evidence from studies of torturers is scanty and may be unreliable, that which is available suggests that torturers are ordinary people behaving in extraordinary ways and using familiar psychological mechanisms to justify their behaviour.[4] In other words, there is little evidence that torturers differ markedly from their peers at the time when they are recruited and trained as torturers.

Based on his studies of torturers employed by the State during the 1967–74 military dictatorship of Greece, the psychologist Haritos-Fatoutos argues that three situational factors foster the creation of a torturer, namely: training, incremental participation and socialisation, and economic and symbolic reward.[5]

Note that, with the widespread interest amongst contemporary writers on organisational behaviour in the management of meaning – particularly the creation and maintenance of specific organisational cultures – these three factors (not, of course, their content) are common to many management development and employee socialisation programmes in large business organisations.[6]

Training

The first phase of training involves group bonding and isolation from the outside world. In the case of torture, this is achieved by placing recruits in remote training camps and putting them through numerous initiation rites. These include psychological and physical assault and humiliation in order to make recruits more submissive and to get them accustomed to violence. Recipients of such brutality are rarely capable of logical evaluation and their isolation from family and friends (and hence from the mores and values of the outside world) encourages an acceptance of the new moral standards established by the trainers.

Haritos-Fatoutos describes how the use of euphemisms by the trainers helped Greek recruits reinterpret their behaviour. For example, 'tea party' referred to a beating with fists and 'tea party with toast' described a beating with heavy wooden clubs. The use of such euphemistic language is, of course, common practice in organisations to put a gloss on unpleasant reality – from the Nazi Party's 'Final Solution', through the CIA's 'executive action', to the 'downsizing' and 'rationalisation' of contemporary business organisations.

Training also requires the recruit to develop a world view that divides people into the torturable and the non-torturable. Through a programme of seminars the recruit comes to believe that the act of torture is a defence of 'good' values against the 'bad' values espoused by the tortured. The latter are viewed as less than human whilst the recruits are seen as guardians of law, order and common decency. Recruits are trained to be loyal not only to the state but to the organisation, which is semi-secret and will protect them:

> Thus they are brutalised, separated from anyone who might remind them of the morality of the outside world, and fed propaganda about the sub-human status of the enemies of the state. In addition, they are assured that they will not have to take personal responsibility for their action. All this makes it possible to induce in recruits the moral shift that is a prerequisite if they are to torture prisoners.[7]

Incremental socialisation

Such a moral shift, or disengagement, is made easier by the gradual introduction of the recruit to the brutal act of torture. A typical process of incremental socialisation and desensitisation goes through the following chronological sequence:

1. Recruits act as guards while others carry out torture.
2. Recruits carry food to the prisoners in their cells.
3. Recruits are ordered to deliver a short beating to the prisoners.
4. Recruits supervise prisoners during prolonged forced standing.
5. Recruits participate fully in torture.

Hence the recruit is pulled inexorably into the torturing process. Having gone through the first two or three steps in the socialisation process recruits find it very difficult to protest about the use of full torture as they have been corrupted by tacit acceptance of earlier (less extreme) examples of torture.

Reward

Once fully socialised, obedient torturers benefit in both symbolic and economic ways. Training fosters in-group bias. The findings of numerous social psychological studies suggests that participation in strenuous initiation rites makes group membership more desirable.[8] Torturers are always encouraged to see themselves as an elite group. Indeed, few of them openly disclose any information concerning their work or even the nature of their employment to members of out-groups. This secrecy increases the torturers' strong identification with colleagues and conformity to the will of the in-group. In addition to the symbolic value of elite group membership, this process also serves to increase prejudice against out-groups (i.e. the prisoners) to the extent that torturers tend to believe that their victims (even children) have in some way deserved their fate.[9]

Finally, Haritos-Fatoutos' research reveals that Greek torturers received economic rewards including free meals in tavernas and guarantees of employment after military service.

Issues to consider

- Despite such training and indoctrination, torturers often suffer intense stress and must find ways to justify their behaviour in order to reduce the cognitive dissonance their work creates.[10]

What psychological processes are likely to be involved in reducing such dissonance and how are these related to the methods and techniques of the management of meaning outlined above?[11]

- How pertinent are these issues to the understanding and management of employee motivation, commitment and identity in business organisations?[12]

Notes

1. Moore (1985).
2. Gibson and Haritos-Faroutos (1986).
3. Gibson (1990), p. 107.
4. Williams (1992).
5. Haritos-Fatoutos (1988).
6. See, for example, Schein's (1961) discussion of management development programmes and Trice and Beyer's (1985) analysis of organisational rites. Also, compare the socialisation process outlined here with the seven-step process employed by large US corporations discussed in Pascale (1989). For a more general consideration of the relationship between organisational socialisation and employee commitment, see Cialdini (1989) and Jones (1983).
7. Williams (1992) p. 306.
8. See, for example, the research of Aronson and Mills (1959) and its replication by Gerard and Mathewson (1966).
9. Amnesty International (1973).
10. Bendfeldt-Zachrisson (1985).
11. For a general overview of these psychological processes, see Breakwell (1986), Eiser (1986) and McClure (1991). More specifically, consult the work of Festinger (1964) on cognitive dissonance; Bem (1972) on self-perception; Kelley (1971) and Hewstone (1991) on attribution; and Abrams and Hogg (1990), Hogg and Abrams (1991) and Tajfel and Turner (1985) on social identity. See Cohen and Taylor (1992) and Van Maanen and Kunda (1989) for a more sociological consideration of how employees learn to cope with unpleasant work. Finally, see Goldstein *et al.* (1975), Reich (1990), Staub (1992) and Storr (1992) for analyses of socialisation in, and commitment to, group violence.
12. For a critical analysis of the ways in which socialisation in business organisations shapes employee behaviour and attitude, see Kondo (1990), Salancik (1977), Van Maanen (1976) and Van Maanen and Schein (1979). For a more general consideration of the role of situational factors in shaping behaviour and attitudes, see Milgram (1974; 1977) and Blass (1991).

    Most chilling of all, see Bauman (1989) for the argument that state-sponsored violence such as torture (and, in its most extreme form, the Holocaust) are direct products of modernity (i.e. efficiency, bureaucracy, rationality and the social production of moral indifference).

Case 3   The job enrichment experiment[1]

Introduction

Martin MacCarthy, a work psychologist on secondment from university, was walking idly through the busy television manufacturing plant. Long lines of half-finished television sets went almost as far as the eye could see. Although the structure of the company was very conventional (i.e. strict division of labour, centralised production planning and control, separate canteens for management and workers, and so forth), he was surprised how receptive senior management had been to his ideas about employee involvement and motivation. In truth, management were concerned about low productivity levels in the factory. The company could not afford to invest heavily in new technology and senior management were interested in exploring the feasibility of any low-cost, low-technology solutions to their productivity problem.

Martin was just about to leave the assembly area when one of the workers beckoned him over. 'Watch this,' he was commanded. 'In about ten seconds there's going to be an almighty smash up on this machine.'

The two of them looked down at the computer controlled drilling machine running through its lengthy automatic work cycle. Everything appeared to be working normally until the drill bit began to oscillate violently. Then, suddenly, it jammed into the base of the workpiece. The volume of sound from the machine's motors increased dramatically and, less than five seconds later, all became quiet except for the soft hiss of leaking cooling fluid.

When Martin asked why the worker hadn't stopped the machine before the breakdown, he was told that in the past, when workers had stopped machines in order to avert mistakes, line management had accused them of deliberately halting work in order to rest or sneak off for a cigarette.

'You could hardly call this a high-trust environment,' the operator explained. 'It's more of a "keep the machines running at all costs" environment. Management only believe that a machine's breaking down if it's already broken down. So, even though I can see problems coming up on the machine quite often, I have to wait until it's too late before I hit the stop button. Mind you, when the machine goes down it gives me a break from mindlessly staring at it all day long and lets me stretch my legs a bit.'

Designing the enrichment experiment

This incident led Martin to explore the possibility of enriching the shopfloor jobs. Clearly, the company was not using the job-based knowledge and skills of the workforce and it seemed an ideal opportunity to enhance productivity and motivation. At the very least, the amount of machine downtime, scrap rate and machine repair could be reduced if operators were allowed to avert and correct basic machining errors. Martin recalled the basic principle of socio-technical job design: 'variances should be controlled as near to their source as possible'.[2] As far as he was concerned, problems (i.e. variances) arising on a machine were best handled by the people working with that machine.

After a series of meetings with line and senior management, Martin was granted permission to undertake a limited job redesign experiment within the drilling section (14 drillers and one supervisor). Using data generated by quality circle meetings held two or three months ago, and in collaboration with managers in production, maintenance and production planning, he identified five areas of responsibility that he felt could be usefully transferred from production planning and maintenance personnel to the drill operators. These were:

1. Basic preventative machine maintenance at the start of each shift;
2. Correction of basic errors arising from worn drills, incorrectly positioned workpieces, and so on;
3. Resetting of machine offsets to compensate for irregularities in workpiece or drill bits;
4. Proving of computer programs before the start of a batch run;
5. Stopping the machine when problems arise and taking limited corrective action; more serious problems would be referred to the maintenance department after consultation with the production supervisor.

Somewhat to Martin's surprise, his suggestions met no overt resistance. Both maintenance and production planning personnel seemed happy to be relieved of responsibility for these five routine jobs. For their part, the drillers were pleased that their skills and abilities were recognised. The personnel director confirmed that the additional tasks fell within the bounds of the workers' existing job descriptions. Consequently no changes in pay scale were warranted. Even the workers' trade union representative expressed support for the experiment.

Research findings

For the next 30 days Martin collected and analysed downtime data from the eight drilling machines. These data revealed that the average downtime per machine caused by malfunction and subsequent remedial action was 42 minutes per 8 hour day (i.e. just under 9 per cent downtime). Owing to the sequential interdependence of the drilling production line, an average of 18 minutes additional downtime per machine resulted from up-stream machines waiting for work delayed by malfunctions to machines down-stream. Hence, he recorded a total figure of 12.5 per cent average downtime per machine. This represented a total of 8 hours lost production time per day across the whole drilling department. Effectively, Martin mused, the eight drilling machines were achieving the work output of seven machines. Management and workers confirmed this to be a typical figure.

During this period he also obtained data on the drillers' psychological reactions, job satisfaction and perceived job stress through the use of short self-report questionnaires (see Appendix).

After completing a short training programme, the drillers began their new tasks. Ignoring the downtime data for the first 2 weeks to allow for 'teething problems', downtime and psychological data were collected over a further period of 30 days.

Analysis revealed a significant reduction in machine downtime – from an average of 12.5 per cent to an average of only 5.8 per cent per machine. This meant that each machine was now running for an extra 28 minutes per shift. Whilst the total number of downtime incidents was not reduced as much as Martin had hoped, it was clear that the improvements in uptime stemmed directly from the increased speed of response to machine malfunction (and subsequent correction) enabled by the job enrichment experiment. On checking for any possible uncontrolled external factors which may have contaminated the data, it was discovered that hours of work, work loads, product types and batch sizes before and during the experiment were identical.

Analysis of the psychological data seemed to offer equally impressive results. The drillers' self-reported job satisfaction had increased significantly from an average score of 24.2 to one of 28.5, and levels of job stress were down from an average of 8.4 to 5.6. Standard non-parametric statistical tests on the data confirmed that the probability of these changes occurring by chance was over 1:100. This corresponded to the 0.01 probability (or confidence) level required, by professional convention, before any causal inferences might possibly be drawn from the findings of psychological experiments of this kind.

Martin couldn't wait to present his findings to university colleagues and to senior management. One thing puzzled him, however. Analysis of the additional psychological measures included in his questionnaire (see Appendix) seemed to contradict the positive changes in worker job satisfaction and stress. As Table 2.2 shows, the drillers reported a decrease in their use of job-related knowledge and skill (i.e. lower knowledge demand) and an increase in their ability to work automatically without thinking (i.e.

lower attentional demand). They also reported an increase in their job routine and no change in their perceptions of being controlled by technology (despite the fact that they did appear to have more control over the drilling machines than before).

TABLE 2.2   **Means and results of statistical analyses for effects of job enrichment on drillers' psychological reactions**

Outcome variable	Pre-experiment mean score	Post-experiment mean score	Confidence level
Job satisfaction	24.2	28.5	<0.005
Job stress	8.4	5.6	<0.01
Knowledge demand	3.9	3.0	<0.01
Attentional demand	3.4	2.4	<0.01
Controlled by technology	3.3	3.4	no change
Job routine	3.2	3.8	<0.05

Note: No significant changes found in control groups.

Martin was at a loss to explain these findings. He had used his psychological measures questionnaire in different sections on the shopfloor to act as an experimental control and found no significant changes on any of the repeated measures taken over the same time period as the experiment. What was it about the experiment that had caused these changes in worker perception, and why weren't they reflected in the satisfaction scores?

His confusion increased when, under pressure from supervisors and line management, senior management refused to permit any extension of the experiment to other parts of the factory. This decision infuriated the shopfloor trade union representatives who were eager for a factory-wide programme of job enrichment.

Martin began to wonder whether his limited experiment was a success after all. Clearly, a lot depended on whose perspective one took.

Issues to consider

- Analyse and explain the apparent inconsistencies in the psychological data.[3]
- Was the job enrichment experiment a success? If so, why were senior management so reticent to extend job enrichment to other parts of the factory?[4]

Appendix: Psychological measures employed in the job enrichment experiment

Job satisfaction[5]

How satisfied are you with:

- Freedom to choose your own method of working?
- Recognition you get for good work?
- The amount of responsibility you are given?
- The opportunity to use your abilities?
- Your chance of promotion?
- The attention given to suggestions you make?
- The amount of variety in your work?

Answers were given on a seven-point response scale:

    1 = Extremely dissatisfied
    2 = Moderately dissatisfied
    3 = Slightly dissatisfied
    4 = Not sure
    5 = Slightly satisfied
    6 = Moderately satisfied
    7 = Extremely satisfied

Hence, the minimum score = 7 (extreme dissatisfaction); maximum score = 49 (extreme satisfaction).

Job stress[6]

To what extent:

- Are you under constant pressure at work?
- Do you find work piles up faster than you would like in order to complete your work?
- Do you find yourself working faster than you would like in order to complete your work?

Note: For this and all subsequent measures, answers were given on a five-point response scale:

1 = Not at all
2 = Just a little
3 = A moderate amount
4 = Quite a lot
5 = A great deal

Hence, the minimum score (low stress) = 3; maximum score (high stress) = 15

Knowledge demand

To what extent do you have to use your own judgement and skill to make the best use of information whilst doing your job?
Minimum score (low demand) = 1; maximum score (high demand) = 5.

Attentional demand

To what extent can you do your own job automatically without thinking?
Reverse scored such that a score of 1 = high attentional demands, and a score of 5 = low attentional demands

Technical control

To what extent do you feel controlled by the machinery/equipment you use?
Minimum score (not controlled by machinery) = 1; maximum score (controlled a great deal by machinery) = 5.

Job routine

To what extent does your work involve repeating the same tasks over and over again?
Minimum score (not at all repetitive) = 1; maximum score (very repetitive) = 5.

Notes

1. This case reflects the author's own experiences whilst carrying out a similar type of study of technological change (see Wall *et al.*, 1990).

2. See Corbett (1989a) for a discussion of the application of this principle to factory shopfloor job design. See Cherns (1976, 1987) for a fuller explanation of this, and other socio-technical work design principles.
3. See Frese (1982), Glick *et al.* (1985), Guest *et al.* (1980), Kelly (1992) and Quarstein *et al.* (1992) for a critical analysis of the concept of job satisfaction. At a more macro-level of analysis, see Neumann (1989) for the argument that many employees automatically adopt a traditional work ideology and subsequently feel uncomfortable with organisational interventions (such as job enrichment) designed to increase responsibility and participation.
4. For a critical perspective on such job enrichment experiments, see Blackler and Brown (1978), Kelly (1982, 1985), and Silver (1987). For a consideration of how technological factors may constrain job enrichment initiatives, see Corbett (1992) and Daniel (1987). See Guest *et al.* (1980) for how workers and managers differ in their perceptions of job redesign.
5. This is the Intrinsic Job Satisfaction scale developed by Warr *et al.* (1979). In this study the average alpha coefficient for the scale was 0.78.
6. Average (alpha) coefficient = 0.73.

Case 4   Smart pills for management ills?

The promotions committee took a well earned rest after completing lengthy interviews with the four short-listed candidates for the post of director of research and development (R&D) at Associated Fast Food and Drink.[1] All four candidates presently held middle management positions within the company and the task now facing the committee was not an easy one.

'It seems to me that Tony Smythe is by far the best candidate,' began Sara Ross, head of personnel, as she returned to the board room with her committee colleagues after their coffee break. 'He's very energetic, full of enthusiasm, and has an excellent track record.'

'That is true,' replied Arthur Schreisheim, the committee chairperson, 'and under different circumstances he would get my vote as well.'

'What do you mean "under different circumstances"?' Ross asked.

'Well, I am reliably informed that the man's virtually a drug addict,' Schreisheim uttered quietly. A shocked silence fell over the room. 'Don't get me wrong,' he continued, 'he's not on cocaine or marijuana or anything illegal like that. He freely confesses to being an habitual user of Hydergine – one of these new "smart drugs" – and I don't believe that a man who needs to take drugs in order to do his job properly should become head of R&D. I think we should promote Tomlins – a good solid candidate.'

'Just a minute, Arthur,' interjected Elaine Perkins, director of the testing department. 'I happen to know quite a bit about Hydergine. It isn't illegal.

Indeed, it's estimated that over 10,000 people take it in the US alone. And Hydergine is one of only a hundred or so smart drugs. I was reading recently in *Fortune* magazine, that many business experts believe the US domestic market for them will be in excess of $41 billion annually by 1994. It will be legitimate big business sooner than you think. Hydergine is simply an extract of rye ergot and periwinkle. It increases oxygen uptake by the brain and increases glucose metabolism – two effects that enhance thinking processes – and it also protects the brain tissues against free radical damage, a major source of ageing.'[2]

'You mean that this drug can make you more intelligent and keep your brain going for longer?' asked Ross in disbelief.

'Effectively, yes,' Perkins replied. 'It was developed by Santoz for the treatment of Alzheimer's disease and is probably the most-researched drug ever. As yet, there is no evidence of any harmful side effects at all. It certainly isn't addictive. Santoz now market it as a smart drug and sell it in the UK by mail order direct from Switzerland.'

'My God, has Smythe got Alzheimer's Disease?' enquired Schreisheim in bewilderment.

'No, of course he hasn't,' replied Ross gruffly. 'But, with respect, Arthur, that isn't the issue here. On what grounds are you arguing that we reject Tony Smythe for the R&D job?'

'On two grounds,' Schreisheim explained. 'First, if he needs to take drugs to do his job, he must be under pressure. If he takes Hydergine to increase his brain power, he presumably hasn't got enough intelligence under normal circumstances to carry out his present job, let alone the job of running the R&D department! What happens if his supply runs out or Hydergine gets banned? Second, I think taking such a drug is cheating – it isn't fair on the other candidates for the R&D job. It's like athletes using steroids to enhance strength and stamina. This isn't illegal, but steroids are banned in the Olympic Games and all major sports competitions because they give the user an unfair advantage over the other competitors.'

'Oh come now, Arthur,' Ross exclaimed. 'Working here is hardly the same as competing in the Olympics! For a start, athletes don't get paid to compete. Except for the basketball and tennis players, all Olympians have amateur status. Here we have a professional culture – albeit a fiercely competitive one. We make a virtue out of hard work and driving our employees as hard as possible by using pay (not imitation gold medals) as an incentive. I'd worry if Tony Smythe had to have three glasses of whisky for breakfast to get him through the day, but taking a couple of smart pills – these smart drug things – seems to be a rational and very constructive way of dealing with life in the company. It may be a short-cut to reaching peak performance but it's not cheating. In fact, I see Tony's use of Hydergine as a sign of tremendous commitment to his job and to the company.'

'I agree,' interjected Perkins.

The fourth member of the committee, Jack Tausky, then offered his view. 'We welcome employees using their initiative in this company and, in a way, Smythe has used his initiative in making his decision to take this smart drug. He's committed to the company and that's one point in his favour. Also, I'm not convinced that drugs are unfair. It's more of a social prejudice based on the perception that all drugs – except government-sanctioned ones – are bad.'

'That said,' Tausky continued, 'I have grave misgivings about promoting Smythe. It may send out all the wrong signals to other ambitious employees. Imagine if the press got hold of the story, for heaven's sake! I can see the headline now: "Associated Fast Food and Drink condone management drug taking". Our public relations department would have a hard time dealing with that sort of publicity.'

Schreisheim nodded in agreement.

'All things considered,' Tausky concluded, 'I favour giving the job to Tomlins, even though Smythe is a better candidate on paper.'

'Thank you Jack,' said Schreisheim.

'On the other hand,' Tausky continued (almost in a whisper), 'if I may speak candidly for a moment as head of marketing? I'm wondering if we ought to start thinking about adding some of these brain-enhancing drugs and nutrients to a small range of our products. We could target white-collar workers and managers with a new line in "smart food" products. Lunch time snacks that recharge the brain. It could be a winner if. . .'

'Thank you Jack,' interrupted Schreisheim with noticeable irritation. 'I can just see *that* headline! "Associated Fast Food and Drink encourage customer drug taking." Now, if we could get back to the issue at hand for a moment? As I see it, two of us are in favour of Smythe and two favour Tomlins. How shall we proceed?'

Issues to consider

- Is Smythe over-committed to the company or is he 'a law unto himself'?
- Which of these two approaches to work may be more appropriate for someone at the head of an innovative research and development department?[3]
- What are the implications of this case for the management of staff commitment and ambition?[4]

Notes

1. A fictitious organisation.

2. For more detailed information on Hydergine and other smart drugs and nutrients, see Pelton (1988) and Dean and Morgenthaler (1991).
3. The relationship between creativity and commitment is considered in Coopey and Hartley (1991), Janis and Mann (1977), Peltz (1967) and Salancik (1982).
4. The advantages and disadvantages of strong employee commitment are examined in Mowday *et al.*, (1982), Randall (1987), Staw (1982) and Whyte (1956). Also see Schaef and Fassel (1988) for a consideration of the similarities between addiction to drugs and addiction to work.

Case 5   B. F. Goodrich Wheel and Brake Company

Introduction

In 1967, the B.F. Goodrich Company was one of the three largest manufacturers of aircraft wheels and brakes in the US. The company's products supported well-known aircraft, such as the Boeing 727 and the F1-11.

On 18 June 1967, Goodrich received a purchase order from the Ling–Temco–Vought (LTV) Aerospace Corporation for 202 brake assemblies for the new Air Force plane – the A7D. The company beat many competitors to the order as its bid was so low that LTV could not turn it down. Goodrich effectively 'bought into the business' in order to benefit from the longer-term benefits of supplying spare linings and other parts during the lifetime of the A7D. But it wasn't just the competitive price that appealed to LTV. The Goodrich bid offered a relatively small brake containing four discs and weighing only 106 pounds. This was very light compared to the five-disc brake designs proposed by other bidders, and LTV realised that the Goodrich brake would allow the A7D to carry a heavier payload.

The brake was designed by John Warren, one of Goodrich's top engineering designers. Warren was named as project engineer for the A7D, and he, in turn, assigned the task of producing the final production design to a young engineer called Searle Lawson. Lawson's job included overseeing rigorous laboratory-based qualification testing of the brake to ensure that it complied with the rigid military specifications. Results of these qualification tests are then delivered to the LTV and various government officials. Passing the tests implies the brake is safe to flight test.

The laboratory tests specified for the brake were divided into two categories: dynamic brake tests and static brake tests. The Goodrich brake passed the static tests but failed all the dynamic tests. The latter involved the installation of a prototype brake in a test wheel and placing it on a large dynamometer in the Goodrich test laboratory at Troy, Ohio. Lawson ran a series of dynamometer tests designed to simulate the physical stresses of landing the wheel and brake assembly at the A7D's landing speed and braking to a stop. Each test required a total of 51 simulated landings.

In the first three tests, the brake assembly glowed red hot and began to disintegrate. Lawson realised that the fault lay with the actual design of the brake rather than with any defect in the materials used in its construction. He calculated that a five-disc brake was necessary. But Warren dismissed Lawson's calculation and ordered him to continue testing the four-disc version using different mixtures of brake lining materials.

Goodrich technical writer, Kermit Vandiver, takes up the story of the subsequent tests.[1]

Brake qualification test 13

Vandiver: The thirteenth attempt at qualification was being conducted under BF Goodrich Internal Test number T-1867.

On the morning of April 11 [1968], Richard Gloor, who was the test engineer assigned to the A7D project, came to me and told me he had discovered that some time during the previous twenty-four hours, instrumentation used to record brake pressure had been miscalibrated deliberately so that while the instrumentation showed that a pressure of 1000 pounds per square inch had been used to conduct brake stop numbers 46 and 47 (two overload energy stops), 1100 psi had actually been applied to the brakes. Maximum pressure available on the A7D is 1000 psi.

Mr Gloor further told me he had questioned instrumentation personnel about the miscalibration and had been told they were asked to do so by Searle Lawson, a design engineer on the A7D. I subsequently questioned Lawson who admitted he had ordered the instruments miscalibrated at the direction of a superior.[2]

Upon examining the log sheets kept by laboratory personnel, I found that other violations of the test specifications had occurred. For example, after some of the overload stops, the brakes had been disassembled and the three stators (or stationary members) of the brake had been taken to the plant toolroom for rework and, during an earlier part of the test, the position of the elements within the brake had been reversed to distribute the lining wear more evenly.

Additionally, instead of braking the dynamometer to a complete stop as required by military specifications, pressure was released when the wheel and brake speed had decelerated to 10 miles per hour. The reason for this, I was later told, was that the brakes were experiencing severe vibrations near the end of the stops, causing excessive lining wear and general deterioration of the brake.

All these incidents were in clear violation of military specifications and general industry practice.

I reported these violations to the test lab supervisor, Mr Ralph Gretzinger, who reprimanded instrumentation personnel and stated that under no circumstances would intentional miscalibration of instruments be tolerated. As for the other discrepancies noted in test procedures, he said that he was aware that they were happening but that as far as he was concerned the tests could not, in view of the way they were being conducted, be classified as qualification tests.

Later that same day, maximum energy stop was conducted on the worn brake. The brake landed at a speed of 161 mph and the pressure was applied. The dynamometer rolled a distance of 16,800 feet before coming to rest. The elapsed stoppage time was 141 seconds. By computation, this stop time shows the aircraft would have travelled over 3 miles before stopping.

Within a few days, a typewritten copy of the test logs of Test T-1867 was sent to LTV to assure LTV that a qualified brake was almost ready for delivery. Virtually every entry in this so-called copy of the test logs was drastically altered. As an example, the stop time for the worn brake maximum energy stop was changed from 141 seconds to a mere 46.8 seconds.

Brake qualification test 14

Vandiver: On May 2 [1968] the fourteenth attempt to qualify the brakes was begun, and Mr Lawson told me that he had been informed by both Mr Robert Sink (project manager) and Mr Russell Van Horn (projects manager at Goodrich) that "regardless of what the brake does on test, we're going to qualify it." He also said that the latest instructions he had received were to the effect that, if the data from this latest test turned out worse than did test T-1867, then we would write our report based on T-1867.

During this latest and final attempt to qualify the four-rotor brake, the same illegal procedures were used as had been used on attempt number 13. Again after 30 stops had been completed, the position of the friction members of the brake were reversed to distribute wear more evenly. After each stop, the wheel was removed from the brake and the accumulated dust was blown out. During each stop, pressure was released when the deceleration had reached 10 miles per hour.

After stop number 48 – the third overload stop – temperatures in the brake were so high that the fuse plug, a safety device that allows air to escape from the tyre to prevent blowout, melted and allowed the tyre to deflate. The same thing happened after stop number 49.'

Preparing the qualification report

Vandiver: While these tests were being conducted, I was asked by Mr Lawson to begin writing a qualification report for the brake. I flatly refused and told Mr Gretzinger, the lab supervisor, who was my superior, that I could not write such a report because the brake had not been qualified. He agreed and he said no-one in the laboratory was going to issue such a report unless a brake was actually qualified in accordance with the specification and using standard operating procedures.

He said that he would speak to his own supervisor, the manager of technical services section, Mr Russell Line, and assured me that both had concurred in the decision not to write a qualification report.[3]

Mr Lawson stated that if I would not write the report he would have to, and he asked if I would help gather the test data and draw up the various engineering curves and graphic displays that are normally included in a report.

I asked Mr Gretzinger, my superior, if this was alright and he agreed. As long as I was only assisting in the preparation of the data it would be permissible.

Both Lawson and I worked on the elaborate curves and logs in the report for nearly a month. Many, many of the elaborate engineering curves were complete and total fabrications, based not on what had actually occurred, but on information that would fool both LTV and the Air Force.

During this time we both frankly discussed the moral aspects of what we were doing, and we agreed that our actions were unethical and probably illegal. Several times during that month I discussed the A7D testing with Mr Line and asked him to consult his superiors in Akron [Goodrich head office] to prevent a false qualification report from being issued. Mr Line declined to do so and advised me that it would be wise to just do my work and keep quiet.

About the first of June 1968, Mr Gretzinger asked if I was finished with the graphic data and said he had been advised by the chief engineer, Mr H.C. Sunderman, that when the data was finished they were to be delivered to him – Sunderman – and he would instruct someone in the engineering department to actually write the report. Accordingly, when I had finished with the data, I gave it Mr Gretzinger who immediately took it from the room.

Within a few minutes, he was back and was obviously angry. He said that Mr Sunderman had told him no-one in the engineering department had time to write the report and that we would have to do it ourselves. At that point, Mr Line came into the room demanding to know 'what the hell is going on.' Mr Gretzinger explained the situation again and said he would not allow such a report to be issued by the lab. Line then turned to me and said he was 'sick of hearing about this damned report. Write the goddamn thing and shut up about it.'

Aftermath

Within two days, Vandiver completed the falsified report. By his own admission, he added a 'meaningless gesture' as a final sop to his self-respect.[4] In the conclusion of the report he wrote:

> The B. F. Goodrich P/N2 – 1162-3 brake assembly does not meet the intent or the requirement of the applicable specification documents and therefore is not qualified.

When the report was published on 5 June 1968, the two 'nots' in the conclusion had been removed. That same day, Vandiver contacted his attorney and was advised to contact the Federal Bureau of Investigation. Lawson took the same action a week later.

Meanwhile, flight tests had begun and brake problems arose on the very first flight. The Air Force rescinded its approval of the qualification report and demanded that Goodrich show them the raw data. Goodrich refused on grounds of commercial confidentiality.

Fearing that the Air Force might force a confrontation, Goodrich management decided to deal directly with LTV. A week before the scheduled meeting with LTV, an internal meeting was held on Saturday 27 July 1968, between Vandiver, Sink, Lawson and Warren. The purpose of the meeting was to review the raw data and to highlight any 'discrepant items' contained in the qualification report. Each point was discussed at great length and a list of 43 separate discrepancies was compiled. Sink claimed that these would be revealed to LTV personnel the following week. However, by the time of the meeting with LTV only a few days later, he had cut the list of discrepancies down from 43 items to three.

Lawson resigned on 5 October. Vandiver resigned two weeks later.

Despite the two men's damning testimony to the Proxmire Subcommittee, and an equally damning report from the four-man team from the General Accounting Office (which declared that the Goodrich brake was unsafe and improperly tested), Goodrich management put up a stout defence to the Subcommittee.

When questioned about the falsification of data and figures in the report, Sink testified:

> When you take data from several different sources, you have to rationalise among these data what is the true story. This is part of your engineering know-how. Changes were made to some data but only to make them more consistent with the overall picture of the data that is available.[5]

For his part, the Goodrich vice-president and general counsel of the company, denied any wrongdoing on the part of the company:

> We have thirty-odd engineers at this plant and I say to you that it is incredible that these men would stand idly by and see reports changed or falsified. I mean, you just do not have to do that working for anybody. Just nobody does that.[6]

Vandiver offered his own interpretation of events:

> I feel in the beginning stages of this program someone made a mistake and refused to admit that mistake, and to hide his stupidity or his ignorance, or his pride, or whatever it was, he simply covered up with more false statements and false information. By the time it came time to deliver the brake, Goodrich was too far down the road that there was nothing else to do. They had no time to start over. I think it was a matter not of company policy but of company politics. I think that probably three or four persons within the Goodrich organisation at Troy were responsible for this. I do not believe for a moment that the corporate officials at Akron knew that this was going on.[7]

The four-hour hearing adjourned without a firm conclusion being reached. The following day, the Department of Defense made sweeping changes in its inspection, testing, and reporting procedures.

Issues to consider

- Analyse the events outlined in the case. In the light of your analysis, assess the relative merits of the interpretations offered by Robert Sink, Kermit Vandiver and the Goodrich vice-president.[8]

Notes

1. Vandiver's version of events is taken from his sworn testimony to Senator Proxmire's Subcommittee on Economy in Government of the Joint Economic Committee of the Congress of the United States, 91st Congress, 13 August 1969. The Subcommittee's inquiry was set up to assess the evidence collated by the Federal Bureau of Investigation (FBI) and others, implicating the Goodrich company in an attempt to defraud the Department of Defense. The FBI were alerted to this alleged fraud by Kermit Vandiver.
2. According to Vandiver (1972), Lawson admitted to Ralph Gretzinger, the testlaboratory supervisor, that this directive had come from Goodrich project manager, Robert Sink.
3. Vandiver changed his account of this incident when he wrote subsequently about the A7D affair. In this later account he states that Gretzinger returned from Line's office in a dejected frame of mind and told him: 'Well, it looks like we're licked. We're to go ahead and prepare the data and when we're finished someone upstairs will actually write it' (Vandiver, 1978, p. 62).
4. Vandiver (1972).
5. Testimony to the Proxmire Subcommittee, 13 August 1969.
6. Testimony, 13 August 1969.
7. Testimony, 13 August 1969.
8. Useful sources here include Bazerman *et al.* (1984), Biggart and Hamilton (1984), Coser (1974), Daneke (1985), Gouldner (1957, 1958), Rotondi (1976), Staw (1976b), Staw and Fox (1977), and Whyte (1986). Braithwaite (1984), Clinard (1990), Clinard and Yeager (1980) and Colesman (1982) offer broader socio-economic analyses of corporate misconduct.

   According to the research of Clinard (1983) and Cousins (1987), falsification of tests by military contractors would appear to be a fairly widespread practice.

Case 6   Commitment as dissent[1]

Inspectors at a Detroit car factory relieved boredom by taking their jobs absolutely seriously. Following a quality campaign by higher management, the inspectors began rejecting something like three out of every four cars under examination, some simply because the engines didn't turn over quietly enough. Management tried to drop hints about the inspectors being perhaps a little too punctilious, but they were naturally reluctant to state it too openly. The inspectors simply ignored the hints, arguing consistently in return that their interests and those of the company were identical, and they had a positive duty to ensure that only products of the finest quality left the factory.

Issues to consider

- What is the relationship between commitment, power and control?[2]
- Is a highly committed employee an asset or a liability to a business organisation?[3]
- To what extent may commitment to one's employer conflict with commitment to one's occupation or work?[4]
- What would you advise higher management to do in this case?

Notes

1. This true story is recounted in Rosen and Widgery (1991). This book and that by Buffo (undated) are excellent sources for such vignettes of anarchic mischief.
2. See Geary (1992), Guest (1992), Knights (1990), Lincoln and Kalleberg (1992), Ray (1986), Salancik (1982), Schein (1961), Silver (1987) and Willmott (1993) for a variety of critical viewpoints on this.
3. See Coopey and Hartley (1991), Guest (1992), Keenoy (1992), Kiesler (1971), Kunda (1992), Randall (1987, 1990), Salancik (1982) and Staw (1982).
4. See Angle and Perry (1986), Fukami and Larson (1984), Koslowsky (1990), Morrow (1983) and Wiener and Vardi (1980).

Case 7   Irresponsible autonomy in the factory

Introduction

'A world of pleasures to win and nothing to lose but boredom.'[1]

Monotony is a subjective psychological condition which is related to objective conditions. Early research discovered that many people found it difficult to carry out the same simple repetitive task effectively over a long period of time.

Monotony rather than fatigue seemed to be the culprit. In these early studies it was discovered that worker monotony could be attenuated through working in closely-knit social groups and/or through the covert injection of variety into the work.[2] Needless to say, these strategies were not necessarily conducive to improved performance or line management control.[3] Yet many adaptive work behaviours, whilst 'against the rules', may actually be functional to the extent that they help the organisation's overall performance.

Hence, 'deviant' work behaviour can be destructive or constructive. It can also take many forms: from sabotage and theft, through drinking alcohol at work, to covert job redesign. Whilst sabotage and similar expressions of worker resistance to managerial control have been researched fairly extensively[4], workers' covert negotiation of increased work autonomy is less well documented despite its widespread practice in work organisations.

Example 1   Covert job redesign on the car assembly line

In almost all machine-paced shopfloor work, employees are expected to do their job without assistance except in special circumstances (e.g. machine breakdown). Yet, in many factories, and usually in violation of shopfloor rules and regulations, it is common for workers to practise covert job enlargement. This may take the form of 'doubling up' or even 'tripling up'.

A typical way of 'doubling up' in a machine-paced work environment is for one person to do his or her own job plus that of another for an agreed period of time. This adds variety to the first person's job and gives the other person a break from the monotony. 'Tripling up' involves three people and allows two of them to rest simultaneously.

Workers argue that such practices increase job variety, allow them more participation, and do not affect quality adversely. However, such practices cannot continue for any length of time unless an implicit bargain is struck between workers and line management (i.e. 'you help me do my job and I'll help you do yours').

As ex-car assembly line worker John Runcie recalls:

> In many cases, workers negotiated with each other to 'trade' jobs for some period of time. In my case, the employee to my left and I often traded jobs for an hour or so as a means of reducing the boredom and monotony. The supervisor on that part of the automobile assembly line indicated that as long as we were sending no repairs and were not causing *him* problems, job trading (although against shop rules) was acceptable.[5]

Another interesting form of covert job redesign described by Runcie involves employees selling merchandise or services to other employees. During

Runcie's employment as an assembly line worker, for example, one coffee-and-doughnut concession had two large coffee urns operating continually throughout the shift. Another of his colleagues (whose official job was to collect litter) acted as a bookmaker and would take bets on horse races and the results of major sporting events.

In all these cases, workers added to the standard behaviours they were paid by the company to do. They created autonomy for themselves through the creation of a second, illegitimate, job within the boundaries of the first, legitimate, job.

Management were content to allow these practices to continue so long as they did not affect productivity or quality. Management turned the proverbial 'blind eye'.

Example 2   Deviance in the 'smile factory'

Disneyland is a huge theme park based in Anaheim, California. The Disney Corporation market it as the 'happiest place on Earth'. But whatever services Disney executives provide to the 70,000–80,000 visitors who flow through the park every day during the peak summer season, it is the employees at the bottom of the organisational hierarchy who must provide them. A number of these employees refer to Disneyland as the 'smile factory'.

Disneyland employees ('cast members' in the corporation's parlance) are trained to demonstrate heroic forbearance and politeness to all customers ('guests') even under the most trying circumstances.[6] The company is very proud of its high standard of customer care and failure to maintain these high standards results in the immediate dismissal of the employee responsible.

The work of the ride operators is fairly monotonous and is governed by strict rules stipulating the exact timing of the ride, the exact words to be used to describe the ride to visitors, and so on. Again, deviation from these rules is punishable by dismissal.

It is the job of the numerous area supervisors in Disneyland to monitor the behaviour of ride operators and other 'cast members'.[7] All employees are aware of the surveillance of these supervisors, and realise well enough that security of employment is most easily achieved if a degree of emotional self-management is practised (i.e. put on the generalised countenance of a happy-go-lucky person and project enthusiasm and dedication at all times).

Generally speaking, the people-processing tasks of ride operators pass good-naturedly and smoothly. Any troublesome visitors are dealt with by the ever-present security staff (disguised as sheriffs in Frontierland, Keystone Kops in Main Street, and cavalry officers on Tom Sawyer's Island). Occasionally, however, the behaviour of a visitor is so personal or extraordinary that a ride operator finds it impossible to ignore or merely inform others and allow them to decide what is to be done. Restoration of dignity and self-respect is called for and routine practices and techniques have been developed for these circumstances.[8] These 'deviant' practices are such that, if carried out with skill, they are virtually undetectable by the omnipresent area supervisors. They include:

The seatbelt squeeze: the rapid clinching-up of a seatbelt so that the target subject is doubled-over at the point of departure and left gasping for breath for the duration of the ride.

The seatbelt slap: the offending visitor receives a sharp, quick snap of the hard plastic belt across the face, legs or arms when entering or leaving a seat-belted ride.

The hatch-cover ploy: this is employed on the submarine ride only; in collusion with colleagues on the loading dock, the submarine pilot drench the offending visitor(s) with water as their units pass under a waterfall.

The brake toss: this is employed on the Autopia ride only; ride operators jump on the outside of the car occupied by the target subject, deftly unfasten the seatbelt and apply the car brake so severely that the subject is thrown onto the bonnet of the car or beyond.

Area supervisors are aware of these rare outbreaks of deviant behaviour. But they experience difficulty in catching offenders 'in the act'. Also, experienced ride operators know the limits beyond which they dare not pass and are careful to avoid exposing themselves to detection or to the public wrath of a customer whilst 'on stage'. It is probably because virtually all 'cast member' exercise this kind of self-management that top management have never explicitly set out to eradicate these covert practices in any heavy-handed way. [9]

Issues to consider

- To what extent do the covert job practices described here represent an attempt to make unchallenging jobs more challenging?[10]
- What are the implications of covert job redesign for management control and authority?
- Both case examples illustrate negotiated indulgency patterns.[11] To what extent may these act as a barrier to the successful implementation of organisational changes such as an official programme of job redesign?
- What do these two case examples tell us about the creation and maintenance of work identity, and about employee motivation and commitment?[12] Do the cases highlight the same issues?

Notes

1. Vaneigem (1983), p. 150.
2. Many of these were carried out by researchers at the National Institute of Industrial Psychology (NIIP) in the UK. See Myers (1920), Vernon (1924) and Wyatt and Frazer (1928). The work of the NIIP is critically reviewed by Hollway (1991) and Rose (1988).
3. Some of the famous Hawthorne experiments were the first to show how work group norms can develop which may be at odds with the wider organisational norms established by management. See Roethlisberger and Dickson (1964) and critical reviews by Franke (1979), Parsons (1974) and Rose (1988).
4. E.g. Collinson (1992), Scott (1985), Taylor and Walton (1971) and Thompson and Bannon (1985).
5. Runcie (1988) p. 133.
6. For a description of the Disney approach to training and human resources management generally, see Blocklyn (1988) and Holmes and Holmes (1988). The film/video 'In Search of Excellence' (produced by Nathan/Tyler Productions and distributed in the UK by Melrose Film Productions London) contains excellent footage of this. For a more critical look at the Disney approach, see Sehlinger (1987) and Van Maanen and Schein (1979).
7. Much of the information contained in this case example is based on Van Maanen's (1991) account of his work experience at Disneyland. He was a 'cast member' at Disneyland for a number of years before being fired for failing to get his hair cut. His description of the theme park conjures up images of a panopticon. It would seem that blind observation posts are located throughout the park. These enable area supervisors to monitor the behaviour of employees at different workstations and on various rides without themselves being seen. In this way area supervisors can oversee a substantial geographical area.
8. These deviant practices are described in detail by Van Maanen (1991).
9. This is not to imply any neglect or unprofessionalism on the part of Disneyland management. Millions of people have visited (and doubtless will continue to visit) Disneyland with no cause for complaint whatsoever. Neither should the focus on the deviant ride operator practices in this case be seen as a general criticism of the conduct of Disneyland ride operators or other park employees. According to Van Maanen (1991), these practices described here occur very infrequently (and then only in response to the most objectionable of customer behaviour).
10. See Morgan (1975) and Runcie (1988). There is also an interesting body of research examining the role of emotional expression (and its suppression) at work. In this view, the case examples touch on important issues of identity and self-esteem. See Ashworth and Humphrey (1993), Ashworth and Lee (1990), Breakwell (1986), Cohen and Taylor (1992), Hochschild (1983, 1990), James (1989) and Van Maanen and Kunda (1989) for details.
11. The indulgency pattern of bureaucracy is described fully in a classic study by Gouldner (1964).
12. You may wish to consider the extent to which the meaning of work, even one's power and status at work, emerges through a process of negotiation. See Berger and Luckmann (1967), Goffman (1959), Harré (1979) and Silverman (1970). Also, see the references above (no. 10) for an examination of the ways in which work identity is negotiated.

CHAPTER 3

The management of meaning, motivation and commitment

Introduction

A key dilemma for organisational decision-makers is how to structure the control of organisational members so that organisational objectives are met without engendering resistance from members who often wish to exercise a degree of self-control and autonomy. If controls are too visible or too strict, employees tend to find ways to overcome them. As a result, even stricter controls are initiated, and so on in a vicious circle of control. On the other hand, if organisational members are left entirely to their own devices, coordination of activities may become a serious problem. An important factor shaping organisational behaviour is thus the extent to which a balance between organisational control and personal commitment or autonomy is achieved and sustained.

Of course, the issue of control is a complex one. Unfortunately, much of the analysis of organisational (usually management) control in OB texts is rather one-sided – taking its starting point from the view that power is bestowed upon managers by those who are managed. Consequently, the covert nature of power relationships and organisational control is largely ignored, despite a growing realisation that commitment and control are not mutually exclusive concepts:

> In the amorphous twentieth-century world, where manipulation replaces authority, the victim does not recognise his (sic) status. The formal aim, implemented by the latest psychological equipment, is to have men internalise what the management cadres would have them do, without knowing their own motives, but nevertheless having them. Many whips are inside men, who do not know how they got there, or

indeed that they are there. In the movement from authority to manipulation, power shifts from the visible to the invisible, from the known to the anonymous. And with rising material standards, exploitation becomes less material and more psychological (Mills, 1951, p. 110).

This passage from Mills raises the question of the role of organisational psychology research in the control of organisational behaviour. It also locates the management of meaning, motivation and commitment firmly in the domain of power relationship within and beyond organisational boundaries. (Note that many of the issues raised by the cases in this chapter resurface in Chapter 5).

The seven cases in this chapter examine the commitment–control dilemma from a variety of critical viewpoints. Case 8, written by Neil Anderson, examines the extent to which changes to a company's selection and recruitment methods (an important component of Mills' 'psychological equipment') can overcome problems of low commitment and high staff turnover. Case 9, prepared by Yasmin Frings and Neil Anderson, again looks at selection and recruitment, but comes at it from the other side of the control–commitment dilemma. This case study of a voluntary organisation reveals how high commitment cannot guarantee high performance or low staff turnover.

Unlike Cases 8 and 9 in which fitting the person to the job is the main problem, Case 10 is set in a manufacturing organisation and focuses on a job redesign programme designed ostensibly to fit the job to the person. The problems caused by the implementation of the programme reveal the importance of organisational factors under-emphasised in narrow psychological theories of motivation and job design.

Case 11 explores the extent to which the manipulation of employee commitment and work identity is within the power of management. The case invites an answer to a vital question: is it possible to obtain a committed workforce whilst increasing, rather than decreasing, managerial control? Case 12 illustrates how important a role is played by management in (de)motivating employees at lower levels of an organisational hierarchy. Although all names have been changed, this is a true story: in my experience the events outlined are by no means uncommon in UK industry.

Case 13, prepared by Margaret and David Collinson, raises the issue of sexuality and gender in organisational life. Again, the scenario described is not uncommon, yet conventional OB texts have kept strangely quiet about this 'irrational' side of behaviour in organisations and the extent to which gender relations are embedded within organisational power relations.

Finally, Case 14 explores the control–commitment dilemma as it applies to a voluntary organisation. Greenpeace feels this dilemma keenly because the vast majority of its members pay for the privilege of organisational membership. In this case, members are committed to radical actions which may undermine the primary strategic objectives of the organisation as a whole.

Case 8   Selection and retention at Compservices Limited[1]

Neil Anderson[2]

Introduction

Compservices Ltd is a local and national supplier of computer hardware and software located in the financial district of the city of Nottingham. The company supplies hardware produced by all major manufacturers, including IBM, ICL, Apple Macintosh and DEC. It holds franchise arrangements to supply a diversity of software ranging from spreadsheets (e.g. Lotus 123) to word processing packages (e.g. Word, Wordperfect and Locoscript) to more specialised applications such as 'Windows' packages and operating systems. Compservices is a well-established supplier and is well known to local businesses in the Nottingham area.

Established in 1972, the company is still owned and managed as a joint partnership by Bill Druxton (Chairman) and Steve Warring (Managing Director). Both remain extremely active within the business and tend to devote long hours to all matters – both strategic and day-to-day – associated with the company. Both men could be described as stereotypical entrepreneurs – committed, ambitious, active and ever-hungry for financial success. Indeed, Druxton recently won the 'Entrepreneur of the Year' award from the local Chamber of Trade and Industry (an award greeted with envy by his partner Steve Warring). At the presentation for this award, Druxton concluded his acceptance speech with following comments:

> If I am asked the reasons for our success, I reply hard work, more hard work, and rigorous cost control to maximise profitability. These are not simply aspects of doing business in our business, they are our life-blood. To get the best out of people at work demands tight control, target-setting, monitoring and performance evaluation. Staff come and go, but our core business has always been, and will always remain, a profitable employer in the local economy.

Business growth

Under the management of Druxton and Warring, Compservices has grown from strength to strength. In 1972, when first established by the two men, the company was run from Druxton's home (from his spare bedroom, to be precise) with the sole support of Druxton's niece as a part-time secretary. By 1980, the company had an annual turnover of over £½ million and employed 15 full-time staff. In 1992, it had grown to total staffing of 35 people (including technical sales staff, warehouse operatives, secretaries, account assistants, and the partners' personal assistant, Julie Barrick).

However, the company has recently developed the reputation of being a hard employer, particularly amongst technical sales staff, and it is in this category of employees that several problems have begun to surface over the last 18 months.

Technical sales staff

Compservices employs a total of 20 technical sales staff, all based in the Nottingham showroom but supporting clients on a nationwide basis. These staff, known internally as 'floggers', are responsible for all aspects of computer sales and after-care support for clients within their geographical region. Of the twenty staff, six cover Greater London, four cover the South East, four the Midlands, two the North West, and one each the South West, Wales, Scotland and Northern Ireland. Floggers are employed largely on a commission basis with a maximum of 20 per cent of earnings being paid as basic salary. The remainder of their pay is dependent upon sales revenue and revenues generated from chargeable support services.

Staff turnover in the last 18 months has been excessive in this job role – no fewer than 15 technical sales staff have left and been replaced. This represents a turnover of 75 per cent in 11½ years, or the equivalent of 112.5 per cent per annum. Leavers have consistently blamed the unrealistically high performance targets imposed by Druxton as a major influence on their decision to leave the company. They also blame the lack of career development opportunities within Compservices and the need to drive up to 50,000 miles a year (albeit in a company car) to visit clients' sites.

Selection and retention issues

These problems have prompted Steve Warring, as managing director responsible for day-to-day sales support activities, to conduct research into the selection and retention of floggers. He has ascertained the following:

1. Nine of the 15 leavers have joined a direct competitor based in Leicester, called Support Systems Ltd. This company pays a relatively generous

guaranteed annual salary and all technical staff are employed as salaried personnel. The other six leavers moved on to similar jobs in smaller computer support companies in the Midlands or London areas.

2. At least 12 of Compservices clients have switched to the new employers of the technical staff after they had resigned. To add insult to injury, for the first time ever in the company's history, a series of complaints have landed on Warring's desk over the last few months. Essentially these complaints concerned over-charging by floggers or of being invoiced for uncompleted work. In one case, a client was invoiced for three personal computers, a lap-top computer, a laser printer, and one full-day support consultancy when the technical sales person had spent a mere two hours at the client's office connecting up hardware for a local area network which had already been paid for!

3. Sales revenue targets have risen rapidly over in recent years despite the economic downturn and recessional pressures affecting the computer industry. 4 years ago, the average target for a flogger was £5000 a month total revenue. 4 years later, Druxton had raised this to £10,000 a month – a target which few sales staff were meeting with any consistency.

4. Druxton selects all floggers personally. He uses only an unstructured interview coupled with a brief telephone conversation with a previous employer as a reference check. Warring has identified a number of personality tests and realistic sales exercises to improve the objectivity of this selection process, but Druxton has steadfastly refused to use them. Druxton claims to be able 'to spot a good salesman as soon as he walks through the door'.

5. The highest performing flogger, Andrew Shales, has been with the company for 2 years and has averaged a total annual revenue of approximately £100,000. At the other end of the scale, David Myers, still in his initial training period, has been averaging around £4000 revenue per month over the past 6 months.

Armed with these facts and figures, Warring has decided to tackle the thorny issue of technical sales staff selection and retention. Currently, he is preparing a short report to Bill Druxton recommending improvements to selection procedures and modifications to the terms and conditions of employment for this category of staff. Given the importance of technical sales to the future profitability of Compservices, Warring is determined to deal with these personnel problems once and for all.

Case resolution

- Outline and analyse the problems confronting Compservices and offer recommendations for their resolution.

Issues to consider

- What would you advise Steve Warring to include in his report to Bill Druxton?
- What organisational, psychological and social psychological theories and models help explain the present difficulties at Compservices?[3]
- What selection methods, other than interviewing, psychometric testing and realistic exercises, could the company consider to make its recruitment decisions more objective?[4]
- What action, if any, should be taken against floggers who intentionally over-charge a client in order to improve their revenue figures?

Notes

1. A pseudonym for an existing company.
2. Neil Anderson is a lecturer in the Department of Psychology at the University of Nottingham, University Park, Nottingham NG7 2RD.
3. See Anderson and Shackleton (1993), Arnold *et al.* (1991) and Smith and Robertson (1986).
4. See Herriot (1989), Muchinsky (1986), Reilly and Chao (1982) and Wanous (1980).

Case 9   Recruiting helpline counsellors: dilemmas in validation

Yasmin Frings and Neil Anderson[1]

The situation

Carole Jones was very concerned. The morning post had just delivered another 124 completed application forms. This brought the week's total to a staggering 1361. It appeared to her that the publicity campaign she had started several months ago was paying off. 'The Carers',[2] a free 24 hour telephone counselling service, had obviously become a household name throughout the country. But if applications kept coming at the present rate, it would take Carole several weeks just to compose a shortlist, and a further two or three months to conduct the interviews.

Carole knew the danger of this only too well. If she did not manage to respond to suitable applicants within the next month, 'The Carers' might lose potential volunteers (as all applicants were indeed volunteer counsellors).

The organisation

It had all started 2 years ago out of a growing awareness that existing UK government counselling services could only cater for a minute fraction of people seeking help. As a result, 'The Carers' had been set up as a free telephone counselling service funded solely by donations from the public. Although these donations were often very generous, organisational overheads had to be kept to a minimum.

'The Carers' advertised for telephone counsellors and immediately recruited 90 volunteers. However, as each volunteer was only able to cover two 4 hour shifts a month, it was soon discovered that it was impossible to have a volunteer by a single telephone 24 hours a day, 7 days a week. It was hoped that the organisation would eventually have up to ten telephone lines open at any one time. Reaching this ultimate target meant having a pool of at least 900 volunteers to draw from. At present, the actual number of recruited counsellors had increased to 372 and had already cost 'The Carers' a crippling £186,000 (@ £500 per recruit) in training costs alone.

The last management meeting had revealed one problem that had come as a shock to the team and to Carole Jones (Director of Human Resources) in particular. Out of a total of 372 recruits, only 290 had successfully completed the 10 week training programme. Worse still, having started the actual telephone counselling shifts, only 161 volunteers could be identified as still playing an active role (i.e. working two shifts a month or more). Hence the organisation was facing two major problems: a 27 per cent wastage through training and more than 50 per cent turnover of qualified counsellors in 2 years.

Put another way, out of the initial £186,000 spent on training over a 2 year period, £105,500 had been spent in vain. The implication of these facts was painfully obvious. After 2 years, 'The Carers' could still only provide a 24 hour service with two telephone lines being constantly monitored, and even that relied on a few very dedicated volunteers working extra shifts. As a consequence, out of approximately 8000 attempted telephone calls each day, only 500 calls (6.25 per cent) were being answered.

The management meeting concluded that urgent action was needed to tackle these issues. Carole Jones was made personally responsible for meeting an agreed target of 300 active volunteer counsellors within the next 6 months.

Carole's immediate reaction had been to intensify the publicity campaign. It was Christmas time and the plea to help those in need was heard by hundreds of 'do-gooders', as Carole called them. A brief look through some of the 1361 completed application forms suggested that, once again, the majority of applicants were middle-aged, middle–class women.

The job

If Carole was honest, she had to admit that she did not really have a clear picture of her ideal candidate. She had never gone to the trouble of conducting a thorough job analysis on what it actually meant to be a telephone counsellor. She had presumed to know what a good counsellor does. With the benefit of hindsight she thought this had probably been a mistake as the lack of job criteria had made her job of composing a shortlist extremely difficult.

In the publicity campaign, potential candidates had simply been told that if they were good listeners, were able to give up 8 hours of their time per month and cared about others, then they should apply for the job. No prior experience was needed as training would be given.

The problem with this approach was that most people think they have these skills and capabilities. What the campaign failed to convey was the demanding and often depressing nature of the work. Also, asking people for 8 hours a month was somewhat misleading. With briefings before and after each shift, Carole reckoned that 15 hours a month was probably a more realistic figure.

Up to this point, Carole had always thought that because she was recruiting volunteers, almost anyone would be adequate. In any case, a comprehensive training programme was given and so poorer candidates could be 'brought up to speed' prior to starting the job. However, with a 20 per cent wastage figure through training, she was clearly quite wrong.

The training

A great deal of effort had gone into the development of the counselling training programme. The actual counselling approach could be loosely described as client-centred, information-giving within a climate of appropriate empathy. Callers came from a wide cross-section of the population, with the youngest caller being 4 years old and the oldest being 72 years of age. Out of all callers the vast majority were either aged between 12 and 19 or between 35 and 43 years.

Problems which callers presented depended to some extent on their age. Two typical scenarios are outlined below.

- Typical problems: 12–19 year olds
  Concerns about sexuality (puberty, masturbation, etc.)
  Pregnancy
  Bullying (e.g. physical or sexual bullying at school)
  Homelessness (e.g. run away from home)
  Concern about others (e.g. friends, parents)
  Physical abuse (e.g. by parents, relatives, friends)
  Sexual abuse (e.g. by parents, relatives, friends)
  Wanting to talk to someone (e.g. feeling bored, unloved)

- Typical problems: 35–43 year olds
  Divorce (e.g. requesting legal information or advice)
  Unemployment (e.g. information about benefits, depression)
  Rape
  Physical abuse
  Being an abuser
  Drug abuse (including alcohol and cigarettes)
  Concern for others (e.g. children, spouse, friends)
  Wanting to talk to someone (e.g. feeling depressed, lonely, suicidal and unloved)

Clearly, this was not a job for the faint-hearted or for the naive do-gooder with little or no experience of life's darker side. To some of these problems there were solutions or options which could be explored during a single telephone conversation, while others were more or less insoluble or required a series of telephone conversations between caller and counsellor. Thus, being tolerant, respectful and non-judgemental are key attributes of counsellors working for 'The Carers'. The organisation are proud of these attributes, which make them different to some other counselling services.

For the past 2 years, the training programme has concentrated firstly on raising self-awareness in new recruits (especially regarding verbal and non-verbal behaviours). Another part of the programme tackled the issue of empathy, the ability to acknowledge and take seriously another person's feelings and thoughts whilst being patient with that person.

Even though a 'natural' human reaction is to switch to problem-solving mode, the training emphasised the importance of leaving the caller feeling in control. Trainees were made aware that their job was to explore options without pushing callers into making their minds up on the spot. A large proportion of calls received by 'The Carers' are victims of abuse, but the organisation also receive a high percentage of calls from the abusers themselves. Therefore, teaching tolerance played a further important role in the programme, as did teaching active listening skills.

Carole Jones had gone through the training programme herself and now, in retrospect, she was surprised to realise how much of a deskilling–reskilling process was actually involved.

The problem in retrospect

Clearly, the first mistake Carole had made had been the way the publicity campaign had been conducted. Then, at the first stage in the recruitment and selection process, a misleading picture of the organisation and the job had been presented. The second stage, the application form, had also created problems as it had only asked candidates to give biographical data such as age, sex, education, profession, time available and how applicants had heard about the organisation. Carole had then shortlisted candidates according to the amount of time available by individuals, giving preference to professionals such a teachers, nurses and social workers.

At the next stage of the selection process, shortlisted candidates had been invited to a 1 hour interview conducted by either Carole or one of her colleagues. This was usually no more than a casual chat based upon application details as well as general commitment and whether the candidate was a 'caring type of person'. Usually, Carole decided during the first few minutes of the interview whether or not the candidate was suitable. Any subsequent offers of training places were made within 1 week of the interview.

Carole had never performed a validation study into the predictive validity of her selection system, but under the circumstances it seemed unlikely that the system she was using was in any way adequate for selecting the right candidates for the posts.

Future scenarios

Against this background, Carole has recently decided that she faces four distinct action plan options:

1. *No Change*
    She could stick to her old selection system while changing the training programme to accommodate candidates' differences in ability.
2. *Modification*
    Parts of the selection system could be changed (e.g. the application form or the interview).
3. *Re-design*
    Carole could perform a thorough job analysis on what it means to be a good and effective telephone counsellor. This would provide her with initial job competencies and valid criteria. The criteria would also give her a better insight into how a more realistic publicity campaign could be conducted.

4. *Assessment Centre Procedure*
    Instead of a 1 hour interview, Carole could put shortlisted candidates through a 1 day assessment centre, comprising, for example, realistic role plays and/or personality and ability tests.[3]

Case resolution[4]

- Based on the information given in this case study, conduct a speculative job analysis on what being an effective volunteer telephone counsellor entails and which attributes you feel are a necessary prerequisite.
- Design a brief publicity campaign for recruiting effective telephone counsellors who will be likely to remain with 'The Carers' even in 5 years' time.
- Which action plan (or combination of plans) would you advise Carole Jones to adopt if she is to meet her target of 300 active counsellors within 6 months?
- Whichever plan you advise Carole to adopt, advise on the establishment of suitable criteria to determine whether a counsellor is doing his or her job satisfactorily. Given that they are volunteers, advise especially on two aspects of management, namely:
    (a) leadership and discipline in cases where counsellors are failing to meet established standards of professional counselling practice;
    (b) wastage rates during and after initial training. What might be the causes of these high dropout rates and how can the organisation reduce this wastage?[5]

Notes

1. Yasmin Frings and Neil Anderson are members of the Human Resources Management Group in the Department of Psychology, University of Nottingham, University Park, Nottingham NG7 2RD.
2. A pseudonym for an existing company.
3. For more information on assessment centres, see Fletcher (1982), Muchinsky (1986) and Smith and Robertson (1986). For a critical examination of their efficacy, see Crawley *et al.* (1990), Mitchel (1975), Robertson *et al.* (1987) and Sackett and Dreher (1982).
4. Useful general references here include Anderson and Shackleton (1993), Brehmer (1980), Brewin (1988), Cook (1988) and Lewis (1985).
5. For a consideration of the differences between voluntary work and paid employment, see Butler and Wilson (1989), Handy (1988), Hassenfeld (1992) and especially Oldham (1979) and Pierce (1992).

Case 10   Job redesign at HBO Computing[1]

HBO Computing is a medium-sized computer manufacturing company, employing approximately 520 people. The company manufactures microprocessors and computer-based control systems for the automatic control of machine tools and other manufacturing process technologies. The company has maintained reasonably healthy profit margins and a good industrial relations record in recent years.

'I just don't understand it,' confessed Jim McHugh, HBO's personnel director. 'I've invested a considerable amount of time and energy this year setting up the job redesign programme throughout the production department and it seems to be falling apart.'

Bill Thompson, HBO's production manager, listened sympathetically to his colleague. He had always felt that Jim's job redesign programme was rather over-ambitious, but he had not expected the first phase of the programme to create so many problems in the factory.

After all, he mused, shopfloor work in this department is straightforward enough (see Figure 3.1). Printed circuit boards, together with the electronic components that need to be inserted and soldered to these boards, are delivered to the production department from the process and stores departments, respectively. The computer programs which run the automatic component insertion and soldering machines are prepared in production planning, loaded up by planning personnel, and the smooth running of production machinery is then monitored by production personnel. Once batches (varying from 10 to 800 boards) are completed, they are 'signed off' to the test department and sent to the modification and repair section if necessary. At present, the production department has 12 automatic component insertion machines and two automatic soldering machines.

Given the simple and routine nature of the production workers' jobs prior to the job redesign programme (i.e. basic machine monitoring and summoning the production supervisor whenever problems arose), Bill assumed they would welcome any form of job enrichment. Certainly, Jim McHugh had assumed as much when designing his programme.

'Let's go over the programme again, Jim, and see if we can uncover the cause of all the trouble out there,' suggested Bill, as he glanced out through his office window at the line of idle production machines. 'Look. The night shift workers haven't started work yet. Right now they're in conference with their day shift colleagues. No doubt they're planning further disruption! We've got to sort this mess out before the board of directors meet next month. The board is expecting the full-blown Just-In-Time production system to be fully

FIGURE 1   The production process at HBO

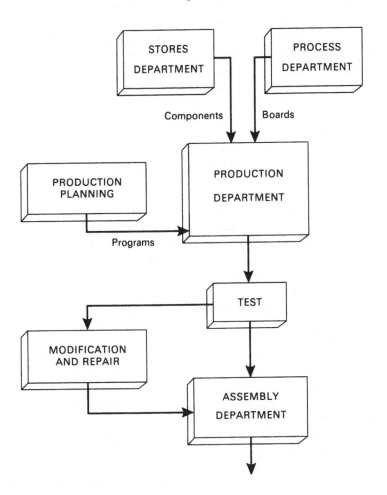

operational by early next year and they're not going to be very pleased with what's going on out there.'[2]

'You're right,' replied Jim wearily. 'Our main problem is that we can't even revert to the original job designs now that the new payment system has been given the go-ahead. There's no way your workers are going to give up the pay increases associated with the new redesign programme. But there's also no chance that the board will agree to the new pay system being scrapped – not after they paid so much to that consultancy firm to set it up. And we certainly can't scrap the programme and let the workers keep their pay rise!'

As the workers' meeting continued outside the office, the two men sat down and went through the details of the job redesign programme.

They recalled how, almost a year ago to the day, Jim McHugh had returned from a conference on work psychology full of enthusiasm for a large-scale redesign initiative throughout the factory. He had seen job redesign as a means to boost worker morale and job satisfaction and had argued the case for the initiative with great passion and skill at the board meeting. Only the factory manager had spoken out against the initiative (because he felt that his own Just-In-Time initiative should have priority) and Jim had obtained the board's formal approval. Somewhat to Jim's annoyance, this approval had hinged on the support given by the financial director, who saw the job redesign programme as an opportunity to cut indirect labour costs in the production planning and maintenance departments. The factory manager, in turn, voted for the job redesign plan (albeit with reluctance) as he felt that such cost savings could be used to subsidise his more ambitious production restructuring plans.

A year ago, shopfloor work in production had always been riddled with informality as far as Bill Thompson was concerned. Despite the routine nature of the work, he often had to 'turn a blind eye' to informal shopfloor work practices in order to get orders out on time and he supported Jim's initiative wholeheartedly because it would allow him to clarify and formally redefine the roles undertaken by his staff. He also saw the success of the programme as crucial to the future of the factory manager's Just-In-Time initiative (which he supported fully).

Bill had worked along with Jim to explore ways of giving production workers more discretion over the pace and methods of work they carried out. After consultation with the head of the maintenance department, Sam Jackson, and with Pamela Jones (head of production planning) it was agreed that production workers should carry out routine maintenance on the automatic component insertion machines, take responsibility for liaising with the stores department over component supplies to the machines, and negotiate daily production targets with their supervisor, Simon Groves, and with a representative from planning. It was decided that workers should be allowed to over-ride or edit parts of the computer programs that ran the machines if and when certain problems were encountered (e.g. component insertion difficulties or missing components). Bill had insisted that the permission of the supervisor must be sought before such actions were undertaken.

Prior to these changes, program writing, proving and editing had been the sole responsibility of the production planning department. Pamela Jones had not taken an active role in working through the details of the job redesign programme and Jim McHugh had taken it upon himself to carry out most of the detailed planning. Pamela was all too happy to devolve responsibility for computer program editing to production as her department was hard at work trying to meet the deadline for completing the complex systems software for the forthcoming implementation of Just-In-Time.

Jim McHugh obtained the agreement of the production workers' trade union representative to his job redesign plans and, after a further round of talks, the new flexible pay system was introduced. In truth, the trade union representative was more concerned with fighting any possible redundancies than she was with the details of Jim's job redesign programme. As it turned out, the new pay system was welcomed by the workforce – not least because it led to an immediate 6.5 per cent pay increase. However, when it came to implementing the new job redesign programme (after training had been successfully completed), the workforce were noticeably less enthusiastic and supportive. Indeed, within 4 days the programme was in danger of collapsing completely.

Bill put this down to the greed of the workers who, as far as he was concerned, wanted more money but did not want the added responsibilities linked to the pay increase. He bemoaned the fact that 'everyone wants something for nothing these days'.

Jim wasn't so sure and, after informal talks with a few of the workers, he realised that the problems went far deeper than the issue of employee motivation. Although it was apparent that some of the production planning personnel resented the fact that their colleagues in production were the sole recipients of the pay increase, Jim did not see this as the root cause of the problems. There was no history of conflict between planning and production personnel at HBO.

One key problem centred around the role of supervision. Production supervisor Simon Groves complained that he could not be expected to supervise machine maintenance or computer program editing when he lacked the necessary technical knowledge.

'My life was pretty straightforward until this stupid redesign programme came along,' Simon complained to Bill Thompson. 'The workers would wait until the planners loaded up the computer program on their machines and then, and only then, they would press the "start" button. I knew when a problem had arisen simply by looking for an idle machine. When that happened the person on that machine had to inform me and I would call up maintenance or production planning to sort it out. I don't know what my job is anymore.'

As soon as the job redesign programme was implemented, the workers began complaining that Simon was continually pestering them to keep the machines running and refusing permission for them to undertake program editing. To make matters worse, personnel in planning and maintenance protested that they could not be expected to take responsibility for machine stoppages and breakdowns now that 'production workers were fiddling with a technology they know nothing about' (as one production planner had put it).

Bill Thompson responded by insisting that all production workers documented precise details of all the maintenance and editing work they carried out. All entries had to be verified and signed by Simon Groves. In this way, Bill reckoned that it would be possible to track down the cause of what he termed 'user-generated breakdowns'. In response, the workers argued that this was a blatant attempt by senior management to increase the formal monitoring of their work. They also argued that it would lead to individual workers being blamed whenever any machine problems or breakdowns occurred.

The trade union representative told Bill: 'If you give us more job discretion, you have to trust us. Otherwise this whole job design programme is pointless. We're doing our bit – now it's up to management to do theirs!' Bill almost lost his temper at what he saw as a questioning of his managerial competence and escorted the union representative, rather unceremoniously, out of his office.

2 hours later matters took a turn for the worse when one of the more sophisticated automatic component insertion machines broke down. This was a serious breakdown which caused thousands of pounds worth of damage to the machine's delicate component insertion mechanism and meant that the day's production target (and probably the agreed target for the week) could not be achieved.

Maintenance personnel were called to the shopfloor immediately and, after a cursory glance at the log book and at the heap of twisted metal in the machine, they accused Simon Groves of failing in his duties as a supervisor in allowing such a serious breakdown to occur. Although Simon had agreed to a minor program change on the machine an hour earlier, he doubted that this had been the cause of the accident. This led him to apportion blame to the worker at the machine who, in turn, accused production planning of supplying him with a defective computer program.

By this time, Pamela Jones had appeared on the scene and it was clear that she took great exception to the machinist's remark. 'We gave you a fully tested and proved program,' Pamela exclaimed. 'You have obviously been fiddling with it. It's nothing to do with my department anymore. If you treat our programs as if they're computer games, that's your affair.' With that, she forced herself through what had become a fairly large crowd of on-lookers and left the shopfloor.

It was this incident that had led to the workers' meeting outside the office where Bill and Jim were reviewing the job redesign programme.

'I don't see that we have any choice but to suspend the programme until this mess is sorted out,' Bill admitted to Jim once they had gone through all the programme records.

'I don't agree,' Jim retorted. 'If your supervisor wasn't so pig-headed and autocratic, everything would probably have worked itself out by now. Change is difficult and requires a change in attitude that your man obviously isn't capable of.'

Bill stood up abruptly from his chair. 'Look Jim, you can't go blaming Simon for the collapse of your half-baked scheme. He's a first-rate supervisor. If you insist on apportioning blame, take a long hard look at yourself. You haven't exactly been a model of participative management yourself! All kinds of rumours about your scheme were flying round months before your formal shopfloor briefing.'

Just as Jim, red-faced with frustration and anger, got up from his chair, the factory manager stormed into the office. 'Just what the devil is going on? There's a wrecked machine out there which maintenance refuse to fix and there's nobody working on the machines that *are* still in one piece because the workers are having some kind of Luddite's convention and plotting a work-to-rule. To top it all, Pamela Jones is threatening to resign!' he shouted.

'It's nothing for you to get worked up about,' retorted Jim. 'Just a few teething troubles. You know as well as I do that change is difficult. It simply requires a change in attitude, that's all. As for Pamela, it's probably just dawned on her that your Just-In-Time initiative will mean job losses in planning. Rumours have been flying around about redundancies for months and you've done nothing to stop them, have you?'

'Listen Jim,' seethed the factory manager. 'You know damned well that any cuts in production planning will come as a result of your initiative, not mine. How do think the company is going to cover the 6.5 per cent increase in direct labour costs without a cut in indirect labour? And don't say something facile like "the workers' pay increase will be re-couped through enhanced labour productivity" because it should be obvious, even to you, that quite the reverse is happening out there!'

Case resolution

- Outline and analyse the problems confronting HBO Computing in both the short and the long term and offer recommendations for their resolution.[3]

Notes

1. A fictitious organisation.
2. The main features of a Just-In-Time (JIT) production system are: (a) to reverse the flow of information concerning parts and sub-assemblies so that the assembly line calls off the parts it needs; (b) to reduce work-in-progress inventory to an absolute minimum; (c) to eliminate bottlenecks and minimise machine downtime; (d) to reduce changeover times that smaller batches become practical; and (e) as a consequence, the production systems handle smaller amounts of parts and materials on a more frequent basis (usually between 2 and 10 deliveries a day). For further technical details see Nellman and Smith (1981). For a critical analysis of the human and social aspects of JIT, see Corbett (1987), Corbett *et al.* (1989), Oliver (1991) and Sayer (1986).

3. For a consideration of the problems surrounding job redesign initiatives of this kind, see Bartunek and Moch (1991), Hackman and Oldham (1980), Hollway (1991), Kelly (1982), and Knights *et al.* (1985). See Burnes and Fitter (1987) for a discussion of the problematic role of the shopfloor supervisor during and after job enrichment initiatives. Finally, Armstrong (1984, 1986) examines the causes of inter-professional competition and conflict in management.

Case 11   Increasing employee commitment at Stewart and Clegg Enterprises[1]

'Ladies and gentlemen of the Board,' announced Gordon Stewart, chairman of Stewart and Clegg Enterprises. 'You know only too well that our company has been witnessing unacceptably low productivity in the past 6 months. Worker motivation and staff morale are at an all-time low. Neither personnel nor production have been able to solve the problem so I have decided to take personal action to sort out the mess. That is why you are all here today and why I have invited Dr Tony Weller to join us. I want you to listen very carefully to what he has to say.'

'Thank you Mr Chairman,' responded Tony Weller. He was a tall man in his mid-forties, wearing an expensive-looking suit and a confident smile. 'My name is Tony Weller. I have a PhD in business psychology and I am a business consultant specialising in motivation and staff commitment. Two weeks ago Mr Stewart contacted me and explained your problem. Today I will outline how my consultancy firm can solve this problem using the very latest psychological techniques.'

'The days of job enrichment and autonomous work groups as solutions to motivation problems are gone (and not before time). Job redesign has always been an extremely radical way of tackling what is basically a psychological problem. Why disrupt power relations and tried and tested working practices when a straightforward programme of attitude change management will do the job just as well (if not better)? Change language and meaning, and behaviour change will follow. I maintain that sharing a language with other people provides the subtlest and most powerful of all tools for controlling the behaviour of these other people to your advantage.'[2]

'In business language, the key to motivation and commitment in the 1990s is contained within a simple formula: Three times IM.' As he spoke, Weller pressed a key on the laptop computer in front of him and the white screen behind him came alive with bright colours and projected the words

INTERNALISED MOTIVATION
IMPRESSION MANAGEMENT
INTERNAL MARKETING

at the attentive audience.

'Work motivation is an attitude or a state of mind which can be controlled and changed by social influence,' Weller continued. 'We all desire to hold correct attitudes. Feeling right fulfils our sense of predictability and control. And we assess how correct our attitudes are by comparing them with those around us. Now let's relate this to your workforce. They want to enjoy their work and enjoy working for the company. Management's task is to help them achieve this through a process of social influence, or what we like to call "cultural management".'

'Ladies and gentlemen, the psychology of attitude change and social influence is extremely well developed in this day and age. Based on experimentation and detailed analysis of such diverse phenomena as the Moonies, wartime propaganda and brainwashing, as well as the technical skills of great salespeople and public orators, my company has devised a complete programme of commitment inducement which we can tailor to your needs. For any psychologists in the room, we employ neuro-linguistic programming techniques coupled with elements of self-justification and social learning theory, plus a sprinkling of operant conditioning.'

'Just a minute, Mr Weller,' interjected Linda Terry, the personnel director. 'Are you suggesting that Stewart and Clegg sets out to systematically brainwash its workers?'

'Our techniques are not brainwashing techniques,' replied Weller calmly. 'On the contrary, they provide the context within which feeling committed to your work is the most rational attitude to hold. Management has tried to achieve this for nearly a century in the West. Pay isn't the answer, employee of the month and job design don't work and cultural change is too sweeping (and in most cases unmanageable). All I'm suggesting is using what we know about the psychology of persuasion to help employees reinterpret their attitudes towards work and to change their work behaviour. There's nothing sinister about that. Goodness me, your sales force must use many of the techniques we employ – the "low ball" and the "foot in the door" are proven ways of gaining commitment to a sale.[3] All I'm suggesting is that you employ the same techniques inside your organisation as you do outside. We call it internal marketing – one of the three "IMs". You sell employees the idea of commitment and they are free to buy or reject that idea. Our techniques help ensure that the vast majority buy – that's all.'

'That all sounds rather calculated, even Machiavellian. As far as I'm concerned, the ethics of your whole approach seem questionable,' Terry confessed.[4]

Weller's face flushed slightly and his voice deepened as he replied in a slow and deliberate tone: 'Surely the role of organisational research is to provide management with the knowledge and techniques to help them manage the company so as to maximise the return on shareholder investment? Is it not incumbent on every executive officer to use all the knowledge and techniques at his or her disposal to achieve profitability and organisational longevity?'

'I think we should keep moral imperatives out of this, don't you?' suggested the chairman, sensing that an argument was about to break out. 'Tony, I think it may help us all if you were to give a simple example of one of your techniques.'

'I don't like to take techniques out of the context of the overall commitment inducement programme,' Tony confessed. 'But perhaps it will allay your concerns (understandable concerns I am sure) about our work if I make an exception in this case.'

'Let me give you a very simple example. Have you ever wondered why big companies are always running those "win a car" or "win a luxury holiday" competitions with a tie-break section requiring participants to explain in less than 25 or 50 words why they like a particular product? What can the company possibly get out of such personal statements? It is not, as some people think, because regulations require a so-called "skill-based" question in these types of competition. So why are these companies happy to incur the huge costs of contest after contest? Let me tell you.'

Tony paused for dramatic effect.

'The personal testimonial contest aims to get as many people as possible to go on record as liking the product. Contestants voluntarily write a sentence or two for attractive prizes that they have only a very slim chance of winning. But common sense tells them that to win they have to write in praise of a product. So tens of thousands of people testify in writing to the product's appeal and they experience a powerful psychological pull to believe what they have written. Research by social psychologists shows that people have a strong drive to appear consistent in their words, thoughts and deeds.[5] The companies simply harness that drive to their benefit. Neither Machiavelli nor ethics come into it!'

'When it comes to achieving motivation and commitment the pen truly is mightier than the sword. The power of the written word is awesome so long as it is written by the person you wish to influence.'

'Let me give you another example. We found that door-to-door sales companies specialising in high pressure, hard-selling tactics were losing sales when the new law came in allowing a "cooling-off" period. Company sales plummeted because far too many customers took advantage of their new right to cancel a sale within 14 days and receive a full refund. The new law was killing off the impulse purchasing behaviour created by high pressure sales techniques. So we advised the companies to get the customer, not the sales person, to fill out the sales agreement. The results were incredible. Sales went back up again. Why? Because people will make great efforts to live up to what they have committed themselves to in writing.'

'Now we use the committing power of public and written statements in many business organisations. As you can see from the documentation in front of you, we have had some tremendous successes. Our techniques work with sales people committing themselves to certain targets. They work with quality commitments in production. They will work for Stewart and Clegg.'

Non-verbal cues from the audience told Weller that his message had got across. He concluded with his favourite aphorism: 'The days of command and control management are surely numbered. The twenty-first century manager will be more person-centred – a manager of meaning.' [6]

The Board members, obviously impressed by Weller's presentation, sat rather nervously in their seats. The idea of deliberate and systematic social influence threw up unpleasant images of 'Big Brother' in the minds of some of them. At the same time, the idea of solving the productivity problem without disrupting the status quo was very appealing.

'Thank you very much, Tony. A most stimulating and eye-opening presentation,' announced Gordon Stewart, smiling.

After Weller had left the boardroom, the chairman confronted his fellow board members across the table. 'Do I take it that everyone is in favour of employing Tony as a consultant and seeing these ideas through?' he asked quietly.

'I would rather like to take advantage of a "cooling off" period, mister chairman,' Linda Terry requested, half in jest.

'That's okay with me Linda,' replied Stewart seriously. 'But if you are thinking of saying 'no' I will have to assume it is because you have your own blueprint for change hidden away and ready for implementation. It's time we steered this company back to full profitability. And if one or two of you are experiencing minor moral qualms, let me remind you that, through our profit-sharing scheme, you stand to almost double your salaries if and when Stewart and Clegg gets back to full profitability.'

Issues to consider

- Assess the empirical evidence supporting Weller's claims for the efficacy of social influence and attitude change techniques.[7]
- What are advantages and disadvantages of utilising such techniques at Stewart and Clegg? [8]
- On balance, if you were a member of the board would you recommend its implementation? Justify your decision.

Notes

1. A fictitious company.
2. This is a verbatim quote from Morris (1949) p. 214.
3. The efficacy of the techniques of the 'low ball' and 'foot in the door' have been demonstrated empirically by Burger and Petty (1981) and Freeman and Fraser (1966), respectively. Also see DeJong (1979).
4. For a critical consideration of the ethical issues in relation to the shaping of employee work behaviour and attitudes by higher management and management consultants, see Schein (1961) and the debate between Locke (1977, 1979) and Gray (1979). In a more positive vein, Manley (1992) presents an analysis of the ways in which some of the top UK firms deal with such ethical issues. Ethical issues are also explored in a more critical vein in the references in n. 8 below.
5. For a good overview see Eiser (1986) or McClure (1991).
6. See Bennis and Nanus (1985), Brown (1978), Gowler and Legge (1983), Pondy *et al.* (1983) and Smircich and Morgan (1982) for a critical examination of this issue.
7. Cialdini (1985), Moscovici (1985) and Zimbardo and Leippe (1991) are excellent source books for such an assessment. At a more macro-level of analysis, some of critical studies of the management of corporate culture may prove particularly insightful. See, for example, Ackroyd and Crowdy (1989), Anthony (1989), Pascale (1985) and Ray (1986).
8. While thinking about this issue, you may wish to consider who are the beneficiaries and who are the losers as far as organisational behaviour research is concerned. For a consideration of the relationship between organisational behaviour research and organisational power, see Baritz (1960), Bauman (1989), Blackler and Brown (1980), Hollway (1991), Nichols (1975), Silver (1987) and Watson (1980).

Finally, see Heller (1991) and Levy-Leboyer (1986) for a discussion of why managers tend to read and utilise poorly conducted (often inaccurate) organisational behaviour research in preference to more rigorous academic research.

Case 12   Managing motivation at Technocraft[1]

Introduction

Technocraft is a small company of 96 employees, based in the South East of England. The company manufacture high-quality sound recording equipment for use in professional recording studios throughout the media industry. The company's main products are high-quality, high-technology sound mixing consoles.

The first stage in the manufacture of these consoles involves the construction of thousands of fairly simple electronic circuit boards. These duplicate boards are then placed in pressed steel console panels and connected together, by hand, using thin insulated wires. Most of the consoles house well over 32 of these boards and the wiring up of the consoles requires considerable concentration and manual dexterity. Once completed, the average console contains approximately half a mile of wiring.

The work, which is carried out by 28 women on the shopfloor, is manual intensive and highly repetitive. The design of the jobs is such that the necessary skills (interpretation of wiring diagrams, manual dexterity and fine point soldering) can be learned in less than a day.

The problem

In recent months, George Newell, the company chairman, has become increasingly concerned about the high labour turnover on the shopfloor and the difficulties the company has been experiencing in recruiting new employees. As a result he has brought in Helen McKiernan, a management consultant, to uncover the reasons for, and provide a solution to, these problems.

'I think it's pretty straightforward,' he told her. 'Unemployment in this area is well below the national average and many of the women are living with husbands who earn a decent living wage or salary. So the money they earn is not for subsistence but for holidays and other luxuries. So they aren't particularly motivated to stay or to do a good job for Technocraft. What I'd like you to do is look around and recommend a new location for the company where workers are more likely to stick with the job.'

'That is your hypothesis, Mr Newell,' Helen replied politely. 'I'd like to cover all the angles before making any recommendations, if that's alright with you?'

'Sure,' George conceded. 'But I think you'll find I'm right on this. I've tried everything I can think of to raise morale here.'

The analysis

Helen's subsequent analysis of turnover rates tended to support George's hypothesis. Technocraft paid its workers similar rates to other companies in the area, its recruitment procedures were not unduly lax, and yet turnover was twice the regional average. This led her to focus on the nature of the wiring job itself.

Helen's visit to the shopfloor confirmed her first impression that the wirers' jobs were unskilled and repetitive. Somewhat to her surprise, none of the women expressed any dissatisfaction with the nature of their work. Indeed, it seemed that it was the routine nature of the work that enabled them to work almost without thinking. This gave them ample opportunity to talk with each other and it was clear to Helen that the informal, social side of the work was an important source of job satisfaction. A pleasant, hard-working yet playful atmosphere pervaded the wiring section. Indeed, she could not get any of the wirers to say anything negative about their work.

The next day, she returned to the shopfloor and asked a number of the wirers what they liked and disliked about the company. The answers to this question opened up a completely different line of inquiry.

Interviews revealed that, whilst the women enjoyed their work, they did not enjoy working for Technocraft. Almost everyone interviewed apportioned blame for this to the same source; namely, management. Unfortunately, no-one was prepared to be more specific despite Helen's promptings. However, over the next 2 days she was able to piece together a short history of managerial practice at Technocraft and this convinced her that George's explanation for shopfloor labour turnover was not only incorrect but actually part of the problem.

Two particular incidents led her to this conclusion.

Incident 1   Dealing with poor performance

During the hot summer the previous year, George noticed that shopfloor performance targets were often not achieved. The problem stemmed directly from the slow work rate of two recently recruited wirers, Elena and Veronica (both in their late teens). George instructed Maggie Francis, the wiring department supervisor, to bring the two women 'up to speed' within a week.

Maggie's efforts were unsuccessful and she explained to George that part of the problem related to the women's inexperience and fear of making a mistake. Indeed, it was not uncommon for some of the older, more experienced wirers to correct Veronica's work from time to time before it left the department.

'Right!' exclaimed George. 'As of next week I'm putting Robert in charge of wiring. You can take his place in packing. Look upon it as job rotation or on-the-job training. You shouldn't let the women get away with hiding shoddy work. You're too soft on them by half. Robert will sort out those two shirkers and then you can both return to normal duties.'

True to his word, George placed Robert Houlden in charge of the wiring department on the following Monday. Robert was a 'meet production targets and no nonsense' type of line manager and his domineering presence in the department was deeply resented by the wiring group. Under instruction from George, he put a stop to all informal working practices and discouraged what he regarded as excessive talking among the women. Things came to a head 2 weeks later when he officially reprimanded three of the women for returning 10 minutes late from their lunch break. Although the women explained that they had finished the morning shift 10 minutes late in order to complete the last of the batch of consoles, Robert refused to reconsider his decision as the women had failed to seek his formal approval for their actions.

Two of the women handed in their notice to George the following morning. Mistaking them for Elena and Veronica, he was only too happy to accept. It was Maggy who subsequently pointed out his mistake. 'You used a sledgehammer to crack a nut,' she told him. 'Elena and Veronica will come into line soon enough. But now you're going to lose two of the hardest working, most experienced women in the department unless you act quickly.'

'There is no way I'm admitting to those women I've made a mistake,' George snapped. 'I'm in charge here. If they get the impression that I'm going soft, they'll never let me forget it!'

Incident 2   The productivity drive

A month before Helen's arrival at Technocraft, the company had enjoyed a record-breaking month of sales. Still smarting from the previous incident, George had decided to tackle the labour turnover problem through a programme of what he called 'employee morale-boosting' and the impressive sales and productivity figures achieved that month convinced him that the programme was a success.

The record-breaking month coincided with the company's high profile at the International Sound and Vision Exhibition in Earls Court, London. The sales team at the exhibition were working wonders and the order book filled rapidly. George's main worry was whether he could deliver the goods in time and he embarked on a series of impromptu lectures around the factory in an effort to boost morale and productivity. He also erected a huge cardboard mock up of a thermometer in the centre of the factory. The red line running up through the middle of this model was extended upwards every morning by George to indicate progress towards the £1 million in completed sales target for the month.

As the end of the month neared, it looked as if this £1 million target would not be met and George persuaded reluctant employees to work overtime and on Saturday mornings in an effort to achieve the necessary rise in productivity. Throughout the last week, he was continually on the shopfloor shouting encouragement and promising that the women would be duly rewarded for their heroic efforts.

On the last Friday of the month, the £1 million target was reached – thanks to a productivity rate 43 per cent above average. George played *Rule Britannia* through the factory tannoy system and gave a rousing 'thank you' speech to the delighted employees. For the first time in the company's history, the workforce were allowed to go home early.

The following Thursday, the employees were dismayed to discover that no bonus payment was included in their wage packets. Before anyone had time to complain, George appeared on the shopfloor and began distributing tee-shirts to all the employees. These were all that remained of the 500 shirts that had been specially designed for distribution at the International Sound and Vision Exhibition. They were slim fitting tee-shirts, in pink and yellow, emblazoned with the company logo.

'I told you you'd get a reward for all your hard work!' George announced proudly.

It was when George examined the productivity figures at the end of the following week that he decided to call in a consultant. The figures revealed a 50 per cent drop in productivity since the thermometer mock up had been removed from the shopfloor. Worse still, his mail included resignation letters from three more wirers.

Case resolution[2]

- Analyse and explain the motivational problems confronting Technocraft. What should Helen do next? What should George do?

Notes

1. A pseudonym for an existing company.
2. In considering the nature of the wirers' motivation and commitment to work, see Staw (1976a) for an examination of the relationship between intrinsic and extrinsic motivation. For the influence of group membership and performance on work attitudes and performance, see Dorfman and Stephan (1984), Goodman *et al.* (1987), Salancik and Pfeffer (1978), Sheridan (1992) and Sykes and Bates (1962) as well as the usual organisational behaviour textbook sources. For the more adventurous, a general theoretical understanding of how individual attitudes relate to the social world of work may be gleaned from the writings on social identity theory by Hogg and Abrams (1991) and Tajfel and Turner (1985).The differing management styles of George Newell, Robert Houlden and Maggie Francis clearly play a part in this

case. See Fiedler and House (1988), House and Baetz (1979), Smith and Peterson (1988), Stodgill (1974) and Yetton (1984) for useful overviews of the leadership and management style literature. You may also wish to analyse the gender issues involved here. See, for example, Bem and Bem (1989), Brittan (1989), Collinson *et al.* (1990), Knights and Willmott (1986) and Pollert (1981).

Case 13 Take your mother not your lover
Margaret Collinson and David Collinson[1]

Introduction

Jenny was the first woman sales representative to be employed by Puffin Insurance,[2] a major UK insurance company. Her appointment to the salesforce in the late 1980s was something of a radical change of policy for the company and a significant break with the past. The job of sales representative in Puffin had always been considered a 'man's job'. Indeed, this stereotyped assumption has been pervasive within the UK insurance industry throughout the twentieth century.[3] Frequently it has been assumed that men are best suited for the 'breadwinner' function of sales, while women are ideally employed in the 'homemaker' support role of clerical work in the office. These assumptions have tended to inform selection practices in the industry.[4]

For many years Jenny had worked in the sales support function but she had increasingly made it known that she wished to pursue a career in sales. She had in-depth knowledge of Puffin's products and had developed very good relationships with the company's clients. As a consequence of her performance record she was promoted to sales representative after applying for a vacant position. Her appointment also reflected Puffin's recently stated public commitment to being an equal opportunities employer. It therefore provided tangible evidence that the company was making progress in that area.

Invitation to the sales convention

During her first year as a salesperson, Jenny was so successful that she sold the highest number of policies in the entire salesforce. Like many other insurance companies, it was the policy at Puffin to organise an annual sales convention, attended by the most successful salespeople, which culminated in an award ceremony for the highest achievers. Seeking to secure an invitation to this all-expenses paid annual meeting was an important motivation for all members of the Puffin sales team. The venue for this elite gathering was invariably somewhere exotic. Its sun-drenched location and the sumptuous facilities of the hotel were heavily emphasised in the company recruitment literature for salespeople and in the monthly newletters distributed to sales staff.

In this particular year, the convention was scheduled to be held in Barbados. All of the high achieving sales representatives and their wives or partners were invited to attend. This was the first convention where a woman sales representative had been invited. When Jenny received her invitation, she advised the organiser that she would be bringing her partner Brian, who worked in a lower-graded post within the sales support function. Yet Jenny's stated intentions began a chain of events which brought her into conflict, not only with the sales manager, but also with the other salesmen.

The sales manager arranged a meeting with Jenny specifically to dissuade her from inviting Brian to Barbados. He raised various objections. First, he implied that as she was unmarried it would be 'more appropriate' if she took her mother, rather than Brian, to Barbados. He explained that it might be 'threatening' for some of the wives of the sales representatives to see Jenny at the meeting with a partner who was a member of the sales support team. He explained that this relationship could give the wives 'cause for concern' in relation to their husbands. The implication was that being unmarried, Jenny might be perceived as promiscuous by the other wives. This in turn could make them concerned, for example, about her presence as the only woman on the many company-sponsored training courses for sales representatives.

Second, he stated that many of the salesmen were unhappy about a member of the sales support staff (who they considered to be junior to themselves) benefiting from a company-sponsored holiday in Barbados. Such rewards were not available to Brian in his support position and he had done nothing in his own work to warrant his presence at the convention.

Third, the sales manager explained that there were various social excursions arranged for the wives during the convention. He felt sure that, as the only man, Brian would feel very uncomfortable participating in these excursions. Fourth, the manager stated that during the prize-giving ceremony, flowers and chocolates would be presented to the wives of the highly successful sales representatives as an acknowledgement of their outstanding contribution and support throughout the year. Of course it would be inappropriate to present Brian with flowers, he elaborated. Hence the manager concluded that Brian was likely to feel excluded and isolated for most of the vacation. It was therefore unwise and indeed unfair to take him.

Jenny rejected the manager's arguments. She believed that the company was trying to influence and regulate an aspect of her personal life which had nothing to do with the management or the other salesforce members. She pointed out that the invitation was for herself and her partner and reassured the manager that there was no reason for him to be concerned since Brian would simply look after himself if he did not wish to participate in the excursions. Jenny added that she had no wish to take her mother, whom she knew would have very little in common with the people on the trip.

The sales manager was unhappy with Jenny's reply and, over the next 3 weeks, he tried on three more occasions to convince her to change her mind about taking Brian. Jenny refused to reconsider her decision.

The sales convention

When Jenny and her partner arrived in Barbados, they found the atmosphere very strained. Throughout the week's stay the salesmen were decidedly cool towards the two of them. The prize-giving ceremony for the top sales representative was held during the dinner on the final evening of the visit. Although the alcohol flowed freely after the ceremony was completed, the evening became increasingly difficult for Jenny and Brian. As the drink began to take its toll on her male colleagues, various ambiguous and suggestive remarks were made to Jenny concerning her sleeping arrangements. Brian decided that as the evening was deteriorating he would go to bed.

Having just received her award, Jenny felt that she should remain at the dinner a little longer. However, as the evening progressed she became more and more uncomfortable. The wives of the salesmen ignored her and even her boss remarked that Brian would be waiting for her to join him upstairs. When the evening finally ended Jenny was extremely upset about the immature way her colleagues had behaved.

The aftermath

On her return to work back in the UK, Jenny discovered that two of the married salesmen who had attended the Barbados convention had been accompanied by their girlfriends rather than their wives and that one of the girlfriends was a secretary in the company. Jenny presumed that the wives of these particular salesmen were unaware that they had been invited to the sales convention, or that their husbands had preferred to take their girlfriends.

Jenny became extremely annoyed and complained about the way that she had been treated both by her colleagues and her boss. The manager replied that she was over-reacting and that she was too sensitive about the situation.

He pointed out that, prior to the convention, he had offered 'constructive advice' which she had chosen to ignore.

The experience of the Barbados convention revealed to Jenny the deep-seated and contradictory character of the highly masculine assumptions embedded both in the occupational culture of the salesforce and in the management practices of Puffin Insurance.

Within 2 years of this experience, Jenny resigned from the company hoping to find a more supportive working environment elsewhere. Puffin had lost one of its most effective and knowledgeable employees.

Issues to consider

- Why did the manager take this view with his most successful sales representative?
- If you had been the sales manager, how would you have responded to the tensions between Jenny and the other sales representatives?
- What does this case suggest about sex discrimination and gender inequality in employment?[5]
- What does the case reveal about the management of men's and women's sexuality in organisations?[6]

Notes

1. Margaret Collinson is a tutor, and David Collinson is a lecturer, in organisational behaviour at Warwick Business School, University of Warwick, Coventry CV4 7AL.
2. A pseudonym for an existing company.
3. For example, see Collinson and Knights (1986).
4. See Collinson *et al.* (1990).
5. See Biggart (1989), Cockburn (1991) Knights and Willmott (1986) and Walby (1986).
6. See Collins (1983), Gutek (1985), Hearn and Parkin (1987), Hearn *et al.* (1989) and Quinn (1977).

Case 14   Greenpeace International

Greenpeace International, an international environmental pressure group, was founded in 1971. 21 years on, it has organisations in 27 countries. These national organisations fund themselves from membership fees and personal donations and donate 24 per cent of their income to Greenpeace International. The biggest single contributor is Germany, with the Netherlands second and Greenpeace (UK), with a membership of 100,000, third.

Greenpeace earned its reputation with exciting and dangerous campaigns of direct action in the 1970s and 1980s. Starting with a protest voyage into the Amchitka nuclear test zone around the Aleutian Islands, the Greenpeace direct action unit has coordinated countless demonstrations and disruptive (albeit peaceful) actions, such as sailing inflatable boats between the armed harpoons of commercial whaling ships and fleeing whales; placing volunteers between seal hunters and seal pups; sealing off toxic waste outfalls; and boarding nuclear-powered submarines. Many of these activities received world-wide media coverage and publicity, and fuelled a rapid increase in both membership and contributions.

The sinking of the organisation's flagship, *Rainbow Warrior*, by the French Secret Service in 1985 led to a further large rise in donations and the green boom of the late 1980s built up membership. Up until 1992, contributions to Greenpeace have risen every year since its foundation.

The flamboyant and often perilous direct actions undertaken by Greenpeace activists have proved extremely popular with young people and, in the view of Alison Reynolds, the administrator of the Greenpeace (UK) direct actions unit,[1] such highly publicised actions have been the key to Greenpeace's thriving membership.

However, in 1992, Greenpeace International suffered a sharp fall in public donations and membership fees, and planned to make up to 25 per cent of its 500 staff redundant. The organisation has cut its budget from $36 to $27 million and its 36-berth ship, *Gondwana*, used in its Antarctic campaigns, has been put up for sale for around $1.5 million.

Part of the reason for this decline stems from the difficulty in maintaining a high profile programme of direct actions. Earlier actions by Greenpeace activists certainly brought publicity and a heightening of public awareness, but now the organisation is finding it more and more difficult to come up with campaigns which can sustain the media interest enjoyed in the early 1980s. Indeed, many staff members of Greenpeace International fear that current actions are more publicity stunts than an embarrassment to polluters, and hence have limited political value.

Many Greenpeace officials now feel that, having raised public awareness, the organisation should concentrate on more conventional forms of lobbying within national and European parliaments and at international conferences in order to bring about change. However, many members joined because of the swashbuckling image of Greenpeace and are likely to resent any sign of the organisation being 'sucked into the establishment'. Herein lies a dilemma.

In order to finance a concerted and effective lobbying campaign, Greenpeace International requires more money from donations and membership fees. Yet, the amount of donations and fees is likely to reduce significantly if such a strategic shift occurs. But it is not just members who may react negatively. The organisation has always experienced difficulty in attracting and retaining good staff within the non-campaigning areas owing to its relatively sedate and unexciting image. Although adopting a policy of paying reasonable salaries (approximately 66 per cent of an equivalent private sector job) has gone some way to solving this problem, staff motivation is not determined by pay but by the thrill of direct action campaigning. As Alison Reynolds puts it:

> The most exciting thing is working among people who are really motivated. When there are campaign highs, the office buzzes and that's incredibly rewarding.

So, decision-makers within Greenpeace must make a difficult strategic choice. Already its place at the radical edge of the green movement is being taken by a more shadowy group called Earth First!, an import from the US, which organises itself into cells, has no leaders, and relies on cell members taking their own direct action.[2] It has an estimated 4000 members in the UK.

Case resolution

- Outline and analyse the problems confronting Greenpeace International in the short and long term, and offer recommendations for their resolution.[3]

Notes

1. As of October 1992.
2. For a description and analysis of the activities of this radical environmental pressure group, see Elsbach and Sutton (1992), and Scarce (1990). For a view from the inside, see Foreman (1990) and Manes (1990).
3. See Butler and Wilson (1989), Handy (1988), Oldham (1979) and Pierce (1992) for a consideration of how managing a voluntary organisation differs from managing a profit-making commercial enterprise. For an examination of employment and commitment as an ongoing two-way psychological contract between employer and employee, see Bowditch and Buono (1990, Chapter 3), Etzioni (1961), Schein (1980, Chapters 3 and 5) and Scott (1972).

PART 2

ANALYSING GROUP BEHAVIOUR IN ORGANISATIONS

CHAPTER 4

Interpersonal relations and group decision-making

Introduction

Interest in interpersonal relations and group dynamics within organisations was awakened by the Hawthorne studies carried out at the Western Electric Company's Hawthorne plant in Chicago during the 1920s and 1930s (Roethlisberger and Dickson, 1964). Following this work, the scientific management view of people as socially isolated and economically rational was gradually replaced by the belief that people are social animals who gain a sense of identity through group membership and interpersonal relationships. Management attention turned on the group rather than the individual and thousands of empirical studies were carried out examining the ways in which leadership and management behaviour can affect group morale and cohesion, and how such group dynamics relate to productivity.

But, as Johnson and Gill (1993) observe:

> in accomplishing this shift away from an analysis of physiological conditions, incentive schemes, work study, etc., to one that concentrated on individuals and interpersonal relations, likely technological, financial and socio–economic constraints bearing on management practice were discounted – an orientation Bennis (1959: 260) subsequently labelled as 'people without organisations' (p. 54).

Social psychology research has tended to follow this trend towards isolating social behaviour from its broader context. To be sure, social psychology has helped us understand the powerful influences that social group membership can have on the way we think and behave as individuals. Social psychologists have also made an important contribution to our understanding of the process of organising (see, for example, Hosking and Morley, 1992).

But it is surely a mistake to see the analysis of interpersonal and intra-group relations as the sole prerogative of social psychology in the way most OB textbook writers seem to do. Whilst it is true that much of organisational psychology has been dependent on the meso-level of analysis offered by social psychology for its theoretical resources, Thompson and McHugh (1990) argue:

> What social psychology actually does is continually to reproduce and repackage the tensions between the dominant competing assumptions about human behaviour. The end product of this process is generally to reinforce the understanding of social problems as residing in the *deficiencies* of individuals (p. 281).

Hence, both the human relations school of management spawned by the Hawthorne studies, and a lot of post-war Anglo–American social psychologists, share an uncritical, often universalistic view of behaviour in organisations. Coupled to this view is the somewhat élitist notion that managers could and should be the disseminators of social and group harmony in organisations.

A more critical analysis of interpersonal relations and group decision-making in organisations necessitates analysis from both a critical social psychological and a broader sociological perspective. The seven cases in this chapter can, perhaps should, be analysed from both these perspectives (i.e. at the meso- and the macro- levels of analysis).

For example, Cases 15 and 16 focus on highly questionable decisions made by groups of professional engineers and managers. Whilst 'groupthink' (Janis, 1972, 1982) and other phenomena of intra-group interaction offer some useful insights into these events, a broader, more sociological level of analysis is also needed to place the case materials in their socio–economic context.

In a more light-hearted vein, Case 17 takes a look at the group dynamics within an orchestra. The case asks two basic questions, namely: is the role of the conductor redundant; and, what lessons for the management of expert groups can be drawn out from the case? The next case – Case 18 – was written by Les Prince, a critical social psychologist. Whilst based on real events, the dialogue in this case is what one might call a creative reconstruction. The issues raised here centre on the problems associated with achieving and sustaining democracy, even isocracy, within a social group. I trust the implications for wider organisational issues are obvious.

Case 19 describes one of the all-time classic studies in social psychology. The implications of the basic findings of these studies for the study and management of organisational behaviour are both profound and disturbing. The person behind these highly controversial studies, Stanley Milgram, believed that a conventional social psychological viewpoint was necessary, but ultimately insufficient, to explain fully the pattern of results he obtained. Personally, I find it hard to credit that the vast majority of OB texts make no reference whatsoever to his work.

Case 20 again explores inter-personal relations in its broader context – this time within the context of top-down organisational change. The case illustrates how members of different groups perceive the same reality in quite different ways.

Finally, Case 21 tells the story of how an organisation came to purchase an expensive management information system without really knowing why or what it was for. In conducting my own research on new technology, I have been amazed at the number of organisations that have wasted considerable sums of money on technology they do not need. Important ideological issues are raised in this case.

Case 15   The rise and fall of the Chevrolet Corvair

Introduction

In 1959, General Motors (GM) launched the Chevrolet Corvair on the American market. The car represented a radical departure from conventional US automobile design. Conceived along the lines of the Porsche sports car, the Corvair was powered by an all-aluminium, air-cooled engine placed in the rear of the chassis and supported by an independent swing-axle suspension system. The car was designed and promoted as a sports car to appeal to young drivers.

Unfortunately, this high performance car proved to be directionally unstable in turns at high speed so that the rear wheels tend to tuck underneath the car and encourage it to flip over. By 1962, a number of Corvair drivers (including the sons of two GM executives) had been involved in fatal accidents of this kind and GM's legal department was inundated with million dollar lawsuits.

However, subsequent investigations by the American consumer watchdog, Ralph Nader, revealed that senior GM management were aware that the car was unsafe well before its launch in 1959.

The decision to launch

In 1957, Frank Winchell, a GM engineer at Chevrolet, drove one of the first Corvair prototypes on the GM test track in Michigan and was lucky to escape injury when the car flipped over during a high-speed turn.[1] Another GM engineer, Albert Roller, tested the car and declared it unsafe. He also informed the head of Pontiac's advanced engineering department that in his previous job as engineer at Mercedes-Benz, similarly designed rear-engine, swing-axle cars had been tested and had been declared too unsafe to build.

As additional tests were carried out on Corvair prototypes, a number of high-ranking GM engineers (including the vice-president of engineering) urged top management to postpone the launch of the Corvair at least until the suspension could be redesigned. However, Chevrolet's general manager, Ed Cole, and a number of his engineering colleagues, were excited by the idea of Chevrolet building America's first modern, rear-engined car and were convinced that the safety risks of the swing-axle suspension were minimal despite growing evidence to the contrary.

As GM manager, John De Lorean recalls:

> Cole was a strong product voice and a top salesman in company affairs. In addition, the car, as he proposed it, would cost less to build than the same car with a conventional rear suspension. Management not only went along with Cole, it also told the dissenters in effect to 'stop these objections and get on the team, or you can find someplace else to work.' The ill-fated Corvair was launched in the fall of 1959.[2]

Aftermath of the decision

When Bunkie Knudsen took over as head of Chevrolet in 1961, he applied for corporate authorisation to install a stabilising bar in the rear of the Corvair to counteract the car's tendency to flip over. He estimated the cost of the modification to be $15 a car. His request was turned down by senior GM management on financial grounds.

But Knudsen then threatened to resign from GM and senior management relented. Even so, it wasn't until 1964 that the Corvair was fitted with a stabilising bar as standard. The following year, a redesigned Corvair was released with a newer, safer independent suspension designed by Frank Winchell (the engineer who had first experienced the 'Corvair flip'). Yet, by this time, sales of the Corvair had collapsed despite GM's strong defence of the car's safety.

In 1969, 10 years after its original launch, the last Corvair was driven off the Chevrolet production line.

In the interim, GM executives took two additional steps to minimise the damage to the company's reputation caused by the Corvair launch decision. First, in the face of the bad publicity following the publication of Ralph Nader's hard-hitting exposé – *Unsafe At Any Price*[3] – GM hired detectives to follow the author with the intention of discrediting him as an anti-Semite and a homosexual. The second decision was to order the destruction of the 19 boxes of microfilmed Corvair owner complaints.

Both actions proved to be counter-productive. The company's decision to hire a former FBI agent in an effort to substantiate completely false rumours about Nader was leaked to the US national newspapers. The publication of the story increased Nader's public profile as a champion of the US consumer and brought more damaging publicity to the company. Also, Senator Ribicoff's Senate Committee on Auto Safety read the newspaper reports and promptly ordered an investigation of GM. Company president, James Roche, was hauled up before the Committee and forced to apologise. The Senator was not impressed. He told Roche: 'Everyone is so outraged that a great corporation was out to clobber a guy because he wrote critically about them.'[4] In response, the GM chairman sacked several executives who were blamed in the media for the incident.

To make matters worse, in the spring of 1971, the 19 (supposedly destroyed) boxes of microfilm turned up in the possession of a Detroit junk dealer who offered to sell the films back to GM for $20,000. Under directions from GM's top management, the customer relations department purchased and then immediately destroyed the films.

Top management, meanwhile, ordered a tightening up of the company's scrapping procedures.

Issue to consider

- Analyse and explain the behaviour of GM's senior management in this case.[5]

Notes

1. Described in Cray (1980). Cray's book offers a comprehensive picture of GM's strong corporate culture. Compare this with Martin and Siehl's (1983) more critical analysis of GM's culture.
2. Quoted in Wright (1979), p. 98.
3. Nader (1972).
4. Quoted in Keller (1989), p. 49.
5. Useful insights into GM can be gleaned from Keller (1989), Levin (1989), Nader (1972), and Wright (1979). For an analysis of senior management behaviour in the US automobile industry, see Clinard (1983, 1990), Eastman (1984), Ermann and Lundman (1982) and Cases 16 and 27 (this volume). For a more psychological perspective see Bazerman *et al.* (1984), Ewing (1983), Janis (1972, 1982), Kohn and Schooler (1983), Staw and Fox (1977), and Whyte (1986, 1989).

Case 16   Death in the Ford Motor Company balance sheet

Introduction

In August 1970, the Ford Motor Company launched its latest car – the Pinto – onto the US market. In a significant move for the company, brought about by fierce competition from smaller, cheaper cars from Japan and Europe, the design of this car was rigidly governed by what Ford engineers termed 'the limits of 2000'. In other words, the Pinto must weigh less than 2000 pounds and cost less than $2000. Sales were buoyant and Ford looked to have a winning product. Nearly 2 million Pintos were sold within 2 years of its launch.

Yet, less than 7 years later, Dr Leslie Ball – former safety chief for the NASA manned space programme and founder of the International Society of Reliability Engineers – publicly declared that 'the release to production of the Pinto was the most reprehensible decision in the history of American engineering.'[1]

So, what went wrong?

The Ford Pinto: unsafe at any speed?

In May 1972, Richard Grimshaw, aged 13, was offered a lift in one of these new Ford Pintos by a friend of his family. Unfortunately, the car stalled on Interstate Route 15 and was hit from behind by another vehicle. Although this vehicle was travelling at only 35 miles an hour, the impact ruptured the Pinto's petrol tank. The escaping fumes mixed with the air in the passenger compartment, a spark ignited the mixture and the Pinto was enveloped in flames. The driver was burned to death and Grimshaw suffered 90 per cent burns and, despite a total of 52 surgical operations, the loss of his nose, one ear and four fingers.

5 years later, Grimshaw's law suit against the Ford Motor Company began. His lawyers sought punitive damages against the company by contending that Ford's decision to locate the Pinto's fuel tank only 7 inches behind the rear bumper showed a 'conscious and wilful' disregard for the safety of people

who bought the car. On 11 February 1978, the jury reached its verdict and ordered Ford to pay Grimshaw $66 million in punitive damages.

The verdict was secured following the damning testimony of a senior Ford designer and the presentation in court of a confidential seven page internal company report from Ford's Environmental and Safety Engineering Division. Both these focused attention on the fact that Ford management were aware of the dangers inherent in the design and location of the Pinto's fuel tank, and yet took no action to remove or minimise these dangers.

The case against Ford

Harley F. Copp, senior design engineer with Ford for 20 years, now retired, told the Santa Anna Superior Court that the company had held numerous meetings to discuss the type of fuel tank to be used in the Pinto. Copp argued for a saddle-style tank of the kind used in the successful Capri range. This type of tank is located either side of the prop shaft and is widely regarded as the safest design possible in a small car. Copp told Ford's senior management that Ford Capris with saddle-type tanks had come through crash tests successfully. The following day, Capris with modified tanks placed, like the Pinto's, under the floor and behind the rear axle, were crash tested and leaked petrol in every case.

However, Copp testified that Ford's 'corporate management' insisted that the fuel tank be located 7 inches behind the rear bumper as this would provide a cost saving of approximately $9 dollars per car when compared with the more expensive saddle-tank design. The 'limits of 2000' could not be transgressed and the Pinto kept the rear tank design. Ford executives argued that a $9 increase could price a compact car like the Pinto out its market, as could a marginal reduction in sales features such as the size of the boot. As one Ford engineer told the US magazine, *Mother Jones*: 'Do you realise that if we put a Capri-type tank in the Pinto you could only get one set of golf clubs in there?'[12]

Copp then told the court that the hazards presented by the design and positioning of the Pinto's fuel tank had been investigated by several independent organisations. A study in 1973 by the University of Miami's Accident Analysis Unit, examining 4 years of car crashes, had singled out the Pinto for comment. Under the heading 'Gas Tank Integrity/Protection (Ford Pinto)', the Unit observed:

'In each case the gas tank was buckled and gas spewed out. In each case the interior of the vehicle was totally gutted by the ensuing fire. It is our opinion that three such conflagrations (all experienced by one rental company in a six month period) demonstrates a clear and present safety hazard to all Pinto owners.'

The most damning evidence against the Ford Motor Company was the report entitled 'Fatalities associated with crash-induced fuel leakages and fires', written by the company's own Environmental and Safety Engineering Division (ESED).

By mid-1972, public concern about the safety of the Pinto prompted political action. US Congress set about drafting a set of tougher fuel tank safety standards to prevent tank explosion after an accident. Whilst these proposals were being debated, Ford senior management commissioned the confidential ESED report. On p. 5 of the report, the authors outline their analysis of the price of building fuel tank safety into Ford vehicles against the expected benefit derived from saving Ford owners from death or injury by burning.

The analysis produced the following figures:

Benefits:
Savings – 180 burn deaths, 180 serious burn injuries, 2100 burned vehicles
Unit cost: $200,000 per death, $67,000 per injury, $700 per vehicle
Total benefit: (180 x $200,000) + (180 x £67,000) + (2100 × $700) = £49.5 million

Costs:
Sales – 11 million cars, 1.5 million light trucks
Unit cost – $11 per car, $11 per truck
Total cost – (11,000,000 × $11) + (1,500,000 × $11) = $137.5 million

In drawing up these figures, Ford's experts doubted the US government's statistics on fatalities from crash-induced fuel leaks and fires which estimated that between 2000 and 3500 such deaths occurred every year. Ford's research suggested that most of the deaths in 'fire-accompanied crashes' were due to injuries caused by the initial crash impact rather than by the flames. They concluded that a figure between 600 and 700 fire deaths a year 'is probably more appropriate'.

The report pointed out that the chance of petrol spilling out from a ruptured tank was significantly greater when a car was hit from behind than from the front, side or after being rolled over. Nonetheless, Ford's engineers based their calculations of the sums at stake (if new fuel tank safety standards being proposed by Congress were adopted) on the less common hazard of 'static roll-over'. This reduced the number of burn deaths per year to 180.

Ford's calculations of the value of a human life were based on a 1972 study by the National Highway Traffic Safety Administration, which sought to establish the cash cost of death in a car crash by breaking down and valuing 10 separate components, including future productivity losses, insurance administration, losses in income tax revenue, and so forth. The sum of $10,000 was established for 'victim's pain and suffering'. The overall cost to society came to $200,000. Ford also allowed $67,000 for non-fatal burn injuries.

In addition to their conservative estimate of 180 burn deaths a year, Ford safety engineers reckoned that 180 passengers a year would survive such accidents with severe burns. Adding an allowance for the cost of damaged cars, the company put the total benefit of a design change at just under $50 million. In the ESED report, this was set against the $137 million costs associated with undertaking fuel tank design modifications to its cars and light trucks.

Ford safety engineers observed that the cost to the Ford Motor Company was almost three times greater than the benefits to society 'even using a number of highly favourable benefit assumptions'. The report concluded by stating that the ESED could not envisage any development which 'would make compliance with the roll-over requirement cost effective'.

No changes were made to the fuel tanks on any Ford vehicle as a result of the ESED report. It wasn't until September 1976 (in response to revised rear-impact standards imposed by the US government) that the Ford Motor Company moved the Pinto fuel tank to a safer position under the car.

Postscript

Responding to the Grimshaw case verdict, a spokesperson for Ford stated that the company would fight against 'this unreasonable and unwarranted award'. Immediately after the court hearing, the company formally appealed against the jury's decision.

Subsequently, on 7 April 1978, a Santa Ann Superior Court judge ordered the $66 million punitive damages originally awarded by the jury to be reduced to $3.3 million. The judge ruled that the ratio of punitive to actual damages was excessive.

Issues to consider

- Analyse and explain the decision-making process undertaken by the engineers in Ford's Environmental and Safety Engineering Division (ESED).
- To what extent does this case reveal the Ford Motor Company of the time to be a socio-pathic organisation?[3]
- What are the roots of organisational socio-pathology?[4]

Notes

1. Quoted in *Sunday Times*, 12 February 1978, p. 4.
2. *Sunday Times*, 12 February 1978, p. 5.

3. See Daneke (1985) for a theoretical discussion of organisational socio-pathology. The work of Clinard (1990, Chapter 2), Cullen *et al.* (1987), Eastman (1984), Farberman (1975) and Reppy (1979) places the Pinto case in the historical context of widespread socio-pathic and criminal activities within the automobile industry.
4. For an argument that the roots are psychological, see Kets de Vries (1989), Kets de Vries and Miller (1984a), Olins (1978) and Staw and Fox (1977). On the role of group processes, see Biggart and Hamilton (1984), Janis (1972), Kaplan (1987), Larson and Christensen (1993), Pryor and Ostrum (1987) and Whyte (1989). For the impact of organisational structure and culture, see Acar and Aupperle (1984), Baucus and Near (1991), Clinard (1983), Colesman (1982), Hill *et al.* (1992), Kets de Vries and Miller (1984b), Merton (1938; 1940), Salancik (1977) and Whyte (1956).

    The role of broader socio–economic, legal and cultural forces is considered in Clinard (1990), Lane (1991), Olson (1983), Saul (1981), Schneider and Dunbar (1992), Stone (1975) and Vaughan (1983).

Case 17   Take it away, maestro!

Introduction

Not for the first time, the rehearsal ended in uproar. As on previous occasions, the musicians in the Organisation Theorists' Symphony Orchestra[1] were at loggerheads with their guest conductor.

'I'm not convinced we need a conductor at all,' shouted Jim Hansard (trumpet). Turning to the person in question, he continued: 'Why on earth do you continue to conduct past the first few beats of the march we've been playing? The percussionists' rhythm combined with the tuba and the French horns provide a clear rhythmic core to the piece. Our orchestra has an inner pulse and rhythm and we don't need some idiot with a stick to remind us of it.'

'I suppose you would recommend applying organisation theory to the question of conducting an orchestra,' retorted Tim Peters the conductor, somewhat taken aback by the trumpeter's harsh words.

'I see no reason why not,' exclaimed Hansard.

'Very well then,' Peters conceded. 'According to conventional theory, a symphony orchestra of over 100 players should have several group vice-president conductors and perhaps a half-dozen divisional directors. In this orchestra we have a flat structure which many a business organisation would envy.'

'With respect Tim, that shows how conventional your thinking is,' suggested David Silver (violin). 'Each of us is a highly skilled specialist –

you can't force us to play. Our motivation comes from a love of music and the thrill of playing with like-minded others. Not only that, the system of authority in an orchestra is more than a pattern of static roles and statuses. It's a network of interacting people each transmitting information to the other, sifting their transactions through an evaluative screen of standards and sanctioned ways of doing things. If anyone is conducting the orchestra, I suppose it is the composer of the score.'

'I believe that my role, at the very least, is to identify and correct errors and increase the scope of collaborative consensus,' Peters replied.

Hilary Knights (tuba) could not agree: 'If that's so, why do you spend whole concerts standing on a rostrum waving a baton. We're experts and you should trust us to come in at the right time and in the right place. To be honest, I'm not sure why you attend concerts at all. Your role seems entirely superfluous after rehearsals are completed. To the "inner pulse" Jim referred to, one should add "inner autonomy". We can plot our own way through a complex musical composition, but the modern-day conductor insists on doing it him- or (more uncommonly) herself by framing and defining the musical and social reality of the orchestral players.'

'I agree,' interrupted Harry Jones (percussion). 'A deskilling process is evident here. Early conductors never assumed ensemble intonation as their responsibility. These conductors were usually the composer or sometimes a member of the orchestra. They would guide and facilitate the expertise of the ensemble. They didn't stand on a rostrum – they didn't control.'

'There is certainly an inherent danger in abdicating control to a power outside the self,' opined Gareth Morton (harp). 'The presence of a well-defined leader will often decrease the ability of the group to experiment and consider alternative course of action. Different musicians read the same musical score differently – so experimentation is possible in classical music. If (to distort Muktananada) "there is a great mirror in the conductors' eyes in which everything is reflected", then what Tim's eyes reflect is our sense of diminishing autonomy and learned helplessness.'[2]

'These days the idea of a symphony orchestra without a conductor is inconceivable to most people,' he continued. 'When I've told people about experiments with leaderless orchestras in the USSR in the late 1920s (and far more recently in the Netherlands), their usual reaction is disbelief and the question: how do the musicians know when to start?'

'You credit me with far too much power, Gareth,' said Peters. 'My authority as conductor is not situationally approved (as this discussion proves!). It is socially created and maintained. As a collective body of musicians you have considerable expertise. I cannot play your instruments as well as you. You have an additional expertise in assessing my interpretive and communicative powers. And, if you so wish, you can remove me from the podium. I cannot make you play. But you make me step down. Hence, you have power over me.'

'As for the conservatism of symphony orchestras,' he continued, 'it is true that (conductorless) chamber orchestras can boast a far longer legacy of musical compositions. These ensembles improve and mature as they accept the problems and challenges of the old and the new. Many are active in commissioning new works. Chamber ensembles are open, receptive and accepting. Perhaps all these attributes must be incorporated into symphony orchestras. Successful musical (and conducting) techniques can and do transcend the boundaries between different ensembles.'

'You're missing the point, Tim,' replied Gibson Cooper (double bass). 'The problem is not one of leadership style or technique, but one of a structural imbalance of power and the institutionalisation of alienation.'

'Well I'm glad it's not all my fault,' the conductor confessed, flippantly. 'Same time next week, everyone?'

Issues to consider

- Critically assess the different views expressed in this case.
- What are the implications of this case for the management of team-based skilled work?[3]
- Does leadership necessarily entail an emotional and/or intellectual deskilling of followers? [4]
- Peter Drucker (1988) maintains that the typical large business of the early twentyfirst century will have a structure and management problems and concerns which resemble those of the symphony orchestra. What are likely to be the main problems confronting management attempting such a transition?

Notes

1. A fictitious organisation. This case was inspired by the thoughts of the conductor Dennis Johnson and the research of R.R. Faulkner (1973).
2. Muktananada (1980) actually states: 'There is a great mirror in the Guru's eyes in which everything is reflected' (p. 34).
3. In addition to conventional management textbook sources, see Hollander (1964), Hosking and Morley (1992), Raelin (1986) and Vroom and Jago (1988).
4. This is the view taken by Gemmill and Oakley (1992). Some support for this view is offered by Maslow (1971), Milgram (1974), Smircich and Morgan (1982), and Ulman and Abse (1983). For a psychoanalytic view, see Jacques (1955), Pedigo and Singer (1982), and Smith and Berg (1987). Also see Cases 2 and 25 (this volume).

Case 18   Crisis Line
Les Prince[1]

Introduction

Crisis Line is a telephone help line service for victims of rape and sexual abuse which operates in Sewerham, a large, previously highly industrialised, city in the Midlands. It was set up in 1975, by a group of graduates from the local university, as an offshoot of the Sewerham Women's Group (SWG). From the outset it was a consciously political project, and its founders saw it not only as a service to the women of Sewerham, but also as a practical and theoretical contribution to the Women Against Rape Movement (WAR).

It was initially supported wholly by SWG, who provided and raised its financial base; supplied volunteers for telephone duty and counselling; and arranged premises.

In the early days it often operated out of individual members' homes, but later, with the support of the Gay Community Centre, where it stayed until finding its own offices in 1980.

Almost as soon as Crisis Line was set up it was inundated with calls and referrals from other agencies. It quickly became an important part of the social and counselling services of the city, performing important functions that other agencies, such as the Samaritans, were less well equipped to supply. It also became obvious, fairly rapidly, that its precarious financial base would not be able to support it for long. As a consequence, the members of the Crisis Line Support Group, in effect its policy forum, agreed to approach the local Social Services and Council for Voluntary Organisations, with a view to arranging regular grant aid and other material support. Both responded with considerable interest, and although there was always some doubt about how long the support would last, Crisis Line began to receive regular financial support from about 1978 onwards. When the local City Council set up a Women's Committee in 1980, it seemed that the future of Crisis Line's support was secure.

But money always remained a problem, and Crisis Line was never able to survive for very long without voluntary donations. This became a severe problem in the mid-1980s when local authorities came under considerable pressure from central government to reduce expenditure. Like many other services Crisis Line first had its grant frozen, and then effectively cut. Nevertheless the service continued and has survived until the present day.

Philosophy of organising

Crisis Line's relationship with the local Council, and Social Services in particular, was always to some extent ambiguous. Members of the group worried from the outset whether accepting money from the Council would compromise Crisis Line's autonomy. They were particularly concerned that Council officers and members would attempt to force the group to abandon its own ideas about organising in favour of a traditional hierarchical committee structure. This issue was of considerable importance to them.

Crisis Line was a consciously feminist initiative, and the support group of volunteers and workers were ideologically committed to finding ways of maintaining the service without recourse to "leaders", "managers", "committees", and all the other trappings of power and status. The members were always acutely sensitive to any process or incident which appeared to compromise their attempts to be, and remain, "leaderless". This resulted in numerous arguments, both within the group, and between the group and local Council representatives, particularly when the latter insisted on dealing only with "the Head of Project" or her representative.

It was with considerable difficulty that they were able to maintain sufficient independence to organise in the way that they wished to. But they succeeded to the extent that they had no formal titles, no differentials of pay, and in the way that all members of the support group were, theoretically, given an equal hearing at policy meetings. When asked, the members of the support group always maintained, although sometimes defensively, that Crisis Line was completely democratic and without leaders.

Current organisation

It became clear soon after Crisis Line began to function fully that it could not depend forever on casual volunteers. There were two main reasons: first, the workload of cases was considerable, and second, the need to liaise regularly with the City Council and other bodies. These made it almost impossible for volunteers, who all had commitments in addition to Crisis Line, to cope with all the jobs necessary to the survival and functioning of the service, particularly within recurrent deadlines.

In 1980 it was decided that Crisis Line would need to recruit a full-time worker. By 1985 this had increased to three. These undertook the routine day-to-day jobs on behalf of the service, including correspondence, paying the bills, and so on.

Nevertheless, Crisis Line, particularly the telephone lines, continued to depend heavily on volunteers, who undertook tasks on a rota system. This worked well. Regular volunteers filled timetable slots on a weekly basis, and more casual helpers offered support and filled in where regulars were not available. The service also offered training in telephone counselling for those who intended to contribute on a regular basis.

Members of Crisis Line were, however, insistent on one point. The full-time workers were recruited to fulfil very particular, and essential, functions for the project. But they were not, therefore, given any greater status *within* the project than even the most casual of volunteers.

In essentials the service was run by the monthly meeting at which policy was established and important decisions taken. Anyone connected with the service, full-time workers and volunteers alike, was entitled to attend. Theoretically at least, no-one who attended these meetings was more important than anyone else, and there were strenuous attempts to ensure that everyone who wanted to speak was given a hearing, and treated equally with others. But it was always at these meetings that tensions within the project became evident.

Crisis within Crisis Line

Things came to a head during a particularly stormy monthly meeting. Carole Lambert and Jayne Carter, two of the three full-time workers, were present. The third, Linda Bartlett, was on holiday, but it was to some extent her actions which precipitated the dispute.

She had been involved in some very difficult negotiations with the City Council over their recurrent grant. Council officers had made it clear that the grant was under threat of complete withdrawal unless Crisis Line accepted new conditions. These included the establishment of a Service Level Agreement with the Council; the adoption of the Council's recruitment policy wholesale; and the toning down of the political element of Crisis Line's work. The Council was especially concerned that Crisis Line had been publicly critical recently, particularly with regard to the poor provision of street lighting in areas of the city which were known to be dangerous to women walking alone. Through the local press they had deprecated the Council's record on this and similar issues.

Linda had been faced with a difficult set of choices. The Council had pressed for the new agreements to be concluded, but the next monthly meeting was not due for another three and a half weeks. In the end she consulted Carole and Jayne, the other full-time workers, and signed the new agreements on behalf of the project without waiting for the next meeting.

Some of the volunteers, especially those who had been with Crisis Line for a long time, were incensed. Among these Christine Oliver was most angry, and it was around her that the 'opposition' clustered. She had been involved with Crisis Line since shortly after it had been established. She had also been the full-time worker for 6 months in 1982.

At first she had been too angry to speak at the meeting, but she listened to the explanations from Carole and Jayne with unconcealed contempt. Finally she broke her silence:

'You have no *right* to make decisions on behalf of Crisis Line without asking the meeting. That power is not part of your job. You are employed *by us* to attend to routine matters.

You are not *allowed* to run things as if this were your own private business!'

Uproar ensued. The meeting became extremely noisy. People were shouting at each other. Accusations were swapped. And several people left the meeting in obvious distress. The whole affair became extremely bad tempered.

Carole and Jayne tried to reply, but it was clear that they felt uncomfortable. Neither of them, in point of fact, had endorsed Linda's actions. They had discussed the issues with her, but at no point did she suggest that she should sign anything. As far as they had been concerned she had simply wanted to clarify what was happening. But now that her actions were under attack they felt unclear about their responses.

On the one hand they both accepted the criticisms that Christine was making. Like everyone else involved with Crisis Line they believed that open democracy was essential. On the other hand they could understand the dilemma that the Council had created. Decisions had to be made quickly, and both thought, like Linda, that they had sufficient knowledge and experience to make them, independently if need be. But the argument began to raise other issues and concerns.

By attacking Linda's actions, Christine also appeared to be attacking Linda. Carole and Jayne, by association, also felt under personal attack. For several months the three of them had felt that they were being given insufficient credit for intelligence and initiative within the project, and consequently their morale was particularly shaky. They also felt that their opinions were not treated seriously enough. From their point of view it was they who dealt on a regular basis with other agencies; they who were up to date on the latest information and legislation; in short they who knew what was going on. But at the monthly meetings their comments were frequently ignored, and in their view decisions were often made on the basis of comparative ignorance. Taken together it had become an extremely frustrating set of circumstances.

From Christine's point of view the situation appeared quite different. To some extent she felt proprietorial towards Crisis Line, and was determined that the ideals upon which it was based should not be compromised. The three full-time workers, however, appeared to be adopting the stance of 'experts' within the project, whose decisions and conclusions should be accepted without question. More than once she thought that she had detected some contempt from them for the volunteers, especially the newer and more casual ones.

More worryingly, she had also noticed a tendency for the monthly meeting to 'rubber stamp' more and more of the full-time workers' actions and decisions. Meetings had therefore become boring, and as a consequence fewer and fewer volunteers attended. At present probably less than a third attended regularly, and some of those quite openly treated it simply as a social event.

This turn of events, she considered, had to be challenged, otherwise Crisis Line might end up like any other hierarchically structured organisation. As far as she was concerned this was too much of a deviation from the ideological basis of the project. And she was not alone in thinking so, as the scale of the argument at the meeting demonstrated.

There were others, however, who couldn't understand what the fuss was about. For the most part these were the newer and more casual helpers. One of these approached Christine on the way out from the meeting. She spoke for several when she asked:

'What was all *that* about? Why all the anger and aggression?'

Case resolution

- Outline and analyse the problems facing Crisis Line in the short and long term and offer recommendations for their resolution.[2]

Notes

1. Les Prince is a lecturer in organisational behaviour at the Institute of Local Government Studies, Birmingham University, Birmingham B15 2TT. The case is based on real events, although pseudonyms are used throughout.
2. For an analysis of the problems associated with achieving and sustaining democracy or isocracy in groups and organisations, see Brown and Hosking (1984), Herbst (1976), Mechanic (1962), Paton (1978; 1983) and Pierce (1992). See also Robert Michels' (1949) classic analysis of the 'iron law of oligarchy'.

Case 19   Obedience to authority

Introduction

It is some 30 years since the social psychologist Stanley Milgram began his study of the dynamics of obedience to authority.[1] Yet the prominent position of his work in psychology has not diminished during this time. Psychologist Thomas Blass attributes the continuing salience of the series of obedience studies to a number of its distinctive features.[2]

1. The enormity of the basic findings – that 64 per cent of a sample of average American adult men were willing to punish another person with increasingly higher voltages of electric shock when ordered to do so by an experimenter who possessed no coercive power to enforce his orders.
2. The studies represent one of the largest integrated research programmes every conducted in social psychology (Milgram conducted over 20 variations of his basic experimental design and used over 1000 subjects).
3. The studies generated intense debate about the ethics of psychological research.
4. Milgram's studies have fundamental and far-reaching implications for our understanding of human behaviour and, more particularly, the extent to which a person's behaviour is determined by particular situational and organisational factors.

The basic experimental design of Milgram's studies

A typical male subject volunteering to take part in Milgram's early experiments at Yale University in 1963 is greeted by a stern-looking experimenter in a white coat. He finds that another subject has already arrived. The experimenter informs the two men that they are to take part in an experiment to discover the effect of punishment on learning and verbal memory. One subject will be the 'teacher', the other the 'learner' during the session. The allocation of the respective roles is decided by lottery.

The two men are told that the teacher is to read pairs of words to the learner and then test the learner's memory by giving the first word of each pair and asking him to supply the second word. Incorrect answers are punished by an electric shock administered by the teacher by depressing one of 30 switches located on a 'shock generator' in front of him. These switches are arranged in a row and are labelled according to the voltage of electricity they transmit to an electrode strapped to the learner's arm. The first switch is labelled 15 volts, the second 30 volts, the third 45 volts and so one. The final switch is labelled 450 volts. There are also a number of descriptive labels on the switch panel. For example, 'Slight Shock' describes the 15–60 volt range, 'Very Strong Shock' describes the 195–240 volt ranges, 'Danger: Severe Shock' the 375–420 volt range; the 435 to 450 volt range is labelled 'XXX'.

The experimenter tells the teacher that he is to punish the learner's first recall error with an electric shock of 15 volts. The second error is to be punished by a shock of 30 volts, and so on until the learner has correctly memorised the list of word pairs.

Before the session begins, the learner is strapped to a chair, his arm is treated with an electrically conductive paste to which an electrode is then attached. He mentions to the experimenter and the learner that he has a mild heart condition. He is assured that the shocks, although painful, will not result in any permanent tissue damage.

Then the teacher is escorted to an adjacent room where the shock generator is situated. The experiment begins. The experimenter sits a few yards behind the teacher reminding him that every error must be punished by increasingly severe electric shocks.

During a typical session the learner makes an error in approximately three out of four responses and the teacher steadily increases the shock level. At 75 volts the teacher hears the learner moan 'ugh'. At 150 volts the learner calls out: 'Ugh! Experimenter, get me out of here. I told you I had heart trouble. My heart's starting to bother me now. Get me out of here, please. My heart's starting to bother me. I refuse to go on. Let me out!'

The experimenter ignores these pleas and urges the teacher to continue. At 210 volts, the learner demands to be let out. Still the experimenter urges the teacher to continue until all the word pairs are learned. At 300 volts prolonged agonised screaming can be heard and the learner shouts in desperation that he will no longer provide answers. At 315 volts, after a violent scream, the learner reaffirms with vehemence that he is no longer a participant. From this point on, he provides no answers. The experimenter tells the teacher that silence represents an error and must be punished.

In the first two experiments 64 per cent of teachers administered the maximum shock of 450 volts.

In fact, the learner was an accomplice trained to play the role and no electric shocks were administered. However, the actual subjects – the teachers – were completely unaware of this. As Milgram states:

> There is overwhelming evidence that the great majority of subjects, both obedient and defiant, accepted the victims' reactions as genuine. The evidence takes the form

of: (a) tension created in the subjects; (b) scores on 'estimated pain' scales filled out by subjects immediately after the experiment; (c) subjects' accounts of their feelings in post-experimental interviews; and (d) quantifiable responses to questionnaires distributed to subjects several months after their participation in the experiment.[3]

Experimental variations

Greatly surprised by their initial findings,[4] Milgram and his research team carried out numerous variations of the basic experimental design in order to ascertain the key situational factors governing the dynamics of obedience. These are summarised below. Note that, unless otherwise stated, all experiments were based on the basic design outlined above and used male subjects. Full obedience rates refer to the percentage of subjects administering the maximum shock of 450 volts.

- Peer administers shock: similar to basic design except the teacher reads out the word pairs and another volunteer administers the shocks on his behalf. Full obedience rate = 92%.
- Women as subjects: similar to basic design except that both teacher and learner are female. Full obedience rate = 64%.
- Institutional context: the original experimental design repeated in a rather shabby downtown building, ostensibly by an organisation called Research Associates of Bridgeport. Full obedience rate = 48%.
- Increased proximity: similar to basic design except the learner is placed in the same room as teacher at a distance of ½ metre. Full obedience rate = 40%.
- Touch proximity: as above but learner receives shock only when his hand is forced onto a plate by the teacher. Full obedience rate = 30%.
- An 'ordinary' man gives the orders: experimenter selects one of the volunteers (a secret accomplice) to take his place. Experimenter remains in room as silent observer. Full obedience rate = 20%.
- Distant authority: experimenter leaves room halfway through the experiment. He explains he will be gone some time and asks the teacher to continue the experiment in his absence. Full obedience rate = 20%.

- Two peers rebel: three teachers participate. Halfway through the experiment, two of them (secret accomplices of the experimenter) refuse to continue administering electric shocks.
  Full obedience rate = 12%.
- Contradictory authority: two experimenters. One behaves as in basic design, the other expresses concern about the health of the learner and the legitimacy of his colleague's authority.
  Full obedience rate = 2%.
- Subjects free to choose the shock level they administer.
  Full obedience rate = 2%.
- Learner demands to be shocked.
  Full obedience rate = 2%.

Issues to consider

- Why do subjects obey the experimenter?[5]
- Analyse and explain the different full obedience rates associated with the variations of Milgram's basic experimental design.
- What are the implications of such obedience studies for the understanding of interpersonal dynamics and power relations in organisations?
- Are such studies unethical?[6]

Notes

1. For more details see Milgram (1963, 1967, 1974).
2. See Blass (1991).
3. Milgram (1967), p. 62. Indeed, the emotional strain suffered by many of Milgram's real subjects brought about serious moral controversy concerning the right of an experimenter to inflict such suffering.
4. Prior to the first study, Milgram asked 40 psychiatrists at a leading medical school to predict the performance of subjects in the experiment. Consensus was that a majority of subjects would not go beyond 150 volts (i.e. when the learner makes his first demand to be freed). The experts believed that only one subject in a thousand would administer the highest shock on the board (see Milgram, 1967: p. 72).
5. See Blass (1991), Cialdini (1985), Milgram (1974; 1977), Miller (1986), Moscovici (1985), and Zimbardo and Leippe (1991). Also see Cases 2 and 11 (this volume).
6. See Abse (1973), Baumrind (1964), Kaufmann (1967), Kelman (1967), Kelman and Hamilton (1989), Milgram (1964), Miller (1986) and Mixon (1974).

Case 20   Managing change at Byfield Business College[1]

It was generally agreed by members of the administrative and secretarial staff that the central records office was the most sociable and efficiently run office within Byfield Business College. Although it often appeared chaotic and untidy on occasions, the office offered a consistently high standard of service to the college's academic staff and students.

Work in central records involved the coordination of student admissions, course enrolment and attendance records, marks for course assessments and examinations, as well as lecture and seminar scheduling and room bookings, the printing and circulation of lecture notes, examination scripts and results, and the dissemination of all such information to members of academic staff. Given that the college was now running 38 courses to over 1000 full-time, part-time and distance learning students, this coordinating role was an extremely demanding one for the five members of the records office. Yet, students found the five women very helpful in answering their numerous (and frequent) inquiries and the office was often over-crowded in between lectures and during coffee breaks. Members of the academic staff benefited from this activity as the office staff acted as a buffer between themselves and the students. This enabled academic staff to carry out their work without constant interruption.

Jane Hacking, head of central records, had worked in the office for nearly 10 years and prided herself on the participative and supportive style in which she ran the office. As long as the work was done and deadlines were met, she was happy to allow her staff time off (especially on some of the quieter Friday afternoons) and to tolerate the occasional outbreaks of playfulness within the office. Over the years a number of social rituals had emerged which Jane and her staff enjoyed immensely. For example, the staff would take it in turns every Monday to bring in cakes to share with whoever was present at the morning coffee break. This had become very popular with many of the secretaries elsewhere in the college and, as a result, anyone passing by the office on Mondays between 10.30 and 11 a.m. could have been forgiven for thinking that a birthday celebration was in full swing!

George Boon, the newly appointed director of the college, was growing increasingly concerned about what he saw as the 'unprofessional' appearance of the central records office, and these concerns had been increased significantly by an incident at the end of the last academic year.

The incident had occurred on the last Monday of the summer term. On walking past the central records office at 10.45 a.m., George had been alarmed to witness a particularly playful cake party which appeared to involve certain members of the secretarial staff eating doughnuts that were suspended on strings attached to the office ceiling. On demanding an explanation, Jane informed him that it was her birthday and that she didn't mind such an outbreak of high spirits. 'It's good for staff morale, Professor Boon,' she explained.

'It may be good for morale,' retorted the director, 'but it portrays just the kind of childish image that the business college can well do without. Besides, this office handles a lot of confidential documents. You can't tell me that this sort of "open house" is good for security. I'm no kill-joy, but I'm afraid this kind of behaviour has got to stop as of now!'

Within 2 minutes, the office was empty.

During the summer vacation, George Boon decided that central records needed a fundamental restructuring in order to cope with the anticipated increase in student enrolments. It was also an opportunity to bring the office in line with his vision of a professionally-run business college. To this end, he asked Dr Robert Mangers, head of the operations research department, to carry out a full operations and methods analysis of central records with a view to integrating all student and course records.

After 2 weeks, Robert Mangers had completed his formal systems analysis. On reading the report, George had been alarmed to discover that the office had been handling a workload almost 20 per cent beyond its theoretical maximum for the past six months.

'That's all I need to know,' he told Dr Mangers. 'Can you design a new system for the office, Robert? The present system is such a mess that it's bound to collapse as soon as our student numbers increase. In fact, I'm amazed it hasn't done so already.'

Robert agreed and the two men worked out the details of the new system over the next 3 weeks. Under the old system, office staff tended to share out work between them. Jane Hacking would place all incoming work in one of three large trays on her desk. These were labelled 'urgent', 'important' and 'routine'. On completing one job, her staff would take another from the 'urgent' tray until it was empty and would then start on the 'important' work, and so forth, until all the day's work was complete. Sometimes Jane would stay late in order to remove any backlog of work and would often help out during the day if workloads increased unexpectedly or if a member of staff was absent.

The proposed new system required all office staff to take on a more specialised role. Each woman was allocated the administrative work for 5 or 6 particular courses and was required to complete a new set of record forms which cross-referenced all relevant information concerning students registered on the specified courses. This, according to George Boon, would give individual members of the office staff a sense of 'course loyalty and ownership'.

The two men agreed that the appearance of the office had to be improved and that entry to it should be restricted to central records office staff only. Student inquiries would be dealt with using a queuing system common in tax offices and delicatessen food counters in supermarkets. Whenever more than one or two students required information, they would be asked to take a numbered ticket and wait until that number was called before approaching the new inquiries window. In order to avoid disruption to the new office routine, it was decided that student inquiries would be dealt with only between the hours of 11 a.m. and 1 p.m. each day. Office staff would take it in turns to deal with inquiries.

'What about Jane?' Robert asked. 'I'm not sure this new system will be entirely to her liking.'

'She should never have let things get so out of hand in the office to start with,' George replied. 'She will admire the neatness of the new regime and, because it's more formal than her previous haphazard arrangement, it should help her control her staff. She'll like it soon enough.'

A week later, George Boon called the staff of central records to his office and outlined the plans for the new system. No-one asked any questions at the end of his short presentation and George saw this as a very encouraging sign. All the staff were then given a detailed job description and by the beginning of the following week, the new system became fully operational. Everyone was impressed with the speed and ease with which the change was managed.

The new academic year started 2 weeks later. Unfortunately, it wasn't long before complaints about the central records office started to reach the director. Members of the lecturing staff moaned that students were plaguing them with enquiries concerning course administration. For their part, students complained that the central records office staff were unhelpful and uncooperative. Matters weren't helped by the fact that absenteeism rates in the office were 40 per cent higher than the same time last year.

George started making impromptu visits to the office and was pleased to note that all signs of the old atmosphere of playfulness had completely disappeared. He decided the complaints just reflected teething problems and he ignored them. However, complaints rose in number dramatically following a mix up with examination registrations and he summoned Jane Hacking to his office, convinced that she was to blame for degradation of the new system.

When asked about the new system, Jane told the director: 'The old system worked far more effectively than the "Mangers' Mangle" ever will.'

'What the hell is the "Mangers' Mangle"?' quizzed George.

'The new system, of course,' came the reply. 'It's far too rigid. The staff are unhappy, the students are unhappy, the academics are unhappy, and I'm unhappy. What do you intend doing about it?'

George was furious. 'I'll tell you what I'll do about it! I'm transferring Ray Johnston from Conferences and Catering to pull everything back into shape again. You and your staff obviously don't like the new system and I wouldn't be at all surprised if you were all working to rule to slow up the system deliberately.'

'Okay, George,' Jane conceded. 'But if we are working to rule (as you call it) it's because the design of the new system doesn't let us do otherwise, and not out of choice, spite or malice.' She left the office without waiting for a reply.

The following morning, George received a letter signed by all members of the central records office (and a few prominent members of academic staff) expressing strong support for Jane Hacking.

Case resolution

- Outline and analyse the problems facing George Boon in the short and long term and offer recommendations for their resolution.[2]

Notes

1. A fictitious organisation.
2. For the importance of informality and playfulness at work, see the work of Breakwell (1986), Cohen and Taylor (1992), Fine (1988) and Katz (1987). More generally, see Plant (1992) for an excellent overview of Dadaist and Situationist writings espousing the virtues of play as a vehicle of resistance and political/ cultural change.

   For consideration of the problematic role of systems analysts in the planning and implementation of organisational change, see Markus (1983) and Newman and Rosenberg (1985).

   For an overview of the causes of resistance to organisational change more generally, see Beckhard and Harris (1987), Carnall (1990), Guest *et al.* (1980), Lippitt *et al.* (1985), Mirvis and Berg (1977), Neumann (1989), Staw (1982), Tichy (1983) and Wilson (1992a).

Case 21 Automate or liquidate

Scene one: selling the system

Jessica Francis, head of sales and marketing at Craven Breweries Ltd,[1] was not impressed by what she had heard so far. Toby Wilson, a smartly dressed representative from IT Systems Management, had just spent 20 minutes outlining the benefits of implementing a computer-based management information system (MIS) within Craven Breweries.

'So as you can appreciate, Ms Francis,' he concluded, 'information technology will allow you to make quicker and higher-quality decisions. It will enable your organisation to monitor progress against targets quickly and efficiently, it will improve communication around the company, and it will reduce costs. You need to ask yourself this question: Can you afford *not* to harness the benefits of information technology?'

'You're forgetting I'm the head of the sales and marketing department,' Jessica replied. 'I can see through all the hype you're offering. I appreciate IT has great potential benefits for businesses, but I need to be convinced that the particular system you're selling will solve the real problems facing this company.'

'Fair enough,' Toby conceded. 'From the information you sent me a few weeks ago things seem pretty clear. First, given you already have a powerful Praxis mainframe computer in your data processing department, it makes sense for you to use it as the central processing unit in an MIS. Unless you want to throw all your current hardware and software away, you'll have to go for a centralised MIS.'

'That's all very well,' Jessica said. In truth she hadn't really understood what the salesman was on about, but she felt it important to keep the conversation on her terms. 'But, how much will it cost?'

'I thought you'd ask me that,' Toby replied. 'To be honest the cost is not the important issue here. Shuffling paper around, keeping in touch with suppliers and retailers, just keeping the company afloat is costing Craven around £2½ million a year. If you go for our System Seven (with electronic mail, on-line customer and supplier database, file-server and back-up, and diskless terminals on all middle and senior management's desks) you'll reduce that cost by about 20 per cent. If my calculations are correct, you'll recoup the cost of design, implementation and proving in one year. After that the MIS will cease to be a cost on the company balance sheet!'

'That sounds impressive,' Jessica responded. 'But half a million pounds is a lot of money to spend. I can't see the finance and resources committee going for it. We aren't a very big company.'

Privately, Jessica was convinced that the implementation of a sales department-oriented MIS was the perfect solution to the problems facing the company. Also she realised she would need at least one powerful ally on the committee if her plans were to reach fruition. She was to give this a considerable amount of thought over the next few days.

Scene two: in search of support

Jeremy Nichols, head of the information services (formerly data processing) department, had been with the company since it had taken over Bailrigg Breweries some 8 years ago. He was widely recognised as a technical genius – especially when it came to dealing with problems arising from the use of the fairly antiquated mainframe computer hardware in his department. In recent years, he had come under increasing pressure from numerous departmental heads to improve their computing and telecommunication facilities. At the same time, he found it difficult to get the finance and resources committee to agree to any additional expenditure on office technologies. Departmental heads seemed so obsessed with the technical needs of their own departments that they almost always refused to sanction any expenditure on IT provision for an individual department lest the company's meagre IT budget was spent before they had a chance to put in their own bids. To make matters worse, most departmental heads had begun purchasing their own desktop personal computers without any reference to his department.

Jeremy was enjoying a well-earned cup of coffee in his office, when Jessica Francis strolled in.

'To what do I owe this unexpected pleasure?' he asked sarcastically. 'What do the Olympians in marketing want now?'

'Nothing thank you, Jeremy,' she replied. 'In fact, I think I can do something for you this time.' She then outlined her conversation with Toby Wilson the previous week and explained her plans for a company-wide MIS (leaving out all technical details).

Jeremy listened intently and looked none too pleased at what he was hearing. 'My, my. You have been busy haven't you? Why is it that no one sees fit to consult me on these matters any more?' he quipped. 'Anyway, most MIS these days are based on a distributed approach. You know the problems I have been experiencing with departmental managers continually under-mining my position by buying their own systems. I can't possibly support your proposal if it means giving departments even more freedom. It's anarchy already for heaven's sake.'

'I understand perfectly, Jeremy,' Jessica replied coolly. 'Are there any circumstances under which would you support my proposal?'

'I think if you were to stress the need for a centralised approach, with responsibility for running the MIS resting in my department, I could be persuaded,' he suggested. 'But I don't see how any MIS can realistically be expected to pay for itself in one year. I also think half a million pounds is a very optimistic price.'

Scene three (3 months later): the finance and resources committee meeting

Managing director, Joan Vasenka sat back in her chair in the executive board room. 'Ladies and Gentlemen,' she announced. 'You have all had time to see the feasibility study and cost-justification report Jessica has prepared. Before we make any decision on the matter, are there any questions you would like to raise?'

'First and last, I would like to know why this MIS is going to cost so much?' inquired finance director, Mota Singh. 'Aren't there any cheaper technical alternatives or cheaper suppliers than IT Systems Management?'

'We haven't put the project out for competitive tender for two reasons. Firstly, because IT Systems Management are the cheapest suppliers in the country and, secondly, because we can't install different makes of hardware and software anyway.' Jessica replied.

'Why ever not?,' the MD asked in surprise.

'No other supplier can give us compatible equipment,' Jeremy responded. 'If we were to go for a different approach and a different supplier it would mean throwing away most of our existing computing equipment. What a waste! Whilst the mainframe in my department is relatively old in this age of disposable PCs, it has proved to be very reliable. It would be financial madness to sell it for scrap. Perhaps it is best to stick with technology we all know than to go for something completely new.'

'I'm glad to see that you're not telling us to buy the latest state-of-the-art expensive equipment Jeremy. But half a million is still a lot of money!' the finance director insisted.

'That is true,' Jessica conceded. 'But the detailed cost-justification study undertaken by IT Systems Management shows that we will recoup the investment in a year just by saving on administrative overheads. Then there are the benefits to consider. This System Seven will integrate sales, marketing, production, distribution and services. At the touch of a button we can communicate with one another, check on progress and inventories, and the like. Our profits aren't so impressive that we can afford to sit back and relax. Our competitors are looking at office automation. I know that our chief rivals at Allied Brewing and Distilling are installing a large MIS later this year at the cost of £3 million. I don't think we can afford not to take the same technological route. You all know the saying: "automate or liquidate". We aren't talking beer here – we're talking about the future of Craven Breweries.'

'All this sounds fine,' interrupted Frank Spencer, production director. 'But it seems pretty perverse logic to throw new technology at the office and expect me to keep using the same old technology in production. It's no good having a state-of-the-art office if no-one buys our products. Why not invest half a million in production technology that will bring brewing times and labour costs down, for example?'

'With respect, Frank,' retorted the MD, 'production technology is not on the agenda today. It's true that you work wonders with the old equipment. But we can't solve all our problems in one go.'

Questions continued for some time. Most of these centred on the cost-saving potential of the MIS. As a consensus of opinion started to emerge each departmental representative demanded the right to be involved in writing up the system specification if the project was approved.

Eventually, Jessica's closing speech (stressing clerical efficiency, lower costs and the need to move with the times) swung the sceptics around in her favour and the MIS project was approved.

Issues to consider

- With reference to the relevant OB literature, analyse the decision-making process outlined in the case.[2]
- What implementation problems, if any, do you envisage?
- Do you expect the performance of the MIS to come up to expectations?

Notes

1. A fictitious organisation.
2. For a general analysis of organisational decision-making, see Cohen *et al.* (1972), Cyert and March (1963), Hickson *et al.* (1986), Janis and Mann (1977), Pettigrew (1973) and Simon (1960). Also see Danziger (1979), Markus and Bjorn-Andersen (1987), Newman and Rosenberg (1985), Scarbrough and Corbett (1992), Wainwright and Francis (1984) and Wetherbe *et al.* (1988) for analyses of the role of data processing and information service personnel in technical decision-making. Finally, see Dussauge *et al.* (1987) and Grindley (1992) for consideration of the pros and cons inherent in IT investment decision-making.

CHAPTER 5

Leadership

Introduction

It is in the analysis of leadership that the study of organisational behaviour is at its most presumptive and uncritical. OB textbook authors continue to rehash long discredited theories and often fail to locate any of their analyses in the context of power or organisational structure and control. The fact that groups and organisations do not have to have leaders, or that isocratic organisations are possible, is usually ignored completely. The starting point for conventional analysis is that leaders exist, and they are important for effective organisational functioning.

The majority of OB textbooks manage not to address the issue of power specifically in the chapters which deal with leadership. As Barrett and Sutcliffe (1993) note, this is despite the fact that, for example, some of the contingency theories list management authority as problematic. They point out that rarely is any attempt made to discuss the various theories of leadership in terms of their implicit concepts of power and legitimation for leaders. Normative considerations of leadership are excluded from OB discourse in much the same manner.

Barrett and Sutcliffe argue that

> By conceptually separating leadership from power, and by failing to comprehend the central manipulative role that power plays in managing compliance, leadership theories generally, and texts on leadership in particular, can be accused of failing to analytically reveal the true nature of the leadership process, and of leadership, to students of management (1993, p. 14).

A more critical perspective could point up the heresy that leadership is perhaps nothing more than a powerful social myth. Encouraged by a plethora of books with titles like 'How I Saved Company X', written by heads and ex-heads of giant corporations, and liberally scattered in book shops at international airports, OB texts perpetuate a false, essentially romantic, view of leadership. As Meindl *et al.* (1985) observe:

> One of the principal elements in this romanticized conception is the view that leadership is the premier force in the scheme of organizational processes and activities (p. 79).

Yet no good evidence appears to exist to justify such a view. Indeed, it may well be that fundamental attribution bias within the Anglo-American view of business explains the prevalence of such romanticism. For example, content analyses of US business journals, magazines and newspapers reveals that corporate success is commonly attributed to leadership qualities whereas average corporate performance tends to be attributed to other factors, such as market fluctuations or global economic changes (Meindl *et al.*, 1985).

The seven cases represented in this chapter encourage the analyst to take a critical look at leadership from a variety of angles. In Case 22, the issues of charisma and corruption are raised in relation to the activities of a certain John De Lorean. By contrast, Case 23 examines the circumstances surrounding the fall of Singapore during the Second World War. You are asked to consider the extent to which strict hierarchical organisations, such as the military, unwittingly encourage the kind of incompetent leadership which brought about the defeat of an army and airforce defending an apparently impregnable fortress.

Case 24 continues on a military theme and concentrates on leadership from the perspective of those who follow. If one accepts that leadership is not an innate trait or a birthright, it is important to examine the ways in which the leadership process is negotiated. This case reveals the dire consequences which may result when this process collapses.

Case 25 is another gem from Les Prince. We so often assume that someone will become a leader within a group that it can come as quite a surprise when everyone resists the 'call'. This case raises the whole question of how leadership is created and negotiated. It also begs the question: Is leadership necessary or desirable?

Case 26 is written in a more conventional problem-solving format and focuses on the behaviour of three managers (departmental leaders) in a business organisation. The conflict described is certainly not uncommon, but it is important to consider the extent to which it has been caused by factors outside the control of the protagonists.

Case 27 briefly outlines the leadership style of Henry Ford Senior. It raises the critical issue of the power relationship between leader and followers in a very graphic manner. The last case – Case 28 – also alludes to this relationship (albeit in a less extreme form) within a problem-solving case format.

Case 22   John De Lorean

Many people are familiar with the appearance of the De Lorean DMC-12 gull wing sports car. Although the car is rarely seen on the public highway, it featured prominently (as a somewhat unreliable time machine!) in the trilogy of highly successful *Back to the Future* films in the 1980s. Fewer people are cognisant with the story of the birth and decline of the DMC-12 and the company that manufactured it – the De Lorean motor car company – or with the car's originator, John De Lorean.

Having resigned from General Motors, partly as a result of his well publicised outrage over the Corvair scandal (see Case 15), John De Lorean was keen to realise his dream of owning a motor car company. In 1978, using his considerable entrepreneurial flair and personal charisma, he managed to persuade the UK Labour government to invest £35.9 million of tax-payers' money in the design and production of an innovative stainless-steel-bodied luxury sports car. De Lorean believed the DMC-12 could compete successfully against the Porsche 924 in the US car market (even though Porsche car sales were very low in a recession-bound US at that time).

The part of De Lorean's proposal that particularly appealed to the UK government was the intention to locate the factory in Dunmurry, West Belfast within the province of Northern Ireland where unemployment was very high and industrial investment virtually non-existent. The subsequent creation of 2000 jobs at the factory was heralded by the then Secretary of State for Northern Ireland, Roy Mason, as a 'tremendous breakthrough'.

De Lorean had previously considered locating the factory in South America, but he was able to secure generous grants from the UK government and a promise of minimal regulatory interference. No feasibility study was carried out by the government nor, apparently, by De Lorean himself. Nevertheless, the UK government funding was topped up with a $27.2 million equity stake by the Northern Ireland Development Agency in 1980.

In 1978, using the UK government's money, De Lorean paid the Lotus car company the sum of $17.65 million to develop the prototype of the DMC-12. However, instead of using this money for development, John De Lorean and two Lotus executives, Colin Chapman and Fred Bushell, kept it for themselves. The money was funnelled through a Panamanian-registered Geneva-based company, GPD Services. De Lorean kept $8.5 million, whilst

Chapman and Bushell deposited $7.5 million and $1.65 million (respectively) in secret numbered Swiss bank accounts. Unaware of this fraud, the newly elected Conservative government agreed to De Lorean's subsequent appeal for a further $15 million loan to develop the DMC-12 prototype.

This work was eventually carried out by Lotus for the De Lorean motor car company and funded a second time with a direct payment to Lotus cars from the Dunmurry-based factory. Once the prototype had been developed, John De Lorean set to work with immense energy and coaxed productivity rates from his workforce far beyond anything ever achieved by the large multinational car companies. He accomplished this through a combination of organisational and managerial techniques.

First, he made sure salaries were high in an effort to boost staff motivation; second, he encouraged production line management to handle the semi-skilled shopfloor workforce in an autocratic manner; third, he kept delegation and executive consultation to a minimum and used his own power and charisma to ensure that work was carried out as he directed; and fourth, taking a leaf out of the ex-IBM President Tom Watson Junior's management book, he practised a system of 'contention management' – the encouragement of conflict and competition between managers and departments – to foster quicker and cheaper car production.

However, the car was not a success in the American market place and sales were insufficient to cover production costs. John De Lorean blamed his marketing staff for the poor sales, and embarked on a hugely expensive advertising tour of America to promote the car.

On his return to Dunmurry in the late summer of 1981, he confidently stepped up production of the DMC-12. But with the demand in the US for 30,000 identical mass-produced foreign sports cars remaining low (not least because of the cars' high price, lack of performance and lack of exclusivity), De Lorean found himself sitting on a huge stockpile of unsold cars.

Thereafter, De Lorean kept his presence at Dunmurry to a minimum. This created significant problems for the management team who found it increasingly difficult to work effectively owing to De Lorean's refusal to delegate executive decision-making and his habit of withholding information. For example, without consultation with senior management or engineering designers, he decided that the flagging DMC-12 sales could be boosted if the car's lack-lustre performance was improved by turbocharging its 2.8 litre engine. To this end he contracted five separate motor engineering companies to undertake development work. At the same time, he invested considerable sums of company money in another vehicle manufacturing company, antiques, property, a working ranch and a fashion business.

In February 1982, the De Lorean motor car company went into voluntary receivership. The only money to be recouped came from the auctioning of the Dunmurry plant and equipment 3 months later.

Postscript

The UK Director of Public Prosecutions had harboured suspicions about financial irregularities within the De Lorean motor car company since its inception, but had been unable to obtain sufficient evidence to justify criminal prosecution during the company's short life-cycle. Until the introduction of the UK Criminal Justice Act in 1988, the Belfast police – the Royal Ulster Constabulary (RUC) – had not been able to raid premises in Britain seeking evidence. In February 1989, the RUC and the Serious Fraud Squad raided the English home and offices of Fred Bushell (former chief of Lotus cars) and seized thousands of incriminating documents relating to the De Lorean case.

On 19 June 1992, Bushell was jailed for 3 years and fined £2.25 million for his part in the conspiracy to defraud the De Lorean motor car company of $17.65 million. Lord Justice Murray, at Belfast Crown Court, told Bushell he was the brains behind the 'barefaced, outrageous and massive fraud'.

The judge explained that John De Lorean was not before the court because, as a US citizen, he could not be extradited. But both he and the late Colin Chapman would have merited a sentence of 10 years for their part in the conspiracy. He told the court that it was only because of Bushell's late decision to plead guilty and his poor state of health that he received a shorter term of imprisonment.

Issues to consider

- Was John De Lorean a good leader? Was he a good manager?[1]
- Irrespective of De Lorean's leadership qualities, do you think the company would have collapsed?

Note

1. In addition to the usual textbook sources, see Bennis and Nanus (1985), Fiedler and House (1988), Kotter (1990), Schein (1989), Wright (1979), Zaleznik (1977) and Zaleznik and Kets de Vries (1975). For a consideration of the relationship between charisma and effective leadership, the writings of Bass (1985), Bryman (1992), Conger and Kanungo (1987), Hater and Bass (1988), Tichy and Devanna (1987), and Wolpe (1968) are worth a look.

Case 23 Military leadership and the fall of Singapore

Introduction

In the first few weeks of 1942, the supposedly impregnable fortress of Singapore – Europe's strategic gateway to the East and location of important large Allied Forces' naval dockyards and military airfields – was invaded and captured by the Japanese. 138,708 British, Indian and Australian troops either died or went into captivity as a result.

Yet barely two months before Singapore capitulated, the Allied Forces' Order of the Day in the *Malay Tribune* read:

> We are ready. We have had plenty of warning and our preparations are made and tested. We are confident. Our defences are strong and our weapons efficient. . . We have one aim and one only, it is to defend these shores, to destroy such of our enemies who may set foot on our soil.

So what went wrong?

Historical background

The loss of Singapore had its origins in events prior to the Second World War. In 1925, the Army, Navy and Air force chiefs of staff engaged in debate concerning how best to defend the peninsula of Singapore. The Air Force argued that defence was best constructed around a large fleet of aircraft which could repel attacks from sea, air and land. However, the Army and Navy countenanced the deployment of heavy fixed 9- and 15-inch guns facing south to repel a sea invasion.

The debate, which the Air Force lost, had three unfortunate consequences.[1] First, Singapore was left exposed and undefended on its north side (where the peninsula is linked to the Malayan mainland by a narrow isthmus and causeway). Second, senior Army commanders from that time on stubbornly clung to the dogma that the Japanese would never advance through the 'impenetrable jungle' of the Malay Peninsula and attack the north side of Singapore. Third, the ensuing quarrel between the three armed forces resulted in an almost complete lack of coordination between them. For example, the

Air Force constructed airfields in Singapore without any consultation with the Army who would have to defend them. Observers also noted that the three headquarters in Singapore were built as far away from each other as was geographically possible.

The fall of Singapore, 1941–2

After the outbreak of the Second World War, the Allied guardians of Singapore were eager to prevent civilians from discovering anything new that might conflict with military dogma. The rationale seemed to be that the disclosure of true facts was bad for civilian morale, and thus suppression of the truth or the broadcasting of false information was justified on the grounds that it was good for morale.

On 8 December 1941, GHQ issued its first war communiqué. This stated that the Japanese forces had failed to land at Kota Bahru and that all the enemy's surface craft were retiring at great speed. However, this morale-boosting news was untrue. Although it was true that the surface craft were retiring at speed, this was only after the successful disembarkation of the enemy troops they had been carrying. It would appear that the Army commanders simply decided that civilian morale would be severely damaged if news of the successful Japanese landing was broadcast.

Meanwhile, Air Chief Marshal Brooke-Popham was insisting that the hopelessly inadequate collection of obsolete aircraft (known locally as 'peanut specials') under his command was more than capable of dealing with any Japanese air strike on Singapore. Furthermore, despite the obvious risk of air raids, the Air Force made no provision for a night-time blackout or for the 'scrambling' of Allied fighter aircraft during hours of darkness. In the event, the first Japanese night air raid claimed 61 lives and 133 casualties – despite over 30 minutes' clear warning of the approaching aircraft. Brooke-Popham's failure to react stemmed from his refusal to believe that any Japanese aircraft were actually flying in darkness. Official Allied military dogma had always had it that the 'poorly-trained' Japanese pilots were unable (as well as too frightened) to fly at night because of their 'poor night vision'.

Yet it was the Army generals who were the most intransigent commanders on the peninsula. Despite all the warnings and evidence of impending invasion, Major-General Gordon Bennett (commanding the 8th Australian Division) and Lieutenant-General Percival (General Officer Commanding Malaya) steadfastly refused to prepare for a Japanese attack on Singapore.

In early November 1941, Brigadier Simson, the Chief Engineer, had a meeting with Percival to urge him to take some defensive measures. The Brigadier explained that he had the staff and materials at his disposal to put up permanent and semi-permanent defences against a Japanese attack on the north side of Singapore (e.g. anti-tank defences, mines, fire traps, methods of illuminating the sea at night and floating barbed wire). The General refused. Simson pleaded once more:

> Sir. I must emphasise the urgency of doing everything to help our troops. They're often only partially trained, they're tired and dispirited. They've been retreating for hundreds of miles. And please remember, sir, the Japanese are better trained, better equipped and they're inspired by an unbroken run of victories. It has to be done now, sir. Once the area comes under fire, civilian labour will vanish.[2]

Percival still refused to give his permission. He told the despondent Brigadier: 'I believe that defences of the sort you want to throw up are bad for the morale of troops and civilians.'[3]

2 weeks later Percival was visited by the Supreme Commander of Allied Forces in the Far East, General Sir Archibald Wavell. Wavell was convinced that the Japanese would attack Singapore from the north-west and urged Percival to set up defences along the lines suggested by Simson. Percival did nothing at first despite a note from the UK Prime Minister Winston Churchill supporting Wavell's view. When he eventually issued the order it was too late as the necessary civilian labour force was no longer available.

2 weeks before the Japanese attacked Singapore, aerial reconnaissance photographs were shown to Percival indicating Japanese tanks moving quickly and easily through the 'impenetrable jungle' of the Malay Peninsula to the north-west of Singapore. In fact, this 'jungle' was a collection of vast rubber tree plantations in which tanks could move easily between the spacious rows of trees. Other photographs revealed insuperable obstacles to an attack from the north-east. Yet, Percival suggested that the Japanese were playing a complex game of bluff and ordered all defence stores moved to the north-east corner of Singapore. He still could not believe that the Japanese would use tanks, but now wasn't sure what form the attack would take. Consequently, he ordered the majority of his troops to spread themselves thinly over the long northern front. Some were retained on the southern front in case of a sea-based attack (even though there was hardly any ammunition for the large fixed guns located there).

Ten days later Percival learned that the enemy were massing in the north-west. He promptly ordered all the stores moved back again. It was too late.

> For the Allies it was a week of chaos and confusion unrelieved by any vestiges of competent generalship. Thanks to the absence of defences, including a failure to use the searchlights which had been assembled to blind and make targets of the attackers as they paddled their way across the Johore Straits, the Japanese landed almost unmolested. Despite a devastating barrage from Japanese artillery, British guns, instead of pounding the enemy's point of embarkation, remained mute, awaiting orders that never came. Despite the weeks of warning, Allied ground forces were speedily outflanked, encircled, cut off and routed.[4]

Though dwarfed at the time by other world events, the fall of Singapore constitutes a disturbing example of military incompetence. Yet the psychologist Norman Dixon argues that the whole episode gives the lie to any 'bloody fool' theory of history.[5] In fact, General Percival was highly intelligent and had shown himself in previous years to be a brilliant staff officer. What he shared with other incompetent military leaders was passivity, over-courtesy, obstinacy and dogmatism. For Percival (as well as Gordon Bennett), to erect defences would have been to admit the danger in which the Allied forces stood.

Issues to consider

- In his psychological analysis of the fall of Singapore, Dixon is struck by the compulsive element in this refusal of the military to defend itself. He argues that such compulsive behaviour is typical of many who are brought up and socialised in military organisations.
- To what extent, and through what mechanisms, do military organisations generate and perpetuate incompetent leadership and compulsive behaviour?[6]
- Are similar mechanisms in evidence in other formal organisations?[7]

Notes

1. According to Bennett (1944), p. 77.
2. Barber (1968), p. 65.
3. Barber (1968), p. 66.
4. Dixon (1979), p. 143.
5. Dixon (1979), p. 144.
6. The writings of Glad (1990), Josephson (1952) and L'Etang (1969) contain in-depth analyses of the derivation of leadership pathologies in general, whilst the work of Smyth (1971) examines General Percival's leadership in particular. For a detailed analysis of the compulsive elements in military training, see Dornbusch (1953), Johnson (1973) and Smyth (1961). For a consideration of the roots of authoritarianism, see Adorno *et al.* (1950) and Christie and Jahoda (1954). For a more general psychological interpretation of the issues raised in the case, see Dixon (1979), Festinger (1964) and Rokeach (1960).

   By way of contrast, take a look at Gal and Mangelsdorff (1991) to get an idea of what contemporary military psychologists regard as the key issues.
7. See Allinson (1984), Crozier (1964), Hirschhorn (1988), Kets de Vries and Miller (1984b), Merton (1940) and Trice and Beyer (1985).

Case 24   When leadership fails – the case of fragging

In military organisations an important function of leadership is the control of subordinates' aggression so that such dangerous impulses are projected upon legitimate targets while keeping other outlets blocked. Elaborating on this view, the psychologist Norman Dixon believes that armies resemble the authoritarian family group:

> Just as the ethos of an upper-class Victorian family totally forbade any show of aggression by the child towards its parents, but encouraged organised aggression in such school pursuits as boxing and sanctioned bullying, so in the Army the slightest hint of insubordination (i.e. aggression directed towards a superior) is severely punished, while aggression towards the enemy is encouraged and rewarded.[1]

Soldiers are required to suppress aggression and physical violence toward their leaders (whom they may despise) while venting it upon an anonymous enemy towards whom they may have no personal hostility. Thus, a prerequisite of effective military leadership is the ability to maintain this paradoxical state of affairs.[2]

By and large, military leaders are able to maintain order and discipline in the ranks. That said, murders and attempted murders of military officers by rank-and-file soldiers have occurred in every war this century. For example, during the First World War, which involved over 4,700,000 American military personnel, 370 cases of murder and attempted murder of US army officers were brought to courts-martial. But it was the Vietnam war that brought an escalation of such incidents.

In 1970 – a period during which approximately 700,000 American military personnel were in Vietnam – there were 363 reported cases of assault with explosive devices directed at superiors. In the first 6 months of 1971 a further 107 US Army officers were assaulted by subordinates armed with explosives. Most commentators believe the actual number of assaults during this time to be at least ten times higher.

The term given to these assaults is 'fragging'. This term derives from the deadly explosive device most commonly used in these violent incidents – the anti-personnel fragmentation grenade.[3]

But what was it about the Vietnam war that produced such an escalation of fragging? Equally puzzling was the fact that in previous wars the typical fragging took place at the front line, whilst in Vietnam most fraggings seem to have taken place in rear areas a relatively safe distance away from the frontline.

The writer Eugene Lindon argues that although the dangers of being in the rear echelon were minimal, the environment was still one of stress.[4] The enlisted men were the pawns of an authoritarian system designed to deploy soldiers to combat efficiently; yet the dangers that justified its discipline were absent. Thus, in the rear areas the troops became acutely aware of the authoritarianism of the system and the privileges and luxuries enjoyed by officers. Yet they saw little immediate justification for the discrepancies in status because both officers and troops were essentially doing nothing.

Yet this perceived inequity hardly explains why soldiers should have resorted to murder. For their part, the US Army were unable to ascertain why soldiers were attempting to kill their superiors in Vietnam. Out of desperation, the generals decreed that access to explosives on Army bases should be restricted. Also, they initiated a series of lecture tours designed to educate soldiers in the gravity of fragging. In some bases the troops were not even trusted to carry the weapons necessary to fight the war they had been sent to wage.

A number of observers blamed drug abuse among enlisted soldiers for the high incidence of fragging. Apparently, heroin was a fierce contender with a commanding officer for the command of the troops in Vietnam.

> For many GIs, fighting a war in Vietnam is so confusing and unassimilable that when they are there they feel as though they are in a dream, that they are not really themselves. Because life is not real it becomes acceptable to snort skag and frag the sarge.[5]

US Army psychiatrist Robert Landeen believes that most officers who are fragged bring about their own downfall to some extent. In the Second World War the non-commissioned officer (NCO) served the function of absorbing resentment and siphoning off frustrations of the enlisted soldiers before they reached a critical level. Landeen argues that the circumstances confronting the NCO during the Vietnam war were quite different. Because of distrust of the drug-using, anti-authoritarian and comparatively unmotivated US Army draftee in Vietnam, the career NCO often retreated from contact with his men and consorted only with other officers and career NCOs.[6]

This uneasy relationship between NCO and soldier had two important consequences. First, army discipline is designed for the rigours of war – an offence is met with sure and swift punishment. Above all, the system of military justice stresses consistency. All offences are dealt with in the same strict manner. However, during the Vietnam war, NCOs often ignored drug use and minor outbreaks of insubordination until they affected the soldiers' work. Hence relatively minor transgressions were disregarded until they reached a point where the NCO had to act to preserve order. Such explosions of discipline and punishment left many soldiers believing that US Army justice was arbitrary and directed towards enlisted men by a conspiracy of professional military careerists.

A second consequence of the distance between NCO and soldier was the insurgence of psychological terrorism among soldiers to intimidate new officers. The machismo culture of the army helped foster this climate of intimidation. Also the fact that many NCOs would ignore minor outbreaks of insubordination served to lower the status of the NCO in the eyes of increasingly disrespectful and alienated GIs. When a new officer joined a platoon he would pick up rumours about fragging, drug use and racial tension. By the time he saw the soldiers in his unit he may already have felt very intimidated.

Enlisted soldiers, resentful of officers' privileges and their demand for unquestioning obedience and respect, thus looked for any signs of inauthenticity, over-ambition or weakness in the officer – qualities that may cost soldiers' lives. If the officer failed to survive the intimidation and confrontations, he was a prime candidate for fragging.

Issues to consider

- Why is fragging the exception rather than the rule in military life and work?[7]
- In analysing this case, how valuable are conventional textbook theories of leadership?
- What other explanations can you offer for the fragging phenomenon?[8]

Notes

1. Dixon (1979), p. 174.
2. For a consideration of other important skills required of military leadership, see Gal and Mangelsdorff (1991) and Page (1981).
3. Laffin (1973).
4. Lindon (1972).
5. Lindon (1972), p. 13.
6. Lindon (1972), p. 14.
7. See Dixon (1979), Dornbusch (1953), Johnson (1973) and Smyth (1961) for an analysis of the training and socialisation of the rank-and-file soldier. For a more general consideration of the relationship between socialisation and commitment, see Cialdini (1989) and Jones (1983).
8. You may wish to consider explanations derived from theories of operant conditioning (e.g. Kerr, 1975), minority group influence (Mugny and Perez, 1991), escalating commitment (Reichers, 1986; Staw and Fox, 1977; Whyte, 1986), intragroup negotiation (Hosking and Morley, 1992) and deviance (Becker, 1963; Box, 1971; Cohen and Taylor, 1992; Matza, 1969). The work of Bennis (1990) suggests the existence of a broader social dynamic making it difficult for leadership to emerge or function effectively.

Case 25   And some have it thrust upon them: a case study in unwanted leadership

Les Prince[1]

Background

The Souton Anarchist Group was founded in 1974 as part of the upsurge in anti-authoritarian idealism of the period. It has nevertheless survived for nearly 20 years, albeit with a considerable change in its membership. At the time of the case study the group comprised a core of about fifteen members, with a network of between 50 and 70 peripheral members who took part in its activities on a regular basis.

The members were overwhelmingly young and professional, with one or two artisans. Most were graduates, and nearly all of them were in full-time jobs. At different times the group had amongst its members: several journalists; a graphic designer; a Sandhurst-trained ex-Guards officer who had taken up professional writing; an architect; a printer; a miner; several bookshop workers; teachers (including one head teacher); a department store manager; several civil servants; and a collection of artists, writers, musicians, and, in varying numbers, students from the local colleges and university.

Politically SAG reflected a fairly even spread across the spectrum of anarchist thought, with some emphasis on syndicalism, anarcho-feminism, pacifism, anarcho–communism and situationism. Although these views were held neither exclusively nor dogmatically, there were nevertheless some tensions within the group which focused on two loose-knit coalitions.

The *Peace Journal* coalition

Several SAG members were associated with the national magazine *Peace Journal*, either as full-time workers or as volunteers. These were characterised by commitments to anarcha–feminism and, to some extent, pacifism. Those who were not dedicated pacifists, who were in the main also Quakers, were nevertheless strongly in favour of non-violent direct action (NVDA) and non-violent revolution, with the emphasis very firmly on the non-violence.

Mike Farmer, an outspoken Quaker whose abrasive manner often belied his declared beliefs, assumed the role of spokesperson for this group, although he was frequently upbraided for his presumption by two of the other members.

One of these, Ellen Pound, generally said very little in group meetings, but nevertheless had an extraordinary ability at times to summarise a long argument succinctly. She also specialised in bringing a discussion back to earth if she thought it was becoming too abstract or abstruse. In this she had an ally, Alice de Fey, with whom she usually sat in the group meetings, the two of them often knitting and apparently taking no interest in the proceedings.

Alice de Fey had moved from the Peace Shop in Mizzenham, another Midlands city, in order to join the Editorial Collective of the *Peace Journal*. A highly committed and articulate linguist, she operated primarily from her well-developed sense of irreverent humour, which she often deployed to significant political effect. One of her delights was to 'prick the bubble of pomposity', and more than once Mike Farmer discovered first hand the effects of her well-honed and barbed wit. She was well liked within SAG, and generally regarded by everyone as one of the significant contributors to group cohesion and identity. Certainly she played a notable part in maintaining the overall good humour of SAG and its meetings. Nevertheless, like Farmer and Pound, she often found herself at odds with a second coalition within SAG.

The 'Black Banner' group

This second group had a much less focused identity than the *Peace Journal* group, and, significantly, consisted mainly of people whose day-to-day work was outside radical politics. The political emphasis of this group was much more inclined towards syndicalism and to some extent revolutionary anarchism. Although no-one within SAG seriously considered armed revolution or Emil Henry's notorious 'propaganda of the deed' to be genuine options, the 'Black Banner' group nevertheless laid much less emphasis on the necessity of non-violence in the pursuit of political ends, and this frequently resulted in protracted discussions about the ethical necessity of making means and ends consistent with one another. The discussions, although generally fruitful, were largely academic, however, because the members of the 'Black Banner' group were in point of fact no more violent than those in the *Peace Journal* group. What really distinguished them was the fact that they had contacts with *Black Banner*, an avowedly 'revolutionary' paper whose publishers were openly scornful of the *Peace Jounal*, a sentiment which was reciprocated.

Most prominent of this group was Corin Holden, a mining supervisor in one of the nearby pits. Physically imposing, being tall, broad and muscular, he was also intellectually accomplished having two degrees and several professional qualifications. In political terms Corin was probably the most experienced member of SAG. He had a considerable background in political activism on the local scene, and knew most of the significant local left wing activists. In particular he was on very good terms with the local Red Flame organiser, had contacts with the local Trades Council, and was generally well liked and respected by both political friends and opponents. Although he was generally tolerant of differing political views, particularly within SAG, he was very clear about his own beliefs which were often at odds with those of other SAG members, especially on the question of 'armed struggle'. Fundamentally he was a syndicalist, although occasionally flirting with Council Communism, and had contacts with the editorial collective of *Black Banner*, and the Anarchist relief organisation the Anarchist Black Cross. Later he became involved with a local Crass War group.

Alongside Holden, although more by default than design, was the graphic designer Lester Marten, the group's founder. He was studio manager of a local advertising agency, and often surprised group members, particularly new ones, by arriving at group meetings wearing a smart business suit and expensive cologne, and carrying a leather briefcase. Nevertheless his orientation was also basically syndicalist, reinforced by his position on the branch committee of his union, the National Graphic Arts Association (1982). He did, however, have pronounced Situationist leanings. It was he, for instance, who, much to Holden's annoyance, opened the group's bank account under the name of The Teapot Club. Like Holden he also had links with *Black Banner*, and was the art editor of its associated journal *The Cinqdoigts Press Anarchist Review* (*CPAR*).

Despite the generally friendly relations within SAG, it was the editorial policies of *Black Banner* and *CPAR* on the one hand, and the *Peace Journal* on the other, both publicly at odds, which generated some of the tensions within SAG.

The *Liberty* group

Between the two groups already mentioned there was a third much larger and much more diverse grouping based around the founders of the bookshop collective Fungus. In terms of orientation most of this group had an inclination towards the non-violence of the *Peace Journal* group, but were also characterised by the liberal anarchism of the London-based paper *Liberty*, and its associated journal *Anarchism*. In some ways this reflected the personalities of the two founders of Fungus, Kristal Baker and especially, Keefer Feynman. Kristal later defected to Crass War with Holden, but at this stage she was very much associated with a semi-mystical, liberal and ecological anarchism through her association with Fungus and Feynman. Although essentially middle-of-the-road in their anarchism, Chris and Keefer were nevertheless significant actors in the local political scene, having organised, amongst other things, the local ABC Defence Committee, and a campaign against official secrecy. In addition Fungus was, and still is, the focus for broadly left-wing, ecological and peace activism in Souton, and was instrumental in the setting up of the highly successful Federation of Alternative and Radical Bookshops. Within SAG Chris and Keefer made important contributions to debate. These were not confined to taking a middle, conciliatory, line in the arguments between the *Peace Journal* and *Black Banner* groups, although they often performed this function particularly well. Their major interest in ecology and what are now called 'green' issues, gender relations and official secrecy played a large part in shaping the group's direction and activities.

On the whole, however, this 'middle' grouping was constituted mainly of people who were new to active politics, and whose views, therefore, were in many cases not yet fully formed. Typical of this group was Jo Pencross who admitted privately to Marten to having some doubts about being in the group. For such people the group and its activities was new, often exciting, and frequently very confusing.

Group activities

Collectively the group was well aware that its role was limited. Despite the level of political, and in particular anti-authoritarian, activity which characterised the period, it was well recognised within SAG that fomenting revolution, non-violent or otherwise, was not a realistic option. Instead the group opted for an agit-prop role, concentrating on spreading the doctrine of libertarian socialism and, more importantly, doing what it could to ensure that the anarchist view was heard in any major political debates being conducted in the area. Thus the group spent much of its time producing propaganda material and taking an active part in most of the current Broad Left activities.

About this time the group designed and produced a poster and associated badges with the caption 'Guy Fawkes: The only person to enter Parliament with honest intentions'. They used this as part of a highly successful fly-posting campaign within the city, so successful indeed, that 3 years after they had finished the campaign many of the posters were still visible and undefaced. Other fly posters had simply stuck their own posters around them. On another occasion the group initiated the 'Ya boo sucks to fascism campaign' as a corrective to what it felt was SWP dominance of the ANL, thus earning themselves the unremitting disapproval of the local SWP who grumbled that SAG didn't take politics seriously enough.

Occasionally SAG collaborated with other groups, such as the local Red Flame group with whom they produced a series of posters for 'Rock Against Racism'. They also turned out regularly for the annual May Day parade and fair, although the organisers generally contrived to demonstrate their distrust of the group. On one occasion, for example, the SAG stall was isolated from the rest of the festival beyond the refreshments stall, but undeterred SAG set up its 'Random Slogan Generator (Central Committee approval not required)', and a 15-foot-long banner with the slogan 'Create Anarchy Now!' held aloft by helium-filled balloons. This did little to endear them to the more traditional left groups, but their pamphlet 'Better Black and Red than Red or Dead' caused the Marxist–Leninist and Maoist groups to send a delegation telling SAG that they were now showing 'the correct spirit of solidarity'. Significantly, however, it was the SAG stall which excited most interest among the festival goers, partly because group members were wearing fancy dress, giving away balloons and selling comics. The unofficial slogan was 'If we can't dance to it, it's not our revolution'.

Overall the group was very active, very visible and very successful. But underlying the public success were a series of crises within the group. As anarchists the members of SAG faced particular problems around the issue of leadership. Specifically the question of how to organise without leaders. Aside from high anarchist theory about how to achieve the just society, and what such a society would look like, this precipitated a series of intense debates about what limited objectives to aim for, and how to achieve them.

Ideological dilemmas

1. What to do?

Having agreed that SAG had limited options for action, there remained the problem of what, more precisely, it could and *should* do. The group had several discussions about it, of which the following, from SAG's early days, is an illustrative example.

The meeting was held in Holden's house, with ten members present and crammed into the front room. Holden, who had been feeling impatient with the group's apparent unwillingness to act up to that point, complained that most of the meetings were just discussion groups with nothing ever decided about doing anything. Chris Brunel, a mathematics graduate of the local university, spoke for several members of the group when he replied: 'That's OK. I like the discussions. That's why I come'.

'Is that all we're here for then?' asked Holden 'In that case why call ourselves an anarchist group? We might just as well call ourselves a political philosophy group and give up the pretence of being serious about politics.

You know we're a joke on the Left, don't you? They think that all anarchist groups ever do is talk and smoke dope. Are you telling me they're right? Because if you are I'll leave the group now. I want to do more than just talk.'

This caused some embarrassed shuffling amongst those in the meeting. Chris shrugged, 'I hadn't thought about it. I guess you're right.'

De Fey looked at Holden and Brunel, and then addressed the rest of the group: 'OK. But what *can* we do? I mean, we could sell papers, or give out leaflets, or something. But is that the kind of thing we *really* want to do?'

'Hey, great idea' said Brunel

'But *which* papers?' asked Holden

'What about *Peace Journal*?' recommended Pound

'And *Black Banner*?' suggested Marten

'No,' replied de Fey. 'its too violent and unreflective.'

Marten protested: 'No it's not.' But de Fey looked set to argue, so he backed down 'OK. Forget it. Why don't we write a leaflet and distribute it in the market square?'

'OK' responded Holden 'what about, and who's going to write it?'

'Er . . . I don't know. May be we could talk about it.'

'*I* know' interrupted Pencross 'why don't we produce a series of leaflets caricaturing the leaflets put out by other political groups. You know – Trots arguing about where the comma goes; CP worrying about Central Committee directives – that sort of thing.'

There were murmurs of agreement at this, even some excitement. 'Fantastic idea!' said Brunel 'Let's do it.'

'So you think you know enough about those groups to parody what they write do you?' asked Holden

'Er, no' responded Pencross 'but I thought you could . . .'

'Not me. I think it's a crap idea. Anyway I don't know enough to do it either.'

'Oh. OK then, forget it.'

'Why don't we buy up a load of those booklets *About Anarchism*, and give them away in the street?' suggested Baker.

'For what purpose? And whose going to pay for them?' retorted Holden.

'Yes. I suppose it *is* a bad idea.'

The discussion continued like this for some time. Someone would make a suggestion, Holden commented, and the idea was withdrawn. Finally, after an extended silence, Jo Pencross said to Holden: 'Why don't you tell us what you think we should do.' At this Holden lost his temper:

'Listen. I'm not your *leader*. It's not up to me to tell you what to do and what not to do. You seem to think that just because I ask questions about the ideas that I'm somehow telling you you shouldn't do them. I've got a *right* to express my opinions and ask questions, but just because I think an idea is crap or impractical it doesn't mean that *you* have to agree with me. Bloody hell, if you want to do it then *do* it. What are we? The Conservative Party? You've got minds of your own, so use them.

What's been happening here? Every time I express a reservation you back off. Why don't you *think* about how to do things if you want to do them, instead of waiting for someone to give you permission? You shouldn't need approval from me or anyone else. If you *do* then join the Sparts or something, because you're not behaving, or even thinking, like anarchists. It's a bloody farce . . .'

Now Alice joined in: 'OK Corin, we get the point. Don't get so upset about it. We're not all as experienced as you. People here are still trying to find their direction.'

'Sorry.'

The group was silent, and obviously stunned. No-one spoke until Ellen Pound said: 'I'm glad Mike wasn't here. I don't think he would have had so much trouble about being asked what to do.' De Fey snorted, and several of the group relaxed, although the smiles were uncertain. 'I think the meeting is over. Anyone want to come to the pub?'

'Actually,' said Marten 'I think I'd rather have a cup of tea.'

2.   How to do it?

Not every meeting was as tense, of course, and decisions about actions were taken, usually by consensus. But having agreed to do something, the problem was then how to achieve it. The 'Guy Fawkes poster' is a good example in which tensions had run high.

The decision to make the poster had been made peacefully enough. De Fey had proposed it one evening, and the group endorsed the idea enthusiastically. Furthermore, when Marten offered to design it there was no argument. It was generally felt that this was a particular contribution that he could make to the group's activities, beside which if they didn't like it they could always reject it. The real problems arose when the design had been accepted and the decision taken to print it.

Holden arranged with Louise Street, a local printer and Red Flame member, for the group to have access to her silk screen presses, and for her to prepare the screen, while Marten arranged the paper supply. The three of them also arranged the date and time for printing the posters.

All of this the group accepted without argument, although there were one or two grumbles about 'leaders' at the meeting before the posters were to be printed.

At first everything went well. Eight members turned up, and everyone took a hand in printing. Marten, however, began to show visible irritation at the quality of the prints, and was told sharply by several of those present that he was not 'in charge', and that it was not up to him to 'dictate standards'.

Boredom, however, soon set in, and several of them went into a corner to 'have a rest'. Effectively they took no further part in the process, and eventually went to the pub leaving Holden, Marten and Street to carry on. At the following group meeting Marten complained about attitudes towards the printing 'If you're not going to do it properly, why bother at all?,' to which de Fey replied: 'Quality isn't everything, so long as people can read them.'

Holden, meanwhile lectured the group on 'collective responsibility'. Mike Farmer responded with an attack on what he called 'the great unsoundness of the dictatorial tendencies around here', and commented: 'You wanted to do it. It's got nothing to do with us what *you* choose to do.'

Holden replied 'No, but you'll make use of the posters alright. *And* take the credit if you can. Besides, it was a *group* decision to do the poster, and therefore *everyone* should have contributed.'

'Not at all. *I*, for one, wasn't here when the decision was made. So why should I help? And if the rest got bored or wanted a rest, why shouldn't they? You've got no authority to prevent them, or make them feel bad about it even.'

'That's true. But if anarchism means *anything*, it means taking collective responsibilities seriously without *having* to be told. It's about *self*-discipline. We have to be able to rely and *trust* each other to help. 'From each according to ability; to each according to need'. That's what Bakunin said about it, and he was right.'

'Oh come off it . . .'

At this point Pound interjected: 'This is getting silly. The posters are done, and it isn't worth falling out about what happened the other night. If we do it again we can sort it out then.'

De Fey added: 'Right then, that's settled. When are we going to post them up, and when are going to the pub?'

Issues to consider

- What are the main issues raised by this case?[2]
- What does the case tell us about the process of organising and the nature of leadership?[3]
- Is leadership inevitable? Why or why not?[4]

Notes

1. Les Prince is a lecturer in organisational behaviour at the Institute of Local Government Studies, Birmingham University, Birmingham B15 2TT. The case is based on real events, although pseudonyms are used throughout.

2. To examine the relationship between leadership and hierarchy, see Gibb (1958, 1969). For consideration of the importance of experience and knowledge in the negotiation of order in groups see Foucault (1979), Hosking and Morley (1992), Lukes (1974), Paton (1983) and Prince (1988). For a good introduction to anarchism in general (and anarchist theories of leadership in particular) see Rooum (1993), Walter (1984), Ward (1988) and Woodcock (1977).

3. See Brown and Hosking (1984), Gibb (1969), Hollander (1964, 1974), Hosking and Morley (1992) and MacGregor-Burns (1978).

4. In addition to the above literature, see Gemmill (1986), Gemmill and Oakley (1992), and Parker and Shotter (1990) for provocative views of leadership as a myth which serves to reinforce existing social beliefs and structures about the necessity of hierarchy and leaders in organisations.

Case 26   Centaur Office Supplies[1]

Frank Tsoukas, sales director at Centaur Office Supplies, put down the telephone and let out a subdued cry of pleasure. He explained to his somewhat bewildered assistant that his top saleswoman had finally managed to get the lucrative Rocastle University account.

'The University are expanding again and they're having trouble getting deliveries from one of their regular suppliers. If we can fill the order by the end of the month, they'll become regular customers. I needn't tell you what a coup that would be!'

'That really is good news,' replied his assistant, sincerely. 'But will George be able to deliver the goods?'

The 'George' in question was George Bennett, production director. Bennett was in his early fifties and had been with the company for 18 years. Just over a year ago he had successfully masterminded the design and implementation of a large amount of complex new automation technology in the production department virtually single-handedly. It was true that the new system had created considerable disruption to Centaur during its lengthy implementation as Bennett had made few, if any, allowances for the 'knock-on' effects in other departments. He also had a reputation for being uncooperative and had jealously guarded his control of the 'automation project' (as he liked to call it).

8 months ago, and against all the odds, Centaur had won a large order to fit out a new office block. George Bennett had insisted the order could not be completed in the time scale quoted to the customer by the Sales department and a full blown argument had broken out between the respective directors.

The issue was finally resolved following the direct intervention of Caroline Haste, the managing director. She agreed to pay overtime to production workers and told Bennett to keep production going throughout the weekend. The order was filled on time but, privately, both men had resented the fact that the managing director had intervened.

Placing these thoughts aside, Tsoukas picked up the internal telephone. Moments later he was talking to Bennett, telling him about the University order.

'Hold it right there,' Bennett interrupted. 'There is no way we can fill that order. It may be good for your bonus to get these big rushed orders, but my department can't just drop everything. We're in the middle of a large production run. Anyway, the University have a long-term contract with Dorchester Office Supplies. Whatever reason they have for switching to us won't last long. Once they've sorted out the problem with Dorchester, the University will drop us like a ton of bricks. It isn't worth the bother. Ring the University back and cancel the order.'

Tsoukas, red-faced with anger, slammed the telephone down and marched out of his office.

Caroline Haste was just about to leave her office when Tsoukas burst in. Taking a few moments to catch his breath, he outlined the gist of his conversation with the production director.

'The fact of the matter is that although I'm not a production man, Caroline, I could get that order out. Surely the new production system Bennett put in is flexible enough to cope with priority orders? If it isn't, he had no business installing it in the first place,' he concluded.

Caroline listened thoughtfully and then picked up the telephone. After a couple of rings, George Bennett answered. A short conversation ensued. Just before Caroline place the receiver down she said: ' Thanks a lot George. I won't forget this. You're a true company man.'

'There you are,' she told Tsoukas. 'He's agreed to halt the current run tomorrow and will start the university order on Friday if you can get the details to him by tomorrow lunchtime. You have to make George feel important you know. If you flatter him a bit, he stops arguing.'

Frank's face reddened again. 'You might have to flatter him but I certainly don't!' he shouted. 'How can I work properly when an incompetent like Bennett tries to block me every time. What would have happened if you had been away for a week? I can't possibly work in the same company as him. You've got to do something about him!'

He stormed out of the managing director's office, leaving Caroline to consider his last words. She wondered if Frank was seriously demanding she make a choice between Bennett and himself. To discipline or sack the production director at Frank's behest would totally undermine her authority. Yet she felt that his complaints were partly justified. She also felt slightly to blame because she had taken little interest in the work of the production department or the 'automation project'. Her own background was in sales and marketing and she found technical details rather boring.

If she were to make a choice between Bennett and Tsoukas, she would much prefer to keep Tsoukas. He was by far the best sales director Centaur had ever had. She recalled proudly how she had managed to entice him away from a competitor with a generous salary package which, given the man's subsequent performance at Centaur, now seemed a trifle mean! On the down side, he did have an annoying habit of bickering and complaining about production delays to everyone but the production director. It was clear that Frank Tsoukas had taken a personal dislike to his fellow director almost from the moment he joined Centaur.

Then there was George Bennett. For all his faults he was a technical wizard, thought Caroline. He would be difficult to replace and, anyway, the company prided itself on keeping on good staff until retirement. After all, she mused, Centaur culture stressed the importance of company loyalty. She hoped the confrontation between the two men would blow over just as it had done eight months ago.

2 days later, with the Rocastle University order in full production, Tsoukas handed in his resignation to the managing director. The letter detailed the history of his complaints against Bennett. A copy was also sent to the Chair of the Board.

Case resolution

- Outline and analyse the problems facing Caroline Haste in the short and long term and offer recommendations for their resolution.[2]
- To what extent, if any, has Haste's leadership style contributed to the conflict?[3]
-

Notes

1. This case study of a fictitious company was inspired by the short case story written by Alvar Elbing (1978).
2. For a consideration of the possible causes of, and remedies for, the conflict between the departmental heads in this case, see McCann and Galbraith (1981), Neilsen (1972), Pondy (1967) and particularly Shapiro (1977).
3. Useful general readings on leadership include Bennis (1990), Fiedler and House (1988), Smith and Peterson (1988), Stodgill (1974) and Vroom and Jago (1988).

Case 27   The Mussolini of Detroit[1]

Introduction: Henry Ford (1863–1947)

Henry Ford was born in 1863 on a farm near Detroit, Michigan. At the age of 28, Henry decided to become a mechanic rather than a farmer. He had a strong feeling for nature together with a revolutionary determination to lighten the farmer's toil – or, as he put it: 'to lift drudgery off flesh and bone and place it on steel and motors.'

The young Henry Ford loved machinery and detested horses,[2] so aptly enough he spent the 29th and 30th years of his life designing and building a horseless carriage – a quadricycle with an internal combustion engine. It was completed in 1893. He proudly proclaimed that this 'gasoline buggy . . . made a racket and it scared horses'.[3]

7 years later, Ford and eleven associates founded the Ford Motor Company. In 1908 the Model T – the 'car for the great multitude' – was launched. By 1920 every other motor car in the world was a Model T Ford; Henry Ford had bought out his eleven partners and become the sole owner of the Ford Motor Company; he was a millionaire and probably one of the most famous people in the world.

Life on the line

The way Ford managed his car plants was strongly influenced by a missionary zeal based on his belief that he could bring salvation and liberation to the world through machinery. He went so far as to declare machinery to be the 'new Messiah'. Certainly, men in the Ford car plants had to bow down to the demands of Ford's mass production system.

As Ford explained:

> We measure on each job the exact amount of room that a man needs. . . This brings our machines closer together than any other factory in the world. To a stranger they may seem piled right on top of one another, but they are scientifically arranged, not only in the sequence of operations, but to give every man and every machine every square inch that he requires and, if possible, not a square inch, and certainly not a square foot, more than he requires. Our factory buildings are not intended to be used as parks.[4]

Job designs were based on simplification and fragmentation:

> Some of the operations are undoubtedly monotonous – so monotonous that it seems scarcely possible that any man would care to continue long at the same job. [But] the most thorough research has not brought out a single case of a man's mind being twisted or deadened by the work. The kind of mind that does not like repetitive work does not have to stay in it.[5]

Socialising the Ford worker

Unfortunately for Henry Ford, a great majority of assembly line workers did not tolerate repetitive labour of the kind offered at his Detroit factory. Life on the line was too physically demanding and mind-numbing for most people to endure. Even the introduction of the famous Five Dollars a Day scheme in 1914 only managed to reduce annual labour turnover from 423 per cent in 1913 to 215 per cent by 1919.[6] The fact remained that working for Ford not only meant repetition, it meant committing yourself to a system of harsh discipline whilst at work and to a life style outside of the factory gates free from 'any malicious practice derogatory to good physical manhood and moral character'.[7]

Ford believed that an employee who lived 'aright' would also work 'aright' and he focused his missionary zeal on 'making men as well as automobiles'.[8] He was passionately opposed to gambling, drinking alcohol, smoking, and sex outside of marriage. He insisted that any employee discovered indulging in any of these activities should be expelled from the 'prosperity sharing' Five Dollars a Day scheme. Ford established a Sociological Department to administer this new scheme and to monitor the behaviour of his employees. Headed by John R. Lee, this department employed 50 investigators to 'promote the welfare of the workforce and to assist the large numbers of people who converged on Detroit to work for Ford to adjust to their new way of life'.

Employees who did not meet the specifications of the Sociological Department were put on probation. By 1915, 90 per cent of employees were deemed fit to qualify for the Five Dollars a Day scheme, but they could be removed from the scheme at any time if they lapsed into 'bad' ways.

The drive to absolutism

In his autobiography, Henry Ford suggested that a person can best be viewed as a machine. Yet he argued that a business is not a machine:

It is a collection of people who are brought together to do work and not to write letters to one another. It is not necessary for any one department to know what any other department is doing. If a man is doing his work he will not have time to take up any other work. It is the business of those who plan the entire work to see that all of the departments are working properly toward the same end. It is not necessary to have meetings to establish good feeling between individuals or departments. It is not necessary for people to love each other in order to work together. Too much fellowship may indeed be a very bad thing, for it may lead to one man trying to cover up the faults of another. That is bad for both men.'[9]

As far as Henry Ford was concerned, his factories had no formal organisation, no specific duties attaching to any position, no line of succession or authority, very few titles, no conferences, no red tape and as little interpersonal contact between employees as possible. He believed that this enabled maximum labour flexibility. In reality, all work was preplanned and all employees' activities were prescribed. Nothing happened without Henry Ford's personal knowledge and authorisation.

Unfortunately, as the profitability of his company increased, so too did the owner's missionary zeal. No longer content to hide his light under a bushel, he began to glory in self-aggrandisement:

Plot conscious and profoundly suspicious by nature, he could never bring himself to trust even the men who worked with him closely, and had done so faithfully for years. Eventually, Ford came to resemble a feudal lord, ever doubtful of the loyalty of his subjects, actually going so far as to encourage disharmony and bickering among his more important retainers. By such means he expected each rival for his favor to act as a counterweight and an informer against every other member of the entourage.[10]

As his self-esteem continued to soar, he grew more and more sensitive to criticism from any quarter. To help alleviate his feelings of insecurity, Ford appointed Charles Sorensen as factory superintendent and Ernest Liebold as his private secretary. Here were two men with authoritarian personalities even more pronounced than Ford's own.

Among line managers, office workers and shopfloor personnel, Charles Sorensen quickly became the most feared man in the organisation. On the shopfloor he was known as 'Iron Charlie' – master of the speed-up. In 1921, on Ford's orders, he ruthlessly increased the speed of the assembly line by 100 per cent, whilst simultaneously cutting the number of workers by 30 per cent and cutting their wages by 25 per cent.

Management were not spared Ford's ruthlessness. Under his instruction, Sorensen and Liebold carried out a wholescale purge of Ford management between 1919 and 1922. Virtually all the company's senior managers and most brilliant lawyers, engineers and designers were either fired or forced to resign for questioning Ford's supreme authority on all matters.

Some of the tactics employed during this purge verged on the sadistic. For example, during the purge of 50 per cent of all office staff, one large group of clerks returned to their office after a lunchbreak to find that their desks had been chopped to pieces with an axe. A poster on the office wall informed them that their services were no longer required.[11]

At the height of these purges, the Sociological Department was abolished. It was replaced by the more ruthless Service Department. By the end of the 1920s Henry Ford controlled all his employees by fear – aided and abetted by a Service Department which, within a matter of years, was to become the largest private quasi-military organisation in the world.[12]

The reign of fear

Harry Bennett, ex-sailor and lightweight boxer, chief of the Ford private police force by 1928 and head of the Service Department by 1932, personified Henry Ford's passion for one-man management. As Ford's right-hand man, Bennett was given almost unlimited powers to ensure that the business ran smoothly. He continued and expanded the Ford tradition of hiring criminals, disgraced policemen, ex-professional boxers, even known gangsters. Henry Ford enjoyed having 'hard men' around him:

> For something like two decades, the Ford worker was marshaled into submissiveness by his mere knowledge of Bennett's alliance with the underworld and by the appearance of the Servicemen whose profession was written into his face. . . For years after Bennett came to power, it was the proud, undisguised aim of the Service Department to blot out every manifestation of personality or manliness in a Ford plant. Striving for such an end, Bennett's mercenaries finally mastered every tactic from the swagger of the Prussian drill sergeant to outright sadism and physical assault.[13]

No-one was safe from the scrutiny and brutality of the Servicemen. Blue- and white-collar workers, dealers, sales representatives, even top executives found themselves shadowed by Bennett's men inside and outside the Ford plants in Detroit. Midnight raids on employees' homes were not uncommon, especially after the Ford edicts of 1930 (banning the consumption of alcohol in the home) and 1932 (compelling all employees to grow potatoes in their garden or yard). In vain efforts to divert the attentions of the Service away from themselves, employees regularly informed on one other and an air of mutual distrust permeated the entire Ford organisation.

Bennett placed spies in as many departments, sections and sales outlets as he could. On the factory floor, where smiling and talking were strictly forbidden by the owner, workers were always fearful of strangers on the shopfloor:

The spies and stool pigeons report every action, every remark, every expression. When a new man comes into a section he is looked at with suspicion and observed carefully. They try little stratagems to test him. One of them will risk his job and ask him a question. If a look of genuine terror comes over his face, he is all right. He's a Ford worker like the rest. But if he answers and tries to draw his questioner away from his work, he is a stool pigeon.[14]

Ford himself believed that humanitarian or social considerations had no place in the work environment. Within his own organisation (and elsewhere) Ford regarded any signs of humanitarianism or charity with contempt:

I pity the poor fellow who is so soft and flabby that he must always have 'an atmosphere of good feeling' around him before he can do his work. . . Not only are they business failures; they are character failures also; it is as if their bones never attained a sufficient degree of hardness to enable them to stand on their own feet. There is altogether too much reliance on good feeling in our business organisations.[15]

Conclusion

Harry Bennett stands out among Ford's other strong men in having become the most potent of them. Biographer Keith Sward argues that Bennett was the most perfect second self Henry Ford ever produced.[16] In the words of the *Detroit Free Press* newspaper: 'This proud, impulsive bundle of dynamite was developed by Henry Ford just as surely as the motor that drives millions of Ford cars.'[17]

It seems clear that Henry Ford knew a great deal about the activities of Bennett and his Servicemen. Yet Ford himself remains something of an enigma. Was he a simple-minded man with an obsession with machinery and the 'common man', or was he an evil genius? Biographer Jonathan Leonard points to Ford's cruelty, his insensitivity, his intolerance, his hatred of everything related to beauty, freedom, human dignity. While tempted to call him the evil genius of twentieth-century America, Leonard professes that it is easy to forget about the man's excesses and feel only the emotion of pity.[18]

Finally, the Reverend Samuel Marquis, one-time head of the Sociological Department, offers the following observation:

He has in him the makings of a great man, the parts lying about in more or less disorder. If only Henry Ford were properly assembled! If only he would do in himself that which he has done in his factory![19]

Whatever the truth of the matter, there can be no doubt that the structure and culture of the entire Ford organisation in the 1920s and 1930s reflected the personality of the remarkable Henry Ford.

Issues to consider

- In 1923, Henry Ford wrote: 'A great business is really too big to be human. It grows so large as to supplant the personality of the man. In a big business the employer, like the employee, is lost in the mass.' Critically evaluate this statement in the light of the history of the Ford Motor Company.[20]
- To what extent can a founder determine the culture of an organisation?[21]
- How far can the nature and scope of Ford's leadership and power be understood from a psychological perspective? How useful is conventional leadership theory in this regard?

Notes

1. This description of Henry Ford was used by a reporter in the *New York Times*, 8 January 1928. The journalist went on the describe the Ford Motor Company as 'the world's outstanding example of complete autocratic control of a vast industry' (quoted in Sward, 1948, p. 369).
2. According to Bruckberger (1959, p. 182), most horses felt the same way about Ford.
3. Ford (1923), p. 32.
4. Ford (1923), p. 111.
5. Ford (1923), p. 106.
6. Exact figures for turnover are difficult to find. It would seem to depend if one takes Henry Ford's definition of 'voluntary' redundancy at face value. Matters aren't helped by reading his 1923 autobiography, where it states that 30,155 employees were 'let go' in the year 1919, of whom only 90 were actually fired (1923, p. 111). Ford goes on to say that between 1915 and 1922 labour turnover averaged between 3 per cent and 6 per cent per month (p. 130). This figure is Ford's own guess as no official labour records were kept after 1919. He boasted that 'we now think so little of our turnover that we do not bother to keep records' (p. 130). For an evaluation of the causes and effects of the Five Dollars a Day scheme, see Raff (1989).
7. Quoted in Nevins (1954), p. 556.
8. Quoted in Marquis (1923), p. 155.
9. Ford (1923), p. 92.
10. Sward (1948), p. 185.
11. This story and many others were related by the Reverend Samuel Marquis (1923). At the time, he was head of the Sociological Department. He resigned in 1921 – blaming the disappearance of 'justice and humanity' at Fords for his action.
12. New York Times, 26 June 1937. At the peak of the department's trade union-busting activities, over 3000 Servicemen were employed.
13. Sward (1948), p. 306. An insight into the machismo mind of the Servicemen can be gleaned from the fact that a favourite pastime for a few of the more senior men was the keeping of lions. Things sometimes got out of hand – one man was 'practically stripped naked' after being pushed into a darkened room with an uncaged lion during a Service Department party – and Bennett felt obliged to put a lion tamer on the Service Department pay roll in 1937 (see McCarten, 1940).

14. Leonard (1932), p. 235. Any form of communication on the assembly line had been strictly forbidden from the earliest days of Ford assembly line work. Of course, covert means of communication were developed (e.g. the 'Ford whisper'), but the fear of disciplining by a Serviceman restricted even this most innocuous form of identity work.
15. Ford (1923), p. 265.
16. Sward (1948), p. 341.
17. Detroit Free Press, 8 February 1942, p. 10.
18. Leonard (1932), p. 11.
19. Marquis (1923), p. 167.
20. The quote is from Ford's autobiography (1923, p. 263). For more details about the Ford Motor Company, see Beynon (1973), Ford (1923), Jardin (1970), Marquis (1923), Rae (1969) and Sward (1948).
21. See Kets de Vries and Miller (1984a, 1984b) and Schein (1985, 1989).

Case 28   Conflict at Medical Supplies Limited[1]

Medical Supplies Ltd is a medium-sized organisation which supplies materials and equipment to local hospitals and community doctors' surgeries. The company has a bureaucratic structure and includes a number of departments, such as materials ordering, materials stores, transport, accounts and personnel.

Gordon Steele joined Medical Supplies 3 years ago and is currently the manager of the large warehouse where all the company's materials are stored. Aged 42, he is a university graduate who had spent 10 years as a junior officer in the Army before joining the company.

It was Monday morning and Gordon Steele was just welcoming the annual batch of three student trainees who were to be employed on a temporary basis over the summer period. After outlining the work programme for the next 8 weeks, he offered the following advice:

> Be careful how you behave in front of the employees here. They are a pretty rough bunch of people. Their work is simple and routine, and, as a result, we can keep labour costs down by hiring unskilled men of generally low intelligence. Most of them are from the poor part of town and tend to resent students coming in to work with them. Don't lend them any money or get involved in any gambling or all your wages will disappear before you get them. My advice is handle them with care.

For their first 3 weeks, the students were assigned to the surgical stores section of the warehouse, under the supervision of Harry Katama, a man who had been with the company since its inception 17 years ago.

After a few days working under Harry's supervision it became clear to the trainees that he was highly respected by all twelve employees in surgical stores. They were told on numerous occasions that he was 'a hard but fair supervisor'. 'Above all,' the trainees were advised, 'don't argue if he tells you to do something.'

The trainees did their best to follow this advice and by the end of his first week they found that Harry was spending more and more time with them. They were pleasantly surprised when he invited them to lunch in a bar across the street where he and the five other warehouse foremen were regular lunchtime customers. It became obvious during lunch that Harry was the informal leader among this group, and when he summed up the lunchtime conversation in the following manner everyone nodded in agreement:

> Gordon tries hard. He's tried to improve things here but he hasn't doesn't really understand enough about the warehouse business. He's good with the company boss though – look at the money he got us for a new fork-lift truck. But then he messes things up and buys the wrong one! He just doesn't know what to do and won't listen when you tell him. He would rather write a memo than communicate face-to-face.

The trainees began thinking that the cautionary advice Gordon Steele had offered them about dealing with other members of the section was at odds with their experience during the week. All members of the surgical stores section had proved very friendly and cooperative.

On returning from the bar, the trainees discovered that Gordon had circulated a memo to section employees stating that all forms used in the routeing of materials in the warehouse would be changed to enable a more precise location of materials within the warehouse to be recorded. The memo stated simply that the change was to be made and requested that all employees familiarise themselves with the new forms over the weekend so that they could follow the new directive at the beginning of the following week.

On Monday morning everyone in surgical stores quickly went to work distributing the backlog of materials which had been delivered on Saturday, making a note of each consignment's ultimate location. As was the practice in this section, all of the workers met in the section office to give this information to Harry so that he could copy it onto the formal forms which went to the office for inventory control. Harry claimed he used this procedure so that all the forms would be uniformly filled out and not lost or mutilated by the men carrying them around as they worked. It was quite obvious, however, that his main purpose for insisting on this procedure was that he wanted to know where every consignment in his department was located, so that when orders came through from the office he could tell the men exactly where the ordered material was located from memory. Indeed, Harry took great pride in his ability to remember exactly where, within each tier and row, every consignment was located.

At the Monday morning meeting there was considerable difference of opinion among the surgical stores employees as to how the locations should be entered on the new forms. Harry demanded that it should be done in the same way as before, while most of the other men protested that additional information regarding the exact location within each aisle and tier should be documented to keep the surgical section in line with the other five sections in the warehouse. However, Harry ignored all dissenting voices. He was not a man to be argued with, it seemed.

Early the next morning, Gordon Steele stormed into Harry Katama's office and said in a loud voice:

> Harry, you're not filling out the forms correctly. Didn't you read the memo? You're still doing it the old way and that's exactly what we're trying to get away from. The office needs new forms on yesterday's materials – correctly filled out – by coffee break.

Harry retorted:

> Look Mr Steele, this department has never had trouble with its locations before. We've been getting along fine, so why change anything? Why don't you handle the top management and let me handle my department? As long as I get the work done, why should you care how I do it?

Gordon replied with impatience:

> That's the trouble with you, Harry, you think only of yourself and not the company. No other department has complained about the new form. From now on the office wants a complete record of exactly where everything is and as long as I'm running the warehouse we're going to do it that way!

Harry was getting angrier all the time:

> Listen, you may run this warehouse, but I run the surgical stores section. Nobody really needs to know those locations except me, and you know it. Why don't you pick on the foremen who don't get their work done. My section has never created any problems.

Gordon moved around to Harry and put his hand on his shoulder: 'Calm down, Harry, remember who's boss here. Just calm down and stop shouting.' Harry would not be placated:

> Wait a minute. Who started the shouting? You come here and tell everyone that I don't know what I'm doing. I've run this section for over 10 years. Don't tell me to calm down and take your hand off me!

The exchange became increasingly heated and despite continued protestations, Gordon Steele did not remove his hand from Harry's shoulder and continued to insist that the directives outlined in the memo were followed. Finally, Harry lost his temper, turned round quickly and pushed the warehouse manager firmly on the shoulders, knocking him into a stack of pallets.

Gordon recovered his balance and walked away, saying: 'Right, you've had it now. Just wait until the boss hears about this. You may as well pack your bags and leave now!'

Case resolution

Outline and analyse the problems confronting Medical Supplies Ltd in the short and long term and offer recommendations for their resolution.[2]

Notes

1. This study of a fictitious organisation is adapted from 'The Crown Fastener Company Case' prepared by Katz (1978).
2. For a consideration of the possible influence of Steele's military training see Dixon (1979) and Johnson (1973). For a general consideration of the role of personality in this conflict see Schneer and Chanin (1987), Utley *et al.* (1989) and Veroff (1982). See Allinson (1984), Crozier (1964) and Hannan and Freeman (1984) for a consideration of the impact of organisational structure on the protagonists' behaviour. Consult French and Raven (1958), Greenhalgh (1987), Hickson et al. (1971) and Pfeffer (1981) for a political perspective on the case.

   In assessing the importance and appropriateness of the leadership style and change management skills of Gordon Steele and Harry Katama, the research overviews offered by Fiedler and House (1988), Smith and Peterson (1988), Stodgill (1974) and Vroom and Jago (1988) may prove useful.

PART 3

ANALYSING ORGANISATIONAL BEHAVIOUR

CHAPTER 6

Inter-group relations

Introduction

Individuals' allegiance to, and identification with, various social groups can have an important influence on their attitudes and behaviour. The notion of employee commitment can over-generalise the nature of such allegiance and hence overlook the fact that you can be committed to your work, to your colleagues, to your department, to your occupation or profession and/or to the company you work for. But these commitments will vary and will often conflict with each other – the most obvious example being the commitment to a trade union or professional association and the commitment to one's employer.

There are many groups within even the smallest of organisations. It is not only the varying degrees of commitment each group commands amongst its members that can have a significant impact on organisational functioning. The relations between these groups and the relative power each commands can be more crucial in shaping organisational behaviour. Hence, a psychological analysis alone is insufficient to understand fully the complexities of inter-group relations. Sociological theories of power and conflict have much to offer the case analyst here.

Case 29 outlines the background to the fatal launch of US Space Shuttle flight 51-L. The investigation carried out subsequently by a Presidential Commission revealed that the mid-air explosion which killed the crew was caused by a technical fault (a leak in one of the engine seals). The case examines the organisational and political context prior to the disaster and shows how organisational politics and conflicts can create an environment in which technical faults, whilst acknowledged as potentially lethal, can be ignored in the name of 'getting the job done'.

Case 30 discloses how the introduction of an apparently politically neutral technology can expose the underlying tensions and conflicts between different expert and professional groups. This short case illustrates the importance of understanding the relationship between professional groups in organisations for an analysis of organisational change and development. Case 31 – presented in a problem-solving format – describes differences between departments in a large telecommunications company. These differences adversely affect the management of the organisation and company performance generally. Your task is to find ways to alleviate these problems.

Case 32 examines the process of innovation within an office environment and reveals how the process can be helped or hindered by inter-departmental relations. Case 33, another problem-solving case, has much in common with the previous one. This time the innovation is an organisational change rather than the manufacture of a new product or service. The political issues are similar, however.

Case 34 is written in a more critical vein and opens up the issue of gender relations for deeper analysis in the context of an organisation's safety policy. My experience with using this case is that it can generate some particularly heated debate. Perhaps I should give tutors a safety warning on this case!

The final case in this chapter is the longest in the book. Prepared, tried and tested by my colleague Brendan McSweeney, it asks if organisational change is always desirable, or even necessary. The very rich and varied material it contains enables you to analyse the different, often conflicting values, assumptions and biases which lay behind corporate decision-making. Such material also encourages a critical examination of the power relations between different organisational groupings.

Case 29   The launch of space shuttle flight 51-L

Introduction

On 28 January 1986, NASA (the US National Aeronautics and Space Administration) Space Shuttle Flight 51-L ended in disaster when, 74 seconds after launch, the shuttle (the *Challenger*) exploded in mid-air, killing all seven crew members (including a civilian school teacher).

William Graham, head of NASA, immediately set up a commission of enquiry, chaired by William Rogers, with a remit to:

(a) review the circumstances surrounding the accident and establish the probable cause or causes of the accident; and
(b) develop recommendations for corrective or other action based upon the Commission's findings and determinations.

The Commission (containing two lawyers, a technical magazine editor, a military general, four aeronautical engineers and four physicists) was given 120 days to complete its investigations.

The space shuttle

The space shuttle comprises two distinct parts; the orbiter (which travels into space and then lands back on earth with a crew on board) and the larger booster rockets section (which propels the shuttle out of the earth's atmosphere). The booster section has two solid-fuel rockets which boost the shuttle for a few minutes before they separate and fall back into the sea. The booster fuel tank separates from the orbiter a few minutes later – much higher in the atmosphere – and breaks up as it falls back to earth.

Manufactured by Morton Thiokol in their factory in Utah (where 2500 employees work on the space shuttle programme), the individual rocket boosters are made in sections that are held together with joints. The Rogers Commission final report concluded that the immediate cause of the fatal explosion aboard the *Challenger* was a massive leakage ('blowby') of ignited fuel through the seals of one of these joints.

However, the Commission uncovered something quite unexpected during its enquiry and this was to cast new light on the genesis of the joint seals problem.

The seals problem

Professor Feynman, one of four physicists on the Commission, recalled how Allan McDonald, head of Morton Thiokol's Solid Rocket Motor Project, turned up, uninvited, to a closed meeting of the Commission:

> McDonald reported that the Thiokol engineers had come to the conclusion that low temperatures had something to do with the seals problem, and they were very, very worried about it. On the night before the launch, during the flight readiness review, they told NASA the shuttle shouldn't fly if the temperature was below 53 degrees – the previous lowest temperature – and on that morning it was 29. Mr McDonald said NASA were 'appalled' by that statement. The man in charge of the meeting, a Mr Mulloy [NASA's Manager for the Booster Project], argued that the evidence was 'incomplete' – some flights with [seals] erosion and blowby had occurred at higher than 53 degrees – so Thiokol should reconsider its opposition to flying. Thiokol reversed itself, but McDonald refused to go along, saying, 'If something goes wrong with the flight, I wouldn't want to stand up in front of a board of inquiry and say I went ahead and told them to go ahead and fly this thing outside of what it was qualified to.'[1]

Further investigations by the Commission revealed Morton Thiokol had been aware of a problem with its booster rocket section joint seals since the very beginning of the space shuttle programme.

The key problem was the lack of resilience of the 12-feet diameter rubber O-rings which seal the booster rocket sections. In normal usage, such as sealing oil in a car engine, O-rings plug a fixed gap. But in the case of the shuttle, this gap expands as the pressure builds up in the rocket and to maintain the seal the rubber has to expand rapidly to close the gap. In addition, at low temperatures, rubber tends to become harder and expands more slowly than it does at higher temperatures.

When the Thiokol engineers were discovering this problem in the early 1980s, they contacted the manufacturers of the rubber, Parker Seal Company, to ask for advice. Parker Seal informed Thiokol that O-rings were not meant to be used in such a way, so they could offer no advice. Despite this warning, Thiokol retained the O-ring design and developed a number of makeshift improvements (e.g. shims) to reduce the likelihood of seal erosion and blowby. To monitor the effect of these improvements, Thiokol engineers kept a record of every shuttle flight and logged the incidence of any erosion or blowby (see Figure 6.1).

FIGURE 6.1   The correlation between temperature and O-ring incidents

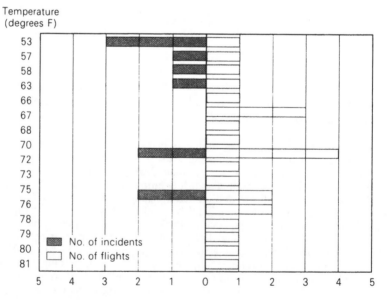

Source: Feynman, 1988.

However, the Rogers Commission discovered that the monitoring of seal erosion and blowby for each shuttle launch, although thorough, never led to any action despite a total of ten incidents of minor seal erosion and blowby since the start of the space shuttle programme (see Figure 6.1). It transpired that the only time the seals problem was ever formally addressed was during the flight readiness review carried out immediately prior to every space shuttle launch.

As a result, the relationship between low temperature and O-ring blowby – stressed by McDonald and suggested by Thiokol's own statistics – was overlooked. Indeed, Thiokol's senior scientist, Roger Boisjoly, testified to the Commission that when he raised this issue during the flight readiness review for Flight 51-E in February 1985, Larry Mulloy and other NASA officials considered the seals problem an 'acceptable risk'.

This was not the first time the O-ring joint seal problem had been highlighted in tests and flight readiness reviews. The Rogers Commission discovered that during 7 years of development and testing (between 1975 and 1981), NASA engineers at Marshall Space Centre found the design of the O-ring joints to be 'completely unacceptable'. It also transpired that by mid-1985, after 19 successful missions, NASA headquarters also acknowledged the seals problem. Yet no flights had ever been cancelled as the seals problem was seen as 'an allowable risk'.

In carrying his own investigations for the Rogers Commission, Professor Feynman was far from impressed by Thiokol's own analysis at this time. He argued that the company's analysis, based on computer modelling, effectively concluded that a little unpredictable leakage here and there could be tolerated, even though it wasn't part of the original design.[2]

However, on 20 August 1985, the company vice-president of engineering, Bob Lund, formally announced the formation of a seal erosion task team. He was spurred into action after receiving an impassioned memorandum from Boisjoly. This memo concluded:

It is my honest and real fear that if we do not take immediate action to dedicate a team to solve the problem, with the field joint having the number one priority, then we stand in jeopardy of losing a flight along with all the launch pad facilities.[3]

Both McDonald and Boisjoly felt that the work of the seal erosion task team was hampered by a lack of financial and human resource support from Thiokol's higher management. The frustration expressed by task team members was clearly illustrated in the following memo to Allan McDonald from task team member Bob Ebeling:

HELP! The seal task force is constantly being delayed by every possible means. We wish we could get action by verbal request, but such is not the case. This is a red flag.[4]

Despite promptings from NASA, the task team made little progress and no change in O-ring design was made prior to the launch of Flight 51-L on 28 January 1986. Indeed, the Rogers Commission were to discover later that Thiokol had written to NASA asking the agency to remove concern about O-ring blowby from its list of critical flight problems. Brian Russell, a Thiokol engineer, testified that because the O-ring was getting so much attention within the company (including the seal erosion task force) it only created more paperwork to keep the topic on the list of concerns being reviewed on a monthly basis:

> One apparent reason for the Thiokol request, which NASA apparently never acted on, was concern by Marshall Space Flight officials that there were too many unresolved issues on a list of technical problems associated with the rocket. The officials asked Thiokol to reduce the number, though it is not clear whether they were to actually fix the problems, or merely scratch them off the list.[5]

27 January 1986

The NASA launch chain of command for Flight 51-L is shown in Figure 6.2.

On Monday 27 January the launch of Flight 51-L was postponed for the fourth time. The previous flight had been the most delayed shuttle flight ever and NASA were eager to restore public (and US Treasury) confidence in the Shuttle space programme. Perhaps more significantly, the *Challenger* flight was to show-case President Reagan's 'Teacher-in-Space' program by carrying the school teacher, Christa McAuliffe. Further, Reagan was scheduled to deliver his annual State of the Union address on the evening of 28 January.

A temperature of 18 degrees Fahrenheit was forecast for the rescheduled launch on 28 January. As a result, a three-way teleconference took place between Morton Thiokol, the Marshall Space Flight Centre (MSFC) and the Kennedy Space Centre on the evening of 27 January.

On reviewing the evidence of a correlation between low temperature and seal erosion/blowby from the seals erosion task team, Thiokol's engineers and management unanimously recommended that the flight be delayed until the temperature exceeded 53 degrees. Larry Mulloy (MSFC) was unhappy with this statement and asked:

> My God, Thiokol. When do you want me to launch? Next April? The eve of a launch is a hell of a time to be generating new Launch Commit Criteria![6]

Both Mulloy and Stanley Reinhartz argued that the evidence was inconclusive and asked Thiokol to reconsider their recommendation. This was the first time NASA had ever challenged a contractor's no-launch recommendation.

FIGURE 6.2   The NASA Launch Chain of Command

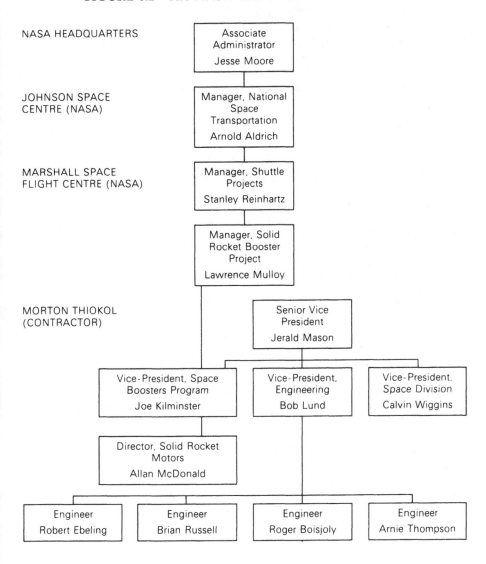

A five minute 'off-line' meeting of Morton Thiokol senior executives was called immediately to allow them to reconsider their position. During the meeting, Mason (senior vice-president) appealed to Lund to 'take off his engineering hat and put on his management hat'. After nearly 30 minutes' deliberation, the four executives went back 'on-line' and informed Mulloy and Reinhartz that they had voted unanimously to recommend *Challenger*'s launch. Aside from the four senior Thiokol executives present at the teleconference (Mason, Kilminister, Lund and Wiggins), all other Thiokol personnel were excluded from the final decision.

The following exchange between the Commissioners and representatives from Morton Thiokol sheds little light on the reason for this change of heart during the 'off-line' meeting:

> *Commissioner Rogers:* How many people were against the launch, even at the last moment?
> *Mason:* We didn't poll everyone.
> *Commissioner Rogers:* Was there a substantial number against the launch, or just one or two?
> *Mason:* There were, I would say, probably five or six in engineering who at that point would have said it is not conservative to go with that temperature, and we didn't know. The issue was we didn't know for sure that it would work.
> *Commissioner Rogers:* So it was evenly divided?
> *Mason:* That's a very estimated number.
> *Commissioner Feynman:* Could you tell me, sirs, the names of your four best seals experts, in order of ability?
> *Lund:* Roger Boisjoly and Arnie Thompson are one and two. Then there's Jack Kapp and, uh . . . Jerry Burns.
> *Commissioner Feynman:* Mr Boisjoly, were you in agreement that it was okay to fly?
> *Boisjoly:* No, I was not.
> *Commissioner Feynman:* And you, Mr Thompson?
> *Thompson:* No, I was not.
> *Commissioner Feynman:* Mr Kapp?
> *Lund:* He is not here. I talked to him after the meeting, and he said, 'I would have made that decision given the information we had.'
> *Commissioner Feynman:* And the fourth man?
> *Lund:* Jerry Burns. I don't know what his position was.
> *Commissioner Feynman:* So, of the four, we have one 'don't know', one 'very likely yes', and the two who were mentioned right away as being the best seals experts, both said no.[7]

Neither Larry Mulloy nor Stan Reinhartz discussed the details of their teleconference with Thiokol with their superior (Arnold Aldrich) because, as far as the two men were concerned, there had been no violation of Launch Commit Criteria and because Thiokol and MSFC had 'fully and openly examined the concern and satisfactorily dispositioned that concern'.[8]

2 May 1986

In his testimony to the Commission on 2 May, Boisjoly stated that on the previous day he had been chastised by Ed Garrison, President of Thiokol's Aerospace Operations, for 'airing the company's dirty laundry' with the memos he had given to Commissioner Rogers.

The testimony of Boisjoly and McDonald had been crucial in uncovering Thiokol's role in the *Challenger* disaster and Chairman Rogers announced that he was 'very upset' on being told that both men had apparently been punished by Thiokol. McDonald had been replaced as head of the company's Solid Rocket Motor Project and made Director of Special Projects. With some bitterness, he told the Commission: 'I was not demoted. They just took my people away and gave me a more menial job.'

After being made a member of (and then promptly removed from) Thiokol's *Challenger* disaster investigation team, Boisjoly had been designated seal coordinator for Thiokol's new task team on seal redesign. However, he told the Commission that he was isolated from NASA and the redesign effort, and that his design information had been changed without his knowledge and presented to NASA without his feedback.

On hearing the testimonies of McDonald and Boisjoly, Chairman Rogers criticised Morton Thiokol's senior management with the following words:

> If it appears that you're punishing the two people, or at least two of the people, who are right about the decision and objected to the launch which ultimately resulted in criticism of Thiokol, and then they're demoted or feel that they are being retaliated against, that is a very serious matter. It would seem to me, just speaking for myself, they should be promoted, not demoted or pushed aside.

Two weeks later, Boisjoly and McDonald requested a private meeting with the Thiokols' three top executives. Both men were eager to heal the rift they perceived developing between engineers and management within the organisation as a result of the bad publicity arising from national media coverage of the *Challenger* enquiry. According to Boisjoly, management was unreceptive throughout the meeting. The CEO told the two men that the company was 'doing just fine' until they had testified about their job reassignments. [9]

16 May 1986

McDonald and Boisjoly were restored to their former assignments within Thiokol.

21 July 1986

Boisjoly found his position untenable and was granted indefinite sick leave from the company.

Issues to consider

- The Rogers Commission concluded that the *Challenger* launch decision-making process was 'seriously flawed'. Who (or what) was responsible for the 'flaw'?[10]
- Analyse and explain the behaviour of Roger Boisjoly.[11]

Notes

1. Feynman (1988), pp. 141–3.
2. Feynman (1988), p. 138.
3. Boisjoly *et al.* (1989), p. 218.
4. Boisjoly *et al.* p. 219.
5. Sanger (1986), p. 7.
6. Boisjoly *et al.* (1989), p. 221.
7. Feynman, (1988), pp. 163–4
8. From Reinhartz's sworn testimony to the Rogers Commission.
9. Boisjoly *et al.* (1989), p. 230.
10. Analyses specific to the *Challenger* disaster include McConnell (1987) and Shrivastava *et al.* (1988). For a more general consideration of the issues see Bazerman *et al.* (1984), Bowen (1987), Janis (1972, 1982), Staw and Fox (1977), Whyte (1956), and Whyte (1986, 1989).
11. See Boisjoly's own account (Boisjoly *et al*, 1989). In addition, the antecedents of 'whistle-blowing' behaviour are discussed in Glazer and Glazer (1989), Miceli and Near (1985), Parmalee *et al.* (1982), Peters and Branch (1972) and Stumpf and Hartmann (1984). See Love (1989) for the means by which organisations can stop 'whistle-blowing'.

    You may also wish to consider the role played by conflicting dual allegiance (to employer and to profession). Cohen (1992), Gouldner (1957, 1958), Norris and Niebuhr (1983), Organ and Greene (1981), Raelin (1986) and Reichers (1986) are good sources for this.

Case 30   'PROMIS' and the politics of expertise[1]

PROMIS (Problem Oriented Medical Information System) was developed in the US during the 1970s in order to apply a technical solution to a number of problems inherent in medical care within large medical hospitals. These problems included the poor organisation of medical records and an over-reliance on the memory of doctors.

PROMIS incorporated computerised relational databases for medical records and automated sophisticated administrative functions. Access to these functions was via a touch-screen terminal. Yet the adoption of the system was extremely slow in the UK. Reasons for this emerged from experimental implementations within a number of hospitals in the late 1970s which indicated the important role played by the politics of expertise.

Nurses welcomed the openness of the system as it expanded their professional discretion and ability to intervene without approval from doctors. Pharmacists and radiographers welcomed the system for similar reasons. It was the doctors – the most powerful expert group within the traditional hospital hierarchy – who proved most resistant to the technology. PROMIS impinged on their sovereignty by codifying elements of their knowledge base and ceding some of their expertise to other expert groups. This conflicted with the fact that medical knowledge is continually expanding and difficult to codify and it is doctors who traditionally cope with this uncertain knowledge base.

Given the strong political positions of doctors in most hospital hierarchies (and the hospitals' dependence on the doctors' expertise) the slow uptake of PROMIS may be seen as a result of the dominant expert group exercising control of that technology – in this case by withholding the resources necessary (i.e. political support and cooperation) to achieve successful implementation.

Issues to consider

- What are the implications of this case for the design and implementation of information systems in organisations?[2]
- What does this case tell us about the potential problems associated with the management and control of professional groups within organisations.?[3]

Notes

1. This short case example is taken from the description of the PROMIS project by Willcocks and Mason (1987, pp. 17–18). For further details see Fischer *et al.* (1980).
2. For an analysis of the relationship between new technology, power and expertise, see Markus (1983), Markus and Bjorn-Andersen (1987), Perrolle (1986), Pettigrew (1973), Scarbrough and Corbett (1992) and Webb and Cleary (1994).
3. For an analysis of inter-professional conflict (especially relating to the introduction of new technology) see Albrecht (1979), Danziger (1979), Haug (1977) and Newman and Rosenberg (1985). For a more general consideration of the problems see Armstrong (1984, 1986), Blau (1979), Child *et al.* (1984), Norris and Niebuhr (1983) and Organ and Greene (1981).

Case 31   Pluto Telecommunications[1]

Introduction

'Just what is going on in this corporation?' shouted Veronica Tsang, managing director of Pluto Communications. Her question – aimed at no particular individual seated around the boardroom table – was provoked by the presentation which had just been given by management consultant, Andrew Wensley.

'Let me get this straight,' Veronica continued. 'Sales, Customer Services and Marketing are not only not talking to each other, on occasions they are actually working against each other. As a result of this, Pluto is losing new orders and getting an increasing number of complaints from existing customers. It's a disaster!'

'That is something of an over-statement, Ms Tsang, but essentially correct,' Andrew admitted.

'Thank you Mr Wensley. Please be so good as to wait outside while I sort this mess out.'

To the three directors sitting round the table, Veronica's request to Andrew sounded more like a threat directed at them. Certainly it was true that integration between their respective departments had become rather loose as Pluto Telecommunications had grown in size quite dramatically during the past year. The company's most recent new products had been launched to customers by Marketing without any advance notice or training being given either to Sales or Customer Services. For example, one customer account manager had been asked by a customer about Pluto's new combined fax, telephone and answering machine. The manager knew nothing about the product and subsequently it took her nearly 3 weeks to locate the relevant information and brochures from the Marketing department.

'Right then, gentlemen,' Veronica announced to the three departmental heads. 'Why is it that Service aren't passing leads they pick up at a customer's premises to Sales? Why do Sales staff promise the installation of a new system to a customer in a non-standard lead time without any consultation with Customer Services?'

'We seem to have three distinct groups within the company,' suggested Matthew Craven, director of Marketing. 'Now, whilst management theorists suggest such differentiation may be indeed be appropriate for the turbulent and uncertain telecommunications environment, they also stress the need for integration.'[2]

'Oh, I see, Mr MBA,' interrupted Veronica, sarcastically. 'So it's not a departmental problem, but a failing of top management. How convenient!'

'You misunderstand me,' Matthew replied. 'I don't know what goes on in other departments because (a) it isn't my job, and (b) I don't have the time to find out. Isn't it possible that personnel in the three departments are motivated by different things, work to different time-scales, virtually work within different organisations?'

In truth, Matthew Craven had hit upon the major problem confronting Pluto Telecommunications. This was conceded, somewhat grudgingly, by the managing director, and over the next hour and a half she sat down with the three men in order to identify and analyse the differences between the three departments – differences which made something of a mockery of Veronica's widely-touted notion of a unitary Pluto culture.

The differences centred on three dimensions – work motivation, time orientation, and work culture. The deliberations of the four executives centred on a comparison of the three departments along these dimensions.

Sales

Pluto's salesforce comprises account managers who are responsible for dealing with customers on a face-to-face basis and who have a portfolio of between 5 and 50 accounts, depending on the size of the customer.

According to Tim Boddy, head of Sales, his staff are motivated primarily by money – the more they sell, the higher the bonuses they receive. Their time orientation is short as they are anxious to boost their income every month. Also, staff have short time horizons, in that once having made a sale they are eager to see it is installed as soon as possible so that they can move on to the next bonus-earning sale.

Sales culture is based on, and perpetuated by, feelings of elitism and individualism. All successful sales staff have company cars, mobile telephones and visibly high incomes. They tend to dress very smartly and walk around company premises in a self-confident, sometimes arrogant manner. They operate very much as individuals and rarely resort to the formal chain of command when a problem arises.

Customer services

This department embraces many functions, but the two main groups of employees are Reception and Engineering. Reception staff process orders taken by Sales and convert them into work orders for the engineers. Engineering staff, in turn, are responsible for the installation and maintenance of Pluto equipment and services. John Buchanan is responsible for overseeing the smooth running of the department.

Customer Service managers are driven by annual service quality targets set by top management. For example, Reception staff are targeted to answer 90 per cent of telephone calls within 15 seconds, whilst Engineering staff are targeted with installing 90 per cent of telephone exchange lines within 6 working days and repairing 90 per cent of faults within 5 hours. Results are monitored daily. Although bonuses are linked to achieving these targets, these are fairly small (a maximum of £1000 per year). In fact, more action is taken when targets are not reached. In these instances, recriminations and formal warnings of poor performance are the norm. Bad news travels faster than good in Customer Services!

Compared to Sales, the work culture in Customer Services is very formal and the structure very hierarchical. A rather bureaucratic ethos persists whereby a manager of a certain grade is often reticent to deal with a manager of a lower grade directly. Written memoranda and E-mail messages are the dominant form of communication within the department.

Marketing

The main responsibilities of Marketing personnel are product launch and withdrawal, the development of marketing programmes and campaigns, competitor monitoring, forecasting and pricing. Performance targets are ill-defined and any bonuses staff may achieve are determined more by overall company performance than by their own efforts. The department's time orientation is fairly long-term compared to Sales and Customer Service. Staff often work on campaigns for delivery in 8 months' time, so they lack the sense of urgency felt by Sales personnel.

Marketing staff usually work in teams and have a strong group identity. This is encouraged by the fact that almost all employees are university business school graduates who have never worked in any other part of the company. Indeed, stories circulating in the department stress how tough and unpleasant the engineering world is and how ruthless the sales personnel can be. Most Marketing department employees are happy to stay in their comfortable London-based office.

Conclusion

'So, we have three quite distinct sub-cultures here, gentlemen,' Veronica concluded. 'Do you have any suggestions as to how we pull them together so that we can all play on the same side?'

The three directors said nothing. They weren't used to being consulted on matters of corporate strategy; internal or external. Indeed, within the Pluto's non-participative culture, Veronica's call for suggestions could easily be interpreted as a call for an admission of middle managerial weakness or failing leadership. All three directors felt that corrective action needed to be taken by senior management. Whilst they each had suggestions to make in this regard, none was prepared to air them in front of the others.

Case resolution

- Outline and analyse the problems confronting Pluto Telecommunications and offer recommendations for their resolution.[3]

Notes

1. A pseudonym for an existing company.
2. See Lawrence and Lorsch (1967) and Lawrence and Dyer (1983).
3. See Brett and Rognes (1986), Martin and Siehl (1983), McCann and Galbraith (1981), Neilsen (1972) and Sykes and Bates (1962) for consideration of how and why departmental loyalties may conflict with loyalties to the organisation. The works of Handy (1992), Galbraith (1977), Pugh (1979), Vieira (1992) and Walton and Dutton (1969) prescribe a variety of remedial integrative mechanisms.

Case 32 Management of innovation at Business Database Company[1]

Business Database Company (BDC) specialises in the creation of large business databases and the formulation of these data into reports that are sold to business organisations and consultancies. These reports include analyses ranging from credit reports to large-scale market research and are highly regarded in the European business world for their accuracy and high quality. BDC's main competitor is Andersen and Clarke.

Company growth certainly has been rapid over the past 5 years, thought Simon Hodges (BDC's recently promoted sales manager) as he examined progress reports on the seven new salespeople who had been added recently to his staff. They were university business school graduates who had been recruited a month or two before he had been promoted. The departments of information services (where data was collected and collated) and information analysis (where the reports were prepared) had seen a similar expansion in the number of university graduates among their staff.

Within a few months of starting work with the company, Angela Johnson (one of the new staff members) approached Hodges with an idea for a new product. Johnson explained that an ex-business school colleague (now working for Bytech Toys) had told her that Bytech urgently needed some specialised data, but did not require BDC to generate a written analytical report to go with it. What they were seeking was a software-based database (on floppy disks) containing specialised data and a reasonably 'user-friendly' database interrogation interface. Such a product would enable Bytech to undertake their own database interrogation and analysis so that they could generate their own internal reports. Bytech were willing to pay a considerable amount of money for such a product (far in excess of what BDC would have charged them for a comparable printed analysis and report). The only condition was that BDC deliver the product within 6 weeks. If this deadline could not be met, Bytech would offer the work to Andersen and Clarke.

Hodges, who had a certain fascination with computers, saw this as a potentially new (and lucrative) market for BDC to enter. Also he felt that to champion such innovation would virtually guarantee him promotion within BDC. With this in mind, he helped Johnson seek permission up the organisational hierarchy to develop the idea.

However, two weeks passed and, despite a number of follow-up telephone calls, permission was not forthcoming. Hodges put this down to the fact that the proposal would have to make a perilous journey up through at least five levels of BDC's bureaucratic hierarchy before it could be formally agreed at board level.

The delay prompted Hodges to consider the establishment of an informal design task force comprising representatives from the departments of sales, information services, information analysis, and finance. Having gained tacit approval from his immediate superior, Hodges sent an internal memorandum to the heads of the other three departments with a view to creating a design task force for a trial period. The memorandum stressed the innovative nature of the proposed group but made no reference to Johnson's new product idea. He thought it better to exploit the *kudos* associated with the phrase 'computer-based innovations' than to spell out details of the product itself at this early stage. He explained later to Johnson that this strategy aligned more neatly with the chairman's recent memorandum encouraging more widespread use of computers among BDC management.

Information services responded positively to the memo and the finance department expressed an interest and a desire to be 'kept informed if, and when, things developed'. However, no reply was forthcoming from information analysis. As a result, Hodges went along to see George Cash, head of information analysis, the following morning.

'What do you think of my idea, George?' Hodges asked as he entered Cash's office waving the memo in the air. He caught sight of the personal computer on Cash's desk. It had obviously never been used since its arrival 6 months before.

'Oh, that computer task force idea,' Cash responded without enthusiasm. 'I had a glance at your memo. I suppose we should make a show of moving with the times. It's hardly BDC's style though, is it? One of my new business school recruits might want to explore the idea of working in a paperless office, I suppose. I'll send Melville Shultz along if that's alright with you? He's a bright lad and is quite friendly with a number of your new recruits anyway. It wouldn't do any harm to encourage a bit of lateral thinking in the system, would it?' he quipped.

'Great,' said Hodges (although he wasn't sure that Cash understood the memorandum correctly). 'I'll call a task force meeting for tomorrow morning at 10 o'clock.'

At the meeting the following morning, Hodges was impressed by the rapport that developed between Johnson and Schultz. Within an hour the two of them persuaded the others that the specialised Bytech database could be generated with little disruption to conventional work procedures and loads. Schultz even gave a demonstration of a suitable user-friendly interface on the computer in Hodges' office. It turned out that he had been developing and using the interface in carrying his work for information analysis for the past 2 months anyway. When quizzed on this, Schultz confessed that Cash knew nothing of this. Hodges, in turn, promised not to tell Cash.

The meeting adjourned after Hodges obtained the agreement of the design task force members to take on the Bytech order.

In less than 2 weeks, the Bytech database and interface software was completed. Not only that, Bytech were very satisfied and, over the next two weeks, several other customers contacted Hodges to inquire whether a similar service could be offered to them.

News of the success of the new product soon spread round the sales department and other new salespeople began to suggest new product possibilities. Soon Hodges had several design task force teams coordinating work on new information products – mainly written reports based on customised variants of existing databases. Hodges was delighted to see that, with one or two notable exceptions, the various new task force products were set to achieve profit margins nearly double those achieved by conventional BDC product lines.

Within the sales department, all seemed well except for the longer-term employees. They were concerned about the procedural changes and the direction sales seemed to be heading. Also, Hodges realised that none of them had come up with any proposals for new products. Consequently, three senior salesmen came to Hodges' office to protest at the pace new databases and reports were being generated. They made it clear that the older workers preferred the traditional method of passing a new idea from one department to the next and getting top management approval before starting. Although this was time-consuming (often taking up to 2 months to get through BDC's bureaucratic system), it gave the salespeople a chance to familiarise themselves with the content of a new report and to update their sales catalogues.

'We don't want to stop change,' said one of the senior workers. 'We just want to do a good job with the products we have. It is wrong that these design teams should force change. I believe that quality is already being sacrificed in the name of speed. Not only that, a lot of customers are interested in these new self-analysis database disks and want a demonstration. We don't know how to run the wretched programs – even if we had a portable computer to run them on!'

Hodges felt in something of a quandary. He was confident that the success of the design task force teams would make him a strong candidate for promotion after the next annual staff review. Yet, if the established sales staff were unhappy, promotion was far less likely and he might lose some of these highly valued employees. However, if he were to disband the design task force teams, some of the more dynamic younger employees might leave the company.

Worse still, Hodges felt that failure to innovate would give Andersen and Clarke a competitive advantage over BDC at a time when both companies' market shares were under threat from European competition.

He could see that tension was growing between the two groups in sales and he wondered what he could do to reduce it. Furthermore, the printing department was beginning to complain about the rush of customised orders from sales and a few of the employees in information services expressed concern privately about the increased pace of work. To make matters worse, Cash had finally realised that some of the new disk-based products required little or no input from information analysis and he was getting agitated at the prospect of his department being 'rationalised'. Historically speaking, the information analysis department had always been the driving force behind BDC and he did not welcome the idea of sales gaining the ascendancy. Indeed, he expressed these same concerns to the finance director when they met, by chance, in the company car park that evening.

Hodges realised that had he opened something of a 'Pandora's Box' when he arrived at work the following morning to see Cash and the finance director waiting inside his office.

'Have you seen the latest memo from the chairman, Simon?' asked Cash with undisguised pleasure. 'It's a lot clearer than the one you sent me a little while ago!' he added. On reading the memo Hodges noted with dismay that it stressed the importance of creating a unified organisational culture and a happy, committed workforce.

'Apparently, it was agreed that these task force teams were for a trial period only,' added the finance director. 'I would suggest that now is a good time to disband them before other departments start complaining. Even I didn't know about them until last week when this Schultz fellow threw my department into chaos by sending in a substantial claim for copyright fees. He reckons he's owed money for every one of your new disk-based products that we've sold so far. Cash says he knew nothing about this. But the bottom line is this: you seem to have forgotten that you have yet to receive board approval for your little venture! It may well be making money, but there are such things as "proper channels" you know.'

'Anyway,' he continued, 'the whole issue is being raised under "chairman's business" at this afternoon's board meeting. Your request to initiate a new product was to have been item eleven on the agenda, but events have moved on since then, haven't they Simon? Has it ever dawned on you that the board might take exception to a sales manager attempting, single-handedly, to steer the company towards a customer-led, new technology-driven strategy?'

'Make sure you're on the premises this afternoon,' the finance director concluded as he turned towards the door. 'We might want to ask you a few questions.'

The two men left and a despondent Simon Hodges began preparing his defence in case he should receive the threatened summons from the board of directors. It did not hearten him to know that the finance director, a close friend of the chairman, wielded considerable power on the board.

Case resolution

- Outline and analyse the problems confronting BDC in the short and long term and offer recommendations for their resolution.[2]

Notes

1. This case study of a fictitious organisation was inspired by the short case story written by Daft (1983, pp. 298–9).
2. For a consideration of the structural barriers to innovation, see Burns and Stalker (1961), Crozier (1964), Drazin (1990), Feldman (1989), Francis and Winstanley (1988) and Hannan and Freeman (1984). See Hickson *et al.* (1971) and Pfeffer (1981) for analyses of the dynamics of inter-departmental conflict.

Case 33   Managing change at Cox's Container Company[1]

Cox's Container Company (CCC) is a large manufacturer of containers ranging from large metal road haulage containers to medium-sized plastic boxes used in the transportation of fragile goods. Its customers range from large transportation and delivery organisations to small specialist manufacturing companies. Since it was established in 1946, the company has steadily expanded and it now enjoys a large volume of national and international sales. The company employs just over 380 people.

Over the years, the ownership and senior managerial control of CCC has remained in the hands of the Cox family. Harold Cox, the founder and managing director, is regarded highly within the local community for his political and financial support for ethnic minorities in the area.

Just over two-thirds of the company's employees work in the production department and a large majority of these jobs are held by people from ethnic minorities. Nearly half of them have worked for CCC for 10 years or more and all senior positions in the department have been filled through the promotion of shopfloor employees. Production personnel jealously guard the autonomy they enjoy under their long-serving manager, Abdul Aziz.

The company has been facing increasing competition over the past 5 years. Although sales remain buoyant, profits have begun to fall because of reduced margins. Harold Cox was anxious to improve the profitability of the company, although he was unsure how to proceed. As managing director he was involved in all strategic decision-making but, in recent years (as he neared retirement), he had begun to insist that operational decision-making be carried out by other managers. Even so, there was little that happened in CCC without his knowledge.

In 1990, Harold Cox asked Erica Wilson, general manager of CCC, to conduct a review of the company's operations. Having carried out the survey entirely on her own and in some secrecy, Wilson concluded that CCC lacked effective operational and cost controls and she believed that the rapid growth of the company had created a managerial vacuum in financial and management accounting. She urged Harold Cox to recruit a number of managerial specialists in order to increase the profitability of CCC. Cox was impressed by the report and asked Wilson to oversee the organisational changes she thought necessary.

In early 1993, Wilson appointed John Straw as manager of CCC's new central administration department. Straw was a chartered accountant who had previously worked for the local government's taxation office. He was the first manager to be recruited from outside the organisation for over 15 years. His first job was to review all CCC's accounting procedures and to explore ways in which cost controls could be tightened.

Wilson planned to develop the central administration department in two further phases. The second phase would be to implement an appropriate budgeting system to replace the rather informal system in operation at the time of her survey whereby each department submitted an annual estimate of expenditures to the company treasurer for approval. The final phase would involve a systematic review of CCC's operational procedures and the implementation of a company-wide information system. This system would require all departments to inform the central administrative department (on a twice-daily basis) of work in progress.

By the summer of 1993, two more central administration managers had been appointed. Eric Long, the new budgeting section manager (previously employed by a large retail organisation) was given the task of developing the budget control system. Simon Pedder, another external appointee, was to use his systems analysis skills in a full review of CCC's operational procedures.

It wasn't long before Eric Long had developed a budget control system (similar to the one used by his previous employer) and he persuaded John Straw to arrange a meeting with all departmental heads so that they could be told the details of the new system.

With the exception of Abdul Aziz, all department managers attended the meeting. No major objections to the new system were raised, although Straw noticed that no-one seemed very keen on the new system. Also, he was a little concerned that the managers did not really understand how the new system would affect current working practices. The meeting decided to set up a steering group, comprising a representative from each department, to oversee implementation of the budget control system.

In the following months, John Straw received repeated complaints from both Long and Pedder concerning the lack of cooperation from Aziz. Eventually, he decided to confront him face-to-face.

'If you expect me to find the time to attend your stupid meetings, you're mistaken' Aziz told Straw angrily. 'From what I can see (and I speak for everyone in my department), your system completely undermines the way we have been working for years. My department achieves zero defects and we always get orders out on time. It seems to me that your beloved central administration department is building its own little empire to run the whole company. But none of you understand the complexities of production. I'll cooperate with you – but not in work time. I'm far too busy keeping this company in business!' Aziz turned his back on Straw and walked off.

Straw decided that, despite Wilson's desire not to be involved in the detailed running of the new department, he would have to enlist her help. He was angry at Aziz's outburst. If there was an empire being built within CCC, it was in the production department, he thought.

Case resolution

• Outline and analyse the problems confronting CCC in the short and long term and offer recommendations for their resolution.[2]

Notes

1. This case study of a fictitious organisation was inspired by the case report on Ward Metal Products Ltd. (Quebec) prepared by Pitsiladis (1983, pp. 300–1).
2. For consideration of the role of accountancy in the control of organisational behaviour see Armstrong (1984, 1986, 1987), Child *et al.* (1983), Hines (1988) and Markus and Pfeffer (1983). See Maas and Schaller (1991), Morley (1992) and Van Knippenberg and Ellemers (1990) for an analysis of the social psychological roots of inter departmental bias and conflict. See Hickson *et al.* (1971) and Pfeffer (1981) for a more sociological analysis. For consideration of the importance of organisational size and growth, see Greiner (1972) and Quinn and Cameron (1983). Finally, see Padsakoff *et al.* (1986) for an assessment of the impact of formalisation on employee attitudes.

Case 34   Making the worker safe for the workplace

Introduction

The past 100 years has witnessed a long and tragic history of employee injuries and deaths due to occupational diseases arising from the manufacture of chemical agents (e.g. silicosis, brown lung and cancer). Industry still takes its toll today. For instance, findings of a 1982 study by the National Institute of Occupational Safety and Health (NIOSH) revealed that 4½ per cent of US shopfloor manufacturing workers are exposed to a potential carcinogen each year. This represents a total of 1.7 million people. NIOSH also estimates that shopfloor exposure to chemicals causes around 30 per cent of all cancers.[1]

An additional hazard associated with the manufacture of chemicals is the risk of congenital (i.e. birth) defects. Of the 28,000 toxic substances listed by NIOSH, 56 are animal mutagens (causing chromosomal damage to the ova or to sperm cells), and 471 are animal teratogens (although harmless to the mother, these cause deformation of the foetus).

The US government requires animal testing of drugs and chemicals to ensure that any new product to which pregnant women may be exposed is harmless to the foetus. Many experts maintain that these tests, although unreliable, are the best available means of establishing toxicity of new substances. The protection of the foetus is complicated by the fact that the human embryo is most sensitive to toxic agents within the first 18 to 60 days of pregnancy. Unfortunately, conventional pregnancy tests are not accurate or reliable enough during these early stages when the foetus is most susceptible to damage.

As a result, many chemical companies have adopted a sweeping policy of prohibiting women 'of child-bearing potential' from all jobs which involve the risk of exposure to teratogenic agents, such as lead. Since a woman is assumed fertile until proven otherwise, this excludes approximately 60 per cent of all working women from these particular jobs.

A question of exclusion: protection or discrimination?

In January 1981, the *New York Times* revealed that a number of female workers employed by chemical companies, including Du Pont, had chosen to undergo voluntary sterilisation rather than give up high-paying jobs which involved the risk of exposure to teratogenic chemicals. The writer of the article, Philip Shabecoff, wondered whether a company should be allowed to discriminate against women in order to protect their unborn children or whether the practice of excluding fertile women was simply another example of sex discrimination in the workplace.[2]

Dealing with teratogenic chemicals at Du Pont

E.I. Du Pont de Nemours and Company, the largest chemical manufacturer in the world, has a long history of concern relating to chemical toxicity and exposure. The company now uses only four hazardous chemicals that require special controls. Its policy on teratogenic (also known as embryotoxic) agents has been clearly specified by Bruce Karrh, company Vice-President for Safety, Health and Environmental Affairs. Du Pont's policy procedure is as follows:

Upon determining that a substance presents a risk to the foetus:
1. Employees who may be affected shall be informed of the possible consequences of exposure to such substances and appropriate handling procedures shall be established and communicated.
2. Engineering controls shall be used to the extent practical to reduce and maintain exposure to embryotoxins to acceptable levels. Such controls shall be augmented by administrative controls as appropriate.
3. Whenever engineering and administrative controls are not practical to keep exposure at or below acceptable levels, personal protection equipment, where

appropriate, and training for its proper use shall be provided to and required to be used by employees who may be affected by such compounds.
4. Females of child-bearing capacity shall be excluded from work areas where:
    a. there is potential for exposure to an embryotoxin for which an acceptable level cannot be set, or
    b. whenever engineering and administrative controls augmented as appropriate by personal protective equipment, are determined to be inadequate to insure acceptable levels of exposure.[3]

A question of policy

It is possible to argue that the 'protective' female exclusion policy practised by Du Pont is a clear example of sex discrimination. This argument is given cogency by four factors. First, the reproductive systems of men are also adversely affected by certain industrial chemicals.[4] Exposure to these toxins can produce mutated sperm and ultimately a malformed foetus. Thus, any policy designed to protect the foetus should include considerations of the sperm and egg that form it.

Second, such exclusionary policies are unusually broad, especially since (contrary to the stereotypical view held by many men) not all women want or plan to have children. The cost of safety should not be inequality and the protection of women against their wishes. Third, there is a lack of accurate scientific data about the embryotoxicity of chemicals used in the workplace. Hence, many women are wrongfully excluded from 'safe' jobs.

Finally, women's advocates take the view that technological solutions to control embryotoxins could and should be developed. For example, management definitions of what is 'appropriate' and 'practical' in the Du Pont policy procedure outlined above are seen as unduly biased. Furthermore, management contentions that acceptable levels of exposure cannot be achieved are viewed with suspicion.[5]

Ultimately, companies such as Du Pont make the worker safe for the workplace (even to the point of exclusion of an entire social group) rather than making the workplace safe for the worker.

Issues to consider

- Is Du Pont's policy of female exclusion (intended to protect the foetus) in fact a policy of sex discrimination?
- Is there a solution to the problem which would satisfy both sides of the argument?

Notes

1. Quoted in Claybrook (1984), p. 78.
2. See Shabecoff (1981).
3. Quoted in Molander (1980), p. 16. For further details, see Elliott and Beauchamp (1989). Du Pont is the subject of this case simply because information about its safety policies are publicly available. The company's inclusion in no way implies a criticism of either the company or the way it is managed.
4. See Hunt (1979) and Whorton (1985).
5. If history is anything to go by, such suspicions have some justification. The research of Berman (1978), Frank (1985), Hills (1987) and Kinnersly (1974) shows how corporations often disregard the health of workers in order to maximise short-term profits and to reduce costs.

Case 35   At the cutting edge: is change necessary at Waterford Crystal?
Brendan McSweeney[1]

Donal Neart, Director and Chief Executive-Operations of Waterford Crystal Ltd is drinking in Power's pub with his old school-friend John Bolger, a skilled worker from the main factory in Waterford city:

Donal: I'm worried about the company's future.
John: What's wrong? Everything's humming at work. There's plenty of overtime. I was tempted to stay and work tonight rather than having a pint with you. But you're worth gassing with!
Donal: The situation is crazy. There's huge unsatisfied demand for the crystal, but volume sales have fallen because we don't make deliveries on time, the quality has deteriorated and we can't get the quantities we want of the popular items.
John: God, Donal you're in a bad mood tonight. Is it because I beat you at squash?
Donal: I'm serious John. Supply should meet demand. But here it's the other way around. I don't begrudge you your overtime, but some blowing and cutting sections have big backlogs while others are underutilised. The demarcations are so rigid and the decisions to do overtime are largely based on personal circumstances and whims, not customer requirements. Your lot – the heavies – are the most troublesome cutters.
John: Well, I keep telling you that it takes a long time to become an experienced heavy, the others couldn't do it. There'd be huge wastage of spoilt items. Anyway, some time in the future when there is less work we'd get less overtime if we share it now.

Donal: Come on John, we're not negotiating! I don't doubt its a skill, which I never learnt, but there are a number of items which buyers are screaming for which others could cut just as well as the heavies. I never quite know whether its just money you lot think about or whether you're just snobs because you think being a heavy is to be the tops.

John: I don't know Donal. I'm just a 'heavy', and yes we are the tops.

Donal: I'm frustrated John. I try my best for the company, but everyone is being short-sighted and selfish. I often think I'll retire and take that part-time University post I'm always being offered. I'm being squeezed on all sides. Its so hard to get the lads to agree to any changes.[2] It wears you down. It wasn't so bad in the past but times are changing. Most of the new directors don't understand the business, its craft nature, and it could be anywhere in the world as far as some of them are concerned. They only want to know the figures. They're not Waterford people. They weren't born here like we were.

John: Well, Mike Ceard and the other union convenors have expected a change since the McGrath family sold their shares to the English investment lot.[3] They're calling the new President, the 'axeman' because he closed down the last place he worked in and the new Director of Human Resources organised large redundancies in his previous outfit. But Ceard and the lads say they are not very worried. The company is making loads of money and we have the whip hand Donal. You can't replace us with machines or cheap labour and Waterford crystal has got to be produced in Waterford. Although, to be honest I know that in the back of his head Ceard does sometimes worry that the President might do something stupid and damage us all.

Donal: Well John, I'm also worried about the new President. He can make things a lot worse for all of us. He sees everything in terms of costs. God knows I appreciate costs – I trained as an accountant. But he sees the lads only as figures on his budgets. He's been amazed at the wage levels, comparing them with Ford's. He's shouting for cost cuts. I'm afraid he may force a confrontation. I don't think he fully appreciates our biggest problem is getting the right stuff of good quality out at the right time. It not just a matter of calculating costs. You've got to get people to do it. The warehouses are overflowing with some items and the buyers are screaming for others. For years we've been bribing the lads to get the items out but you're all so stubborn! I want to improve things, but if that does not work the board will want to start drastic pruning.

John: Have another pint, Donal. You're over anxious. It will all pass. The company is making plenty of money. Everybody does well out of it. Sure, the company could make even more profit, but that's just being greedy.

Donal: I wish I could be as relaxed about life as you John. The new President may not fully understand the business, but events are making his concerns ever more urgent, even if he hasn't a clue how to change things. I was a lot more optimistic last year. I fully backed the generous 3 year wages and benefit agreement, just to get some more items out. But the problems are deep and the world is changing The bottle-necks, the demarcations, the long, long negotiations over the slightest changes continue. Did you know the packers stopped work for 3 hours yesterday because they wanted extra pay to switch from using red to black markers?[4]

John: Yes, Dick Ryan told me about it.

Donal: I had to pay in the end. I'm still trying to get acceptance of laser etching to put the logo on the glass, but the lads want a fortune to agree. The Yanks want the logo to be visible so that they can show off their Waterford crystal to their posh friends. Costs are creeping up all the time but our income is being slashed by the falling dollar, and to add to it a fall in sales volume this year, and there's no improvement in sight. As the dollar weakens we get less pounds for the same dollars. The lads don't understand that. Just to stay where we are we have to sell more, but I can't get the right amount of the right things at the right time. It's crazy. It's not that we couldn't sell more. There are buyers from some of the best stores pleading for more and quicker delivery of some items, but we just can't give it to them. Imagine, we have to ration supply! The board of directors see details of the bottleneck, delivery delays, stoppages and the accounting forecasts every month and they're demanding action. 'How come,' they ask me, 'our competitors don't have these problems?' They don't want history lessons, they want action. If they could move production they'd do it in the morning. We've got to end the ongoing blackmail and get comprehensive change.

John: That was a long speech Donal! Good luck to you, but I'm not sure even I'm convinced. I don't see any signs of the good times ending. You're always pushing for more items, and the company's annual report I got in April sounded very optimistic. I didn't look at the accounts, but I read the President's statement. I see you've just raised £30 million[5] in the United States.[6] Look, we've got to use every opportunity to increase our earnings. The tax is a killer. We're paying almost 60 per cent in no time.[7] That's far worse than in England or the States.

Donal: I know but the company cost is the gross, the full amount!

John: That's no comfort to us. What we get is what's in our pay packets. Anyway, we're the ones who make Waterford crystal. If we don't look for more our efforts just disappear into profits. You call it costs, we call it earnings. You've got to see it from our side also. Management haggles with us, but in the end we make the stuff. The Yanks love it. They enjoy having to wait sometimes. It makes the crystal seem all the more exclusive.

Donal: Times are changing, John. There's a lot more competition now.

John: Maybe you spend too much of your time with your accounts, Donal. The lads will say that there's no crisis and that its just 'axeman' Banham trying to jack up profits.

Donal: You're right John that there's no immediate crisis. The company isn't about to crash. But there will be unless we change now. And all the time the dollar is getting worse and costs are rising. When Banham heard that six of the lads had no work in Dungarvan he hit the roof. We offered them redundancy. I though that at least Joe Riley would take it. His uncle left him the farm, and I know Joe would like to be a full-time farmer.

John: He'd have been treated as a traitor. Its not just the trade union policy against redundancies – every one in the town would think he was selling their son's job. He's got three of his own. They all can't work on his new farm, its too small. The union committee had virtually everyone's support when they vetoed your redundancy offer to the six. Why did you do it? You must have know what would happen?

Donal: Of course, I did. But I had to educate the President in the facts of life here. He's used to being able to hire and fire at will. I'm trying to show him reality is different at Waterford.

John:	Mike, and the other convenors, had some angry words with you.
Donal:	That was to be expected. It's not that I dislike Mike, on the contrary. He's committed to the lads and to their future, but he thinks that things can continue as they always have provided he keeps the pressure up.
John:	Mike's a smart fellow, but he has a hell of a job trying to satisfy everybody.
Donal:	I say this to you in confidence, John. I sense that Mike and some of the other convenors would like more flexibility in cutting rights. After all some are getting much more overtime than others but he does not want to say so too loudly as it would mean isolating you heavies. He wants to keep up the appearance of a united Union. There's little I can do without commitment to change from the lads. If I try and insist that some items be cut by non-heavies you lot will walk out and we will lose major orders. Mike's smart, he knows there is a recession. He was telling me about the factory closures and short time, he heard about at the trade union conference in Blackpool, and he sees what's happening locally. But he thinks we're immune. We can cut costs and produce more of the right items without making anyone redundant and not reducing their income by a penny. But we can only do that by getting the production correct and flexible.
John:	You know, Donal, that if the company tries to impose changes we'd walk out, the rest of the cutters and the blowers, in fact everybody, would be solid. Solidarity is stronger than the bit of extra overtime they would get. From where you sit Donal your changes might seem the right thing, but there is a lot of worry about what might ultimately happen to earnings in the long run if we agree to too many changes too soon. Many of them could not afford a cut. No matter what they earn they find something to spend it on: drink, meals out, bigger houses, holidays. Waterford workers are big spenders. There's a lot of them with debts, but they think they can afford it with their present wages. They're not good at saving and I'm no exception to that myself. You're buying the next round!

Background

Waterford Crystal Ltd, part of Waterford Glass Group Plc,[8] produces handmade (hand(mouth)-blown, hand-cut) full-lead crystal glass stemware (and other crystal glass items including sporting trophies), lightingware (which includes chandeliers and lamps), and giftware (e.g. decanters, vases and corporate gifts). Research has consistently shown that Waterford Crystal's items are regarded by purchasers to be at the top end of the market (see Exhibit 35.3, all Exhibits for this case are on pp. 168–77). US dollar purchases are the most important. In excess of 60 per cent of volume is sold in the US itself, but about another 20 per cent + is bought outside the US by American tourists (mainly in Ireland, UK and the West Indies).

Production is carried out exclusively in the south-east of Ireland in three plants. The main factory (at Kilbarry) and another (at Butlerstown) are located near the city of Waterford. The third (at Dungarvan) is about 30 miles from the city. Notwithstanding the company's turnover (in excess of £77,000,000 in 1985: see Exhibit 35.2) and the large number of employees (about 3000), production has many characteristics of a craft industry with lengthy training and sharp work demarcations.

The work can be demanding, and at times oppressive. For example, blowers (and their assistants) work close to the hot furnaces from which they extract the raw pre-blown glass; some female workers monotonously, and without discretion, open and close wooden moulds to assist the blowers throughout the day. Many cutters wear unsociable sound excluders as the noise made by the cutting wheels is loud and is alleged to have caused hearing difficulties. Although there is no 'closed shop', with the exception of senior management, the entire workforce of the glass division are members of trade unions. Despite the high proportion of 'skilled' and 'semi-skilled' workers there is not, unlike many other companies in the country, a multiplicity of craft unions.

Almost all production workers belong to a single trade union – the Amalgamated Transport & General Workers Union (ATGWU). The two ATGWU branches in Waterford City are dominated by members from Waterford Crystal. Both branches have substantial funds. The union is recognised by management for bargaining purposes and there are a number of full-time shop stewards and union officers paid for by the company.

Both management and the trade union accept that central to the attractiveness of the products is that they are handmade in Ireland – images which are constantly emphasised in the company's advertising. These beliefs have major consequences for management's and the trade union's ability to act. Whilst management believe that technically a much greater proportion of production could increasingly be done by machines, both parties assume that the images, or nature, of the product precludes:

(a)   Substituting labour by technology (as this would undermine the craft image).
(b)   Introducing cheaper labour to reduce wage rates and other payments to employees as both parties believe that blowers and cutters have specific skills which require a long time to develop and are unobtainable in any significant numbers from elsewhere within the country.
(c)   Transferring of production to another location outside of Ireland, or outsourcing parts of the production from other sources such as East European as this would undermine what is assumed by all parties to be a vital product characteristic (especially for US purchasers): that it is an Irish craft product.

These mutually held beliefs about the dependence of achievement on the existing workforce give the employees (and their trade union representatives) substantial influence over work practices and the capacity to veto almost any change in work practices proposed by management.

Management worries

Recently a number of management worries have emerged or grown. Costs are predominantly paid in local currency, but income is largely received in foreign currencies, especially in depreciating US dollars.[9] Under present conditions, costs will rise at a rate greater than inflation largely because an unprecedented wages agreement committed the company to increase wages on 1 February 1985, 1986 and 1987 by 8 per cent, 7 per cent and 7 per cent, respectively, all amounts now known to be above the actual (1985), or anticipated (1986 and 1987) rates of inflation.

To compensate for a declining US dollar, 1986 prices have been increased on average by 9.5 per cent in the US, and UK prices have been increased to reduce the gap between US and UK prices which had encouraged a gray market in Waterford crystal[10] (see Exhibit 35.5). Items destined for sale in the UK have been diverted by customers to the US and sold there at a discount contrary to the company's no-discount policy.

Volume sales, although still high, have dropped in all major markets so far this year (1986) (see Exhibit 35.4). The cause(s) of the drop in demand is variously attributed to: the price increases; decrease in the numbers of US tourists because of the weakening dollar and a reluctance to travel to Europe after the bombing of Libya; inconsistencies in quality; insufficient supply of some popular items, and slowness in introducing new designs.

There is some evidence that the preference of *some* premium crystal purchasers is moving away from extensively cut to leaner styles. There is more intense workplace hostility to the introduction of leaner, simpler designs as these involve less cutting. The quality of Waterford has recently been the target of disparaging efforts by its premium competitors.

Competition is also intensifying in part because technological developments have reduced barriers to entry. An increasing number of producers are using cheaper machine-blown blanks, but more significantly machine cutting is becoming more sophisticated. The difference between hand-cut and machine-cut is becoming less distinguishable – especially in 'blind' tests. Machine-made crystal stemware products have expanded beyond the low end of the market and already have a significant position in the mid-price segment and are even competing in the high end. Machines are already considered unmatchable for product control and consistency and in the longer term their design flexibility and small batch production capabilities will increase. According to one commentator: 'More has happened in glassware production in the last 5 years than in the previous 3,500.'

Additionally, competition is increasingly being defined by Waterford's management not only as other glassware, but any gift item such as video recorders and microwave ovens. Distribution has become more problematic. A number of major stores, especially in the US, which are key sales locations, are threatening to discontinue or reduce sales of high-margin, low-turnover items such as Waterford Crystal. Almost 60 per cent of US sales are made through department stores such as Bloomingdales, Macy's and Marshall Field's. Speciality retailers accounted for about 30 per cent. Management are considering increasing the number of its own exclusive shops in the US and UK.

Management–union meetings

At the monthly management–union meetings, with the exception of quality and the increasing use of machines by some competitors, none of these management concerns have been shared with the trade union representatives. Both parties agree that quality had declined and that there are production bottle-necks (but without much agreement about causes). The trade union acknowledges that certain work practice changes would have to be made if quality is to be improved and productivity increased. But it wants compensation for every employee affected by each change. The company has agreed to no redundancies, no loss of earnings as a result of any work practice changes and promised increased payments for any additional work which resulted. For its part, the trade union consider changes to work practices as unnecessary for the survival of the company which they believe to be very profitable. They argue that in most instances the additional payments offered are insufficient, but as estimating of the precise cost reductions and/or revenue increases which might result from many of the proposed changes is inherently problematic, such calculations are not made and thus not provided for the negotiations.

The union treats each proposed change as an opportunity to bargain for increased wages and conditions regardless of what the specific effects on employees of a change might be. A constraint on union agreement to work practice changes are their consequences for relationships between different sections of employees. The 'heavies' particularly are hostile to changes which might affect their exclusive cutting rights to certain items. Monthly meetings between management and the union to discuss deadlines and other work issues commenced in January 1986. By June only a small number of work practice changes had been agreed.

Management demands change

On 2 July 1986, Donal Neart, on behalf of the company, sent a Strategic Manufacturing Plan (Exhibit 35.1) to the trade union seeking a reply by the

21st July. Amongst other things he stated that unless significant changes were made he held 'great fears for the industry'. The additional exhibits contain information publicly available or obtained by the union representatives from management.[11]

Issues to consider

As the material in this case study uses analysis undertaken at a range of levels both 'within' the organisation, and its contexts, it can be used to consider issues in a number of disciplines, including: organisational behaviour, accounting, marketing, industrial relations, production, and strategy. It is an integrative case which has been written in a manner which encourages consideration of the organisational behaviour significance of many of these disciplines' approaches.

In selecting the data for the case the aim has been to facilitate consideration of aspects of information *in action*. Rather than seeking to advance the notion that in each situation there is absolute truth, with one unavoidable and single meaning, which if recognised leads to inevitable and predictable outcomes, the case suggests the existence (actually and potentially) of multiple, albeit constrained, interpretations through the creation of meaning in specific settings and the constitutive effects of such meaning.[12]

Whilst not essential, using role play in which the class is divided into teams representing, say, the Main Board and Non-board Management; Intra-management Groups, or Management and Union representatives has proven to be very effective in class-room testing of the case.

Notes

1. This case study draws on a participant-observation study of the glass division of Waterford Glass Group Plc, interviews with both management and union representatives, and on analysis of documentation from various sources. The great bulk of crystal glass production takes place within the ambit of Waterford Crystal Ltd. For convenience, and consistent with the practice in the Group, the term 'Waterford Crystal' (capital 'C') is synonymous with, and used interchange-ably in the case, with 'glass division'. Comments on an earlier draft by Sheila Duncan, Gibson Burrell, Francine Le-Saint and participants in the Warwick Full-Time MBA are gratefully acknowledged.

All proper names and job titles of all individuals named in the case study have been altered to preserve anonymity. The discussion between the Chief Executive Operations and the Cutter is not a record of an actual conversation, but it does incorporate a variety of facts and articulates some key differences, alignments, and commonalities in perspectives and values identified by the author to be held by various significant parties in the company.

Brendan McSweeney is Lecturer in Accounting and Finance at Warwick Business School. University of Warwick, Coventry CV4 7AL

2. All the 'skilled' workers are male (as is the majority of the workforce).
3 In 1984, Globe Investment Trust acquired Avenue Investment's 20 per cent shareholding in Waterford Glass Group Plc.
4. Changes which had in the previous 12 months been agreed to in the 'non-craftmanship' parts of the production process have included the automation of transfer of glass of one area of the factory to another, the removal of surplus glass after blowing, the marking of guide lines on the crystal prior to cutting, and the acid dipping and cleaning of glasses after cutting.
5. Unless otherwise stated the sign "£" refers to the Irish pound (Punt).
6. Waterford Glass Group plc had just raised £29.3 million through a share issue in the US.
7. In 1984 a work stoppage at Waterford as part of a nation-wide protest against the levels of Irish income tax brought production to a halt for 5 days.
8. At the end of 1985 the Group's turnover was £255,195,000. In addition to the activities of its crystal glass division it also owns: Aynsley China (products include tableware and objects d'art); John Hinde (printers and publishers, mainly of postcards); Smith Group (principal activities – distribution of Renault cars and commercial vehicles and a retail garage chain) which it intends to dispose of. It (in late 1985) disposed of its 60 per cent interest in the Switzer department store group to the 40 per cent holder – House of Frazer – for £6.43 million in cash.
9. Average annual unhedged exchange rate: ($ US : Irish Punt)

1979	1980	1981	1982	1983	1984	1985
2.05	2.06	1.62	1.42	1.25	1.09	1.07

Source: Central Bank of Ireland.

10. A 'gray market' refers to circumstances in which a manufacturer encounters difficulties in controlling the destination of its products. Customers 'divert' some volume by reselling the products in ways unintended and undesired by the manufacturer. As many as 1500 unauthorised locations have been identified (relative to 4500 authorised).
11. A discussion of what subsequently happened is contained in McSweeney (1989).
12. Studies of accounting in action in specific contexts include Dent (1991), Ezzamel and Bourn (1990) and McSweeney (1989). The theoretical basis of these studies may be broadly described as epistemological constructivism. For a general consideration of some of the constructivist features of accounting see Hines (1988).For a criticism of characterisations of information and choice in micro-economics, *n*-person game theory and statistical decision theory, see March (1987). For a discussion of accounting from a broadly 'labour process' perspective, see Hopper and Armstrong (1991) and Hopper *et al.* (1987).Also see the special edition of *Accounting, Organisations & Society* (1) and (2) 1990 on corporate strategies and organisational accounting.

Case exhibits

Exhibit 35.1   Letter outlining 'Strategic Manufacturing Plan'

WATERFORD CRYSTAL LTD

2 July 1986

Mr. Michael Neart
District Officer
ATGWU
Keizer Street
WATERFORD

Dear Mr Neart,
Both my management and myself have been requested by the Board to prepare the Strategic Manufacturing Plan for Waterford Crystal for the next number of years.

The objects of the plan are:

1. To ensure production facilities will be available to meet an increased demand if required.
2. To Improve Quality.
3. To Institute Cost Reductions mainly by:
   3.1 New Technology
   3.2 Better Factory Layout
   3.3 Elimination of waste – both Materials and Labour

Substantial Cost Reductions are required to combat the decreasing value of the dollar.

During 1983 and 1984 the Company suffered because our products became uncompetitive and we saw a serious build up of unsold stocks and our borrowings reached critical level.

A strengthening of the dollar and a positive response to the introduction of New Technology in the Industry helped to correct the position and sales returned to pre 1983 levels during 1985.

Since 1st January, 1985 the dollar has fallen against the Irish Punt by 35%. The effect of this fall has been cushioned by the Company Policy of selling dollars forward and 1986 is secured at approximately $1.02 per Irish Punt. However, in late 1987 and for all of 1988 we will have to absorb a rate of $1.35 or more, unless the dollar strengthens in the meantime.

The effect of this means that we should increase our Retail Prices in the USA by 35% plus the Cost Increases for 1987, 1988 – say 16% between the two years. This is a total of 51%. During this period the Consumer Price Index in the USA will rise by approximately 9% which is the maximum amount we will be able to increase prices without seriously effecting Sales Volumes and consequently job security in Waterford. The shortfall of 42% must be made up by Cost Reductions. Reductions of the order of 30/35% must be achieved by 1988.

We have carefully studied the work practices at the factory and have noted many factors which are contributing to higher than necessary costs, a random selection would include:

1. Heavy Shops in Blowing finishing at 2.00/2.30 p.m. and not always emptying pots.
2. Spares in Blowing will not work as Shop if not required as Spares.
3. Blowing relief Stemmers – 4 required.
4. No Clocking Cards in Blowing for Craftsmen.
5. Extended Tea and Lunch Breaks in all areas.
6. Performance of Shops on Average
7. Seniority is not a satisfactory basis for selection for promotion, introduction of New Shops or Filling Jobs.
8. Blowing Personnel applying for jobs and not taking up positions, sometimes after 3/6 months training they apply for another job and delay essential expansion.
9. Two additional breaks per day throughout the factory and for example 12 female Spares are required to cover this in the Blowing Area in Kilbarry alone.
10. The Pot Fillers would not help facilitate Overtime in the Blowing Department without further demands.
11. All New Piece rates in Cutting are negotiated at too high a premium over Comparable Piece Rates 10/15 years ago. This has resulted in some items being cancelled because a reasonable rate could not be negotiated.
12. Breaks on Overtime are being abused.
13. Union time is now running at the equivalent of 18 full-time workers.
14. Sickness Scheme gives 100% Net Pay which is not an incentive to come in to work.
15. Absenteeism is totally unacceptable and is running over 15% in some key areas.

16. Despite an agreement guaranteeing No Loss of Jobs and No adverse Effect on Pay, every change is subject to protracted negotiations, for example:

   16.1 Loser Tops machine took over two years to be finalised

   16.2 Transfer of Pre-Markers to other areas of Quality Control

   16.3 Despatch of goods from Dungarvan and Butlerstown.

17. When the company requested Overtime in all sections in March, 1986 the response was very disappointing because of excessive demands.

   The company lost a valued opportunity to balance stocks in readiness for the major selling season. This cost the company considerable Profit.

18. We have the ridiculous situation of strong demand for Machine Items which we could not fulfil, while Pots were left idle in Butlerstown because the interim suggestion to overcome the problem was rejected by the Union. One order alone which we turned down was worth $500,000. I wonder do the Union Members realise that all these actions are losing considerable profit for the Company and affecting their own job prospects and possible expansion.

19. It has taken us almost 12 months to introduce the New Stemware Patterns in the USA, despite the fact that the urgency of the situation was spelled out to the Union and Blowers Committee.

20. Continuous bickering between sections causing production delays and consequent late deliveries, as well as stock build-ups.

21. Employees leaving factory without permission.

22. Numerous minor points, such as:

   22.1 Newspapers for sale in Factory

   22.2 Shops on premises

   22.3 Time lost – Cash Sales and Medical Centre.

It is worth remembering that we are in competition with manufacturers who do not have these problems and also do not have:

- Average Craftsmans' Wages of £400 per week
- 30 Working Days Off Per Year
- 37½ Hour Week
- Blowers who finish at 2.00/2.30 p.m.
- 4 Weeks Bonus Per Annum
- Sickness Scheme equivalent to full pay
- Disability Scheme
- 15 year Bonus
- 30 year Bonus
- Free Transport for visits to Medical Consultants in Dublin, Cork, etc.
- Social & Sports Complex
- Free Medical Service
- Free Medical Service for dependants with choice of doctors
- Subsidised Lunch Canteen

In this regard it is worth comparing Average Wages in the Major Glass Producing Countries in Europe. These figures are from a study by the European Glass Federation and refer to 1984.

	Average hourly wage (Irish Punts)
Belgium	6.85
Germany	6.88
France	6.11
Italy	5.92
UK	5.73
Ireland	8.16

Since 1984 the gap has widened still further.

From this you can see that we have the highest Wage rates of all our Industry – 19% higher than our nearest competitor. Add to this the fact that we work shorter hours and you can see the extent of the problem.

To compete with this it is essential that we address the problems 1–22 listed above and that we institute further Major Cost Reductions.

In conclusion Mr. Neart, with an outdated factory layout, the malpractices that are rampant the industry, together with a mentality that a lot of the workforce seem to have which is so out of touch with reality it is very difficult to justify any major investment in the industry in the future. The Management can and intend to fix the physical layout of the factory immediately, the rest can only be rectified by the Union and its Members. In other words the hour has arrived when everyone has to decide whether they are genuinely committed to bringing the industry into the 21st Century on a competitive footing with the rest of the crystal world or just pay lip service to the problem. If it is the latter then I hold great fears for the industry.

Since there is such urgency about the matter, I would appreciate a written response by July 21st.

Yours sincerely,

Donal Neart
Director & Chief Executive – Operations

cc Mr Mike Ceard, Convenor
Mr B. Murphy, Chairman 11/64 Branch ATGWU

Exhibit 35.2   Glass Division's accounts

ACCOUNTS SUMMARY	1984	1985	Notes
Actuals £000	Dec 31	Dec 31	a
Property	4,645	5,242	
Other tangible FA	5,851	7,623	
Investments	60,968	65,075	
Total Fixed Assets	71,464	77,940	
Stocks	21,210	25,576	b
Debtors	6,231	5,267	
Cash & Securities	954	1,304	
Current Assets	28,395	32,147	
Total Assets	99,859	110,087	
Shareholders' equity	32,379	36,025	
Long & medium loans	17,452	15,199	
Short term loans	1,879	1,365	
Amount due to holding company	35,465	35,247	
Capital grants deferred	2,312	2,396	
Creditors/provisions	7,226	13,297	c
Current tax due	468	380	
Proposed dividends	2,678	6,178	
LIABILITIES & EQUITY	99,859	110,087	
Sales	71,562	77,062	d
Cost of Sales	(50,395)	(52,684)	e
Operating Profit	13,542	12,262	
Dividends	1,019	6,491	
Profit Before Tax	14,561	18,734	
Taxation	(1,658)	(2,659)	
Extraordinary items	–	(7,272)	f
Dividends Paid/Payable	(2,756)	(5,178)	
Retained Profit	10,148	3,645	

Notes to accounts

a. (i) The financial statements are prepared under the historical cost convention modified by the revaluation of properties.

(ii) The Irish Punt value of overseas income is protected where appropriate by means of forward currency sales contracts entered into to fix the exchange rates applicable to estimated future sales revenue. No account is taken of unrealised profits or losses arising on such forward exchange contracts.

(iii) Stocks are stated at the lower of cost and net realisable value.

b.

| | *Stocks* | |
	1984 (000)	1985 (000)
Raw materials & stores	3,250	3,615
Work-in-progress	10,738	12,691
Goods for resale	7,222	9,270

c. 1984 (Creditors: £7,225,951; Provisions: Nil)
   1985 (Creditors: £8,253,265; Provisions: £5,044,000)

d. (i) Includes sales to, but not by, overseas subsidiaries such as Waterford Crystal Inc. (US) and Waterford Crystal SA (Belgium),

(ii) 1985: Giftware 50%; Stemware 40%; Other 10%.

(iii) A nine page document sent to all shareholders (which includes most employees) in May 1986 about the proposed share issue in the US stated that Waterford Crystal turnover had declined in the first quarter of 1986.

e. Costs of Sales includes:

	1984 (000)	1985 (000)
Wages and related costs	38,570	45,622
Raw materials	6,073	6,792
(Increase)/decrease in stocks	2,293	(4,001)

Under the 1985–8 wage and benefits agreement there was an 8% salary increase but there were additional costs because of improvements to the pension scheme and purchase of shares for employees. Between 1981 and 1986 pay and related costs per operative increased at Waterford by an annual average of 14.2% compared with 11.1% for Irish Manufacturing as a whole.

f. Net amount of (i) profit on sale (ii) write-off of cost, and (iii) provision for future finance commitments of/to divestments.

Exhibit 35.3   Some marketing information

Features that recent focus group research suggests attracts crystal purchasers include: design, craftsmanship, elegance, beauty, light reflection, weight, hand-cut, the 'ping', the excitement of crystal, the feel, the reputation/name, the sentimentality, and where it's made. Waterford was clearly viewed as a superior brand of crystal among all segments of participants.

The features that participants mentioned as characterising Waterford crystal were its excellent reputation, distinctive and intricate designs, its nice sound and good weight, its clear and beautiful patterns, its hand-cut and art-like patterns, and its being an investment.

Waterford focuses on affluent householders in general, and the bridal giftware sector in particular. A US profile of Waterford crystal purchasers placed them far above the national average in virtually all major demographic and psychographic categories. These included the following features: upper middle-class, well educated, extravagant, discriminating, selective, entertains a great deal, and someone who likes heavy crystal. Waterford is by no means seen as a product exclusively purchased by older people, the Irish, and women. Approximately 60 per cent of purchases are for self, and the remainder (40 per cent) are bought as gifts.

The durability of patterns is declining. During 1983 to mid-1985 new patterns accounted for about 60 per cent of industry sales but were a much lower percentage of Waterford's sales. Six new Waterford patterns were introduced in the same period. Of these five have become best sellers. One of the new patterns has become one of the fastest selling stemware patterns in the US. Twelve patterns account for over 90 per cent of Waterford's sales.

Between 1982 and 1985 Waterford's giftware sales increased from 39 per cent of total glass sales to 50 per cent. Waterford dominates the over $30 segment of the US stemware market with over 90 per cent of this business. 75 per cent of the total stemware market is under $30 per stem. Waterford offers only two patterns under $30.

There are 26 competitors in the full-lead crystal category, offering more than 600 different crystal patterns.

This tremendous diversity has been made possible by relatively recent improvements in technology. Machine-made crystal has brought down the average price per piece and, consequently, broadened the customer base.

The low-priced competitors have inherently similar products, so they have sought to create product differences by constant introduction of new patterns. As a result, there is a high degree of attrition and discounting as patterns are phased in and out each year (see Exhibit 35.6).

With constantly shifting product lines, brand awareness or brand image is unimportant to these competitors. They are in the game of bringing enough attractive designs to market at a low enough price.

To date this strategy has worked quite well, particularly for Mikasa.

However, it is a short-term approach which relies almost entirely on scoring hits every year.

To maintain and enhance its brand image Waterford advertise extensively and by a significantly greater amount than its competitors. Its 1985 national media advertising expenditure in the US was $3,240,100 (about 5 per cent of US sales) and expenditure is expected to be increased by over 20 per cent in 1986. The second highest crystal advertising expenditure was $1,236,800 by Lenox. The lowest was by Mikasa ($7,900) which does not focus on building brand image.

Extract from the 1985 *Annual Report and Accounts* (published in May 1986)

Crystal demand outstripped production, testifying again to the strong demand for the product. Waterford lightingware products are becoming highly prized and the development of this business should be helped by the installation of Waterford chandeliers in very prominent locations during 1985 – the President's room in the London Stock Exchange, the trading floor of the Dublin Stock exchange and the grand staircase of the National Concert Hall, Dublin

Ten new stemware patterns for the US market are being introduced in 1986. These patterns feature shapes and designs which are suited far more to contemporary tastes.

A major sales and marketing drive in mainland Europe is planned with particular emphasis on Germany, Switzerland, Belgium and France. This follows a strategic market study of these countries, completed during the first quarter of 1986. This study helped to establish the best distribution, marketing and advertising methods of penetrating these markets.

A major new, state-of-the-art showroom was opened at the Waterford factory in April 1986 ... The Waterford factory hosts over 100,000 international visitors annually.

Exhibit 35.4   Nine years sales volume index (1984 = 100)

Year	United States	United Kingdom	Ireland	Total
1977	76	94	73	78
1978	77	87	74	78
1979	87	82	66	82
1980	83	43	62	74
1981	84	54	103	84
1982	77	57	90	77
1983	82	82	85	83
1984	100	100	100	100
1985	103	101	93	101

Exhibit 35.5　Average price increase versus inflation

	United States		United Kingdom		Ireland	
	Price Increase	Price Infl.	Price Increase	Price Infl.	Price Increase	Price Infl.
	%	%	%	%	%	%
1978	12.5	7.6	17.5	8.3	17.5	7.6
1979	17.5	11.3	24.0	13.4	22.5	13.2
1980	19.8	13.5	21.5	18.0	25.0	18.2
1981	14.0	10.4	0.0	11.9	12.5	20.4
1982	5.6	6.1	20.0	8.6	22.7	17.2
1983	1.9	3.2	5.0	4.6	11.3	10.4
1984	0.0	4.3	8.8	5.0	11.7	8.6
1985	2.1	3.5	6.3	6.1	20.0	5.4
1986(a)	9.5	1.9	10.6	3.4	19.3	4.0

Note: (a) At the beginning of 1986.

Exhibit 35.6　Stemware US market share percentage: Dollars ($), Pieces (P)

Manufacturer	1982		1983		1984		1985	
	$	P	$	P	$	P	$	P
Waterford	26.4	12.7	25.7	11.3	23.6	9.9	23.9	10.3
Mikasa	26.7	39.2	20.6	33.7	25.1	40.4	29.5	48.8
Lenox	18.4	20.4	18.8	17.1	17.5	14.9	15.7	12.5
Gorham	6.4	5.8	7.4	6.9	7.3	7.1	8.8	8.6
Sasaki	4.8	5.3	6.0	6.2	5.4	4.9	5.8	5.0
Orrefors	4.2	3.2	4.8	3.5	4.7	3.2	3.6	2.5

Mikasa: A US selling organisation which commissions production from factories in West Germany and Eastern Europe. Products are 24% lead; half range is cut, half is plain, coloured or etched. About 50% of volume under $10, the remainder sold at between £10 and $20 per stem. Also a leading china brand.

Lenox: A US company producing glass in Pennsylvania. Over 24% lead. Very limited range. Often discounted.

Gorham: The US selling arm of Nachtmann of Germany. Mostly pressed and machine cut. Designs mostly 'knock-offs' of best selling Waterford patterns.

Sasaki: Japanese, good quality, poor design. Entered the US market in 1980. Regularly discounted.

Orrefors: Swedish manufactured. Hand-blown and hand cut. Very modern designs. High prices – little discounting. Opened image-building retail store/showroom off 5th Avenue (New York) in 1985.

CHAPTER 7

Organisational design and change

Introduction

The variety of ways in which organisations are structured and managed, and how they change over time, provides the basis of much OB research. Also it is the domain of almost all so-called management gurus. Issues of organisational design and change are inextricably bound up with issues raised in previous chapters, especially those of power, personal and social identity, and the nature of control.

For instance, Salaman (1981, p. 143) observes that 'organisations are structures of control'. Given that organisational structures include management and worker organisation, control and reward systems, and job design, they clearly involve political issues, as well as decisions and strategic choices.

Despite this, much of the conventional OB literature on organisational structure and design concentrates, somewhat uncritically, on information flows, work structures, job design and cultures as entities designed and controlled by a management élite. The relationship between structure and performance also predominates in the textbooks – a common theme being that the correct structure is the key to good performance.

The cases presented here illustrate the problems, conflicts and contradictions inherent in hierarchical organisations. As such, the cases expose some of the financial, technological and socio–economic constraints placed on organisational behaviour.

Case 36 examines the strategic options facing those who control International Business Machines. Undoubtedly a 'successful' business company for many years, business commentators now feel that IBM must change the way it is structured and managed if it is to remain a key player in the multi-million-pound computer industry. The case exposes the way in which structural repertoires of design which have previously generated huge profits can become millstones.

Case 37 takes a look at two organisations which form part of the UK National Health Service and the problems arising from the need to restructure. The case was prepared by Louise Fitzgerald who has worked as a consultant for the NHS for many years.

Case 38 outlines the problems confronting a new manager eager to implement a relatively simple and straightforward change to a company's operating procedures. The issues highlighted here include problems of controlling a divisionalised organisational structure and the nature of intra-organisational communication.

Case 39 focuses on problems facing a voluntary organisation during a period of structural and strategic change. During your analysis you may wish to ponder how relevant conventional OB theories are to this particular type of non-profit-making organisation. The case was prepared by Dave Wilson.

Cases 40 and 41 are written in problem-solving format and require the user to consider the respective advantages and disadvantages associated with centralised and decentralised organisational designs. The final case in the chapter, Case 42, explores the world of the business franchise. Body Shop International is often heralded as one of the great business success stories of the 1980s. Case 42 reveals that controlling such an organisation is not without its problems!

Case 36   Redefining coporate strategy at IBM

In 1992, many observers argued that IBM was facing a major crisis. In 1988, the company had a stock market value of $105 billion. By the end of 1991 this had dropped by over 50 per cent to less than $52 billion.

Consequently, on 26 November 1991, IBM Chairman John Akers publicly announced what he called a 'fundamental redefinition of IBM's businesses'. He promised a shift in power within the company away from corporate bureaucrats at the headquarters in Armonk to the people actually making and selling products. Faced with increasing competition from DEC, Tandem, Convex and Apple, Akers hoped to oversee the creation of a more flexible corporate structure capable of moving faster to grasp new products and markets. Akers' planned reorganisation involved pushing decision-making down the steep IBM hierarchy inherited from former chairmen Thomas Watson Senior and Thomas Watson Junior.[1]

Under the Watsons, IBM strategy was based on gaining and holding a near-monopoly market share in which any short-term profitability was often sacrificed. Methods employed to achieve these ends were regarded by some observers as vicious, monopolistic and of dubious legality.[2]

With Akers' announcement, this aggressive sales-driven strategy of changing the customer's mind to fit the product is to be replaced by a market-driven strategy in which IBM's products are changed to fit into the customer's own strategy. Crucial to this change is a successful marriage of marketplace and innovation – a rapid commercialisation of innovations.

Historically, IBM have a rather poor track record on this front. For example, although the company were one of the first to design a high-powered RISC microprocessor, they were only fourth to commercialise such a device – and IBM's share of the fast-growing market for computer workstations suffered accordingly.

Part of the reason for this track record undoubtedly stems from the tendency for good product ideas to fall between marketing (which understands customers) and research (which understands technology) within such a large bureaucracy:

> In fact, IBM's top management is not good at absorbing technical detail. The well-defined managerial hierarchy that IBM is based on may make an otherwise ungovernable corporate sprawl manageable, but it creates a terrible information bottle-neck at the top. The minutiae of innovation are hard to fit into the hour-long slots available to the neatly typed schedules which each top executive is handed by his secretary every morning.[3]

The position has not been helped by the fact that all but one of IBM's chairmen (up to and including Akers) served their apprenticeships in sales and marketing. Indeed, some two-thirds of IBM's employees are in sales and marketing.

By 1992, Akers realised that a new-look IBM would need to push technological decisions down the hierarchy and view its research division as a profit-maker rather than a cost centre. This may require a fundamental shift in responsibility so that the research division is placed more directly in charge of the commercial fate of its own ideas. Yet such a shift runs counter to the conventional bureaucratic 'IBM way' in which senior management tell middle managers exactly what to do on a day-to-day basis.[4]

Once again the legacy of the sales-driven strategies of past chairmen makes such a change problematic. Not only has the IBM bureaucracy served to stifle personal research initiatives and resources, Thomas Watson Junior (aka Terrible Tommy) pioneered what he termed 'contention management' whilst company chairman. This approach was based on the view that the best way to motivate people and to boost productivity was to pit them against one another.[5] Under such a system, lateral communications and cross-fertilisation of ideas – key aspects of organisational innovation – were hardly a trademark of IBM's corporate culture!

Indeed, Watson Junior admits that:

> in the history of IBM, technological innovation often wasn't the thing that made us successful. Unhappily there were many times when we came in second. But technology turned out to be less important than sales and distribution methods. Starting with Univac, we consistently outsold people who had better technology.[6]

IBM's problems are heightened by the fact that Akers will have to wean the company away from its dependence on the declining Mainframe business as smaller, but increasingly more powerful computers enter the market. The recession has not helped matters, with companies putting off investing in IBM's bigger and expensive machines. To make matters worse, computer prices are continuing to fall. As John Tysoe, of stockbrokers Strauss Turnbull, put it:

> Given the structure IBM has, it is going to be increasingly difficult to make money out of what it does, which is selling hardware. The decline in hardware prices is so rapid that it is going to have to make every gesture larger and larger. If you take 10% off the top line you've got to do something pretty dramatic to keep up.[7]

Within IBM, employees have had to come to terms with 'getting into bed with Apple' in recent years. Recent collaborative ventures between IBM and Apple would scarcely have seemed possible a few years ago. Historically, arch rivals in the cut-throat world of computer sales, each company would often motivate their employees by decrying the shoddy products, human resource policies, and so forth, of their competitor.

All in all, IBM employees confront a radical shake-up of the company's deeply-embedded culture. Many observers doubt that Akers can successfully manage such a radical change without IBM losing a considerable number of its most valued employees. Many of these employees were attracted, and remained committed, to the corporation because of its world-renowned qualities of size, power, and market dominance. Yet, it is the gradual yet increasingly visible loss of these very qualities that have persuaded Akers to champion a radical organisational change.

Case resolution

- Outline and analyse the problems confronting Akers and IBM in the short and long term and offer recommendations for their resolution.[8]

Notes

1. See Belden and Belden (1962), Rodgers (1969), and Watson and Petre (1990) for fascinating accounts of IBM under the Watsons.
2. See, for example, DeLamarter (1988) and Case 51 (this volume).
3. McKenna (1989), p. 96.
4. Deal and Kennedy (1988), p. 78.
5. Schofield (1990), p. 31.
6. Watson and Petre (1990), p. 168.
7. Manchester Guardian, 1 October 1992, p. 15.
8. For background to the case, see Mallik (1975) and Sobel (1981). See Baur *et al.* (1992) for details of IBM's experiences with new product management techniques and associated organisational changes made during the planning and launch of the company's AS/400 minicomputer. In addition, more critically-oriented writings on the problems inherent in cultural change may prove useful here. See, for example, Harrison (1970), Johnson (1987), Kanter (1977; 1989), Pettigrew (1990), Schein (1985), Staw (1982) and Wilson (1992a).

Case 37   Restructuring of medical physics departments[1]

Louise Fitzgerald[2]

The National Health Service (NHS) in the UK[3]

There are three key tiers in the organisational hierarchy of the NHS, namely: regional, district and unit. Broadly, they relate as shown in Figure 7.1 below.

Formally, District General Managers report to their respective District Health Authority, with only a dotted line of responsibility to the Regional General Manager. In practice, this relationship is much stronger, with many executive decisions and all District strategy plans and resource allocation having to be approved by the Regions.

Some of the key features of the NHS culture are:

1. There is a service orientation, employees value 'caring'. People opt to work for the service for a variety of reasons, but pay is low on the priority list. Many employees rate service to the community or a useful role higher than pay as a motivator.

FIGURE 7.1 Organisation structure of the UK National Health Service (1990)

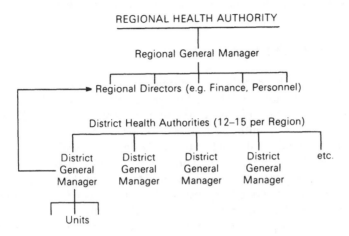

2. The NHS is an organisation in the public sector. Accountable to government, it operates in the political arena and is highly influenced by political pressure. Actions taken in the health service have a high public profile. Also, decisions can have extreme outcomes (i.e. death or life) and this generates high levels of emotion.

3. Uniquely, the NHS is an organisation consisting of a large number of professional groups. On the whole, it employs a highly skilled workforce. The purpose of professional bodies is to set standards, regulate entry through training and to protect members' rights. This is good for training and quality standards, but bad for flexibility and the interchangeability of work. It develops a segmentalist organisation. The NHS consists of many such 'tribes'.

4. As one of the largest organisations in Europe, the NHS is a national organisation on a grand scale. There are huge numbers of employees. The scale of the enterprise is vast and there is no strategic apex (except the Department of Health). The Regions employ between 50,000 and 80,000 people. The management are not treated as equivalent to their counterparts in private industry. In fact, until relatively recently, the organisation was not seen as requiring 'managing' (i.e. hospitals had 'administrators').

5. Because of history (i.e. the development of the medical professions and professions allied to medicine and then the setting up of a public service in 1948), there is widely differentiated status between professions. There are also gender differences. The older professions, such as the doctors, have well entrenched positions and considerable power. There is therefore much to be lost or gained through change.

Currently, the high cost of providing a service and government policies have led to financial restraint. This produces great pressure for change through resource control and resource allocation mechanisms.

Background to the case

The background to this case is the merging of two previously separate London Health Authorities into one. This is now to be called Central London District. Created on 1 April 1985, it is one of the biggest Districts in the UK. It serves a population of 286,400 within 13 square miles of central London. It has a number of large hospitals including St James' Hospital (with 760 beds), Church Hospital (413 beds) and Central Hospital (368 beds). There are also two smaller acute/general hospitals with 216 and 148 beds respectively.

In addition, there are two large psychiatric hospitals with 671 and 952 beds respectively. One of these latter hospitals is also in the process of closing. In total, there are 18 hospitals and 945 doctors and dentists in the District. The St James' Hospital and the Church Hospital are geographically close to each other in an urban area with a declining resident population.

As part of the background scenario, the Church Hospital was proposed for closure. This proposal was so strongly contested that it was agreed to postpone the plan. The hospital remains under some threat, however, though not of immediate closure. The St James' Hospital is a much more modern hospital, opened in 1973 and has since undergone improvement. The Church Hospital moved to its present building in 1939 and is therefore much older.

At present, the District faces the problem of rationalising or restructuring a number of functions which are currently duplicated on more than one site. This is exactly the issue which management face with the Medical Physics function which currently consists of 2 departments, one based at St James' Hospital and one at Church Hospital.

Cost constraints suggest that such duplication of sites can be tolerated only in the short term. Additionally, major technical advances in this area have revolutionised the nature of the work (e.g. through linear accelerators and gamma cameras). However, these advances require a higher level of capital investment and a consequent higher utilisation of equipment is necessary for cost effectiveness.

The medical physics departments

1. Functions of medical physics

Broadly, the functions of any medical physics department might include three strands of work.

Medical

- Radiotherapy: the support and provision of treatments using radiation (e.g. on cancers). The diagnosis and development of treatments by the radiologist in conjunction with the physicist.
- In nuclear medicine, the development, testing and interpretation of images.
- The provision of a specialist service on Radiological Protection to all hospitals, including surveys and planning rules.

Scientific

- Development of the understanding and of the use of radiation, workings of the atom and of alpha and gamma rays to aid medicine.
- Also the development of techniques and computer software to aid diagnosis, interpretation and instrumentation.

Technical

- Preventative maintenance work, particularly on the electronics side, including making new parts.
- Mechanical work includes the making of moulds to protect patients from radiation.

2.   Current organisation of medical physics

The departments in question are structured according to the organisational charts shown in Figures 7.1 and 7.2. These departments have one or two unique features to which attention is now drawn.

Despite the size of Medical Physics department at St James' Hospital, there is no formal manager, nor is there a Top Grade Physicist in charge (see Figure 7.1). Such coordination as exists is performed by one of the section leaders, a Principal Physicist. The Nuclear Medicine section is particularly large and well developed. This section under Dr N M has expanded its role and is doing work which is at the forefront of developments in this field. Regional Audiology is based in the department purely as a matter of convenience.

The Medical Physics department at Church Hospital has four sections (see Figure 7.2). A special group of duties have developed under Dr R P C, who has established a unique computerised cancer registry which services the whole Region (and elsewhere). Note that the head of the Nuclear Medicine section, Dr Nic, is also head of the overall department at Church Hospital.

FIGURE 7.2 Medical Physics Department, St James' Hospital

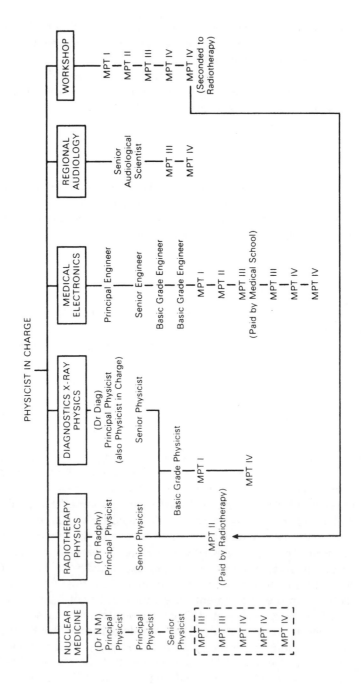

Also, one full-time Research Physicist (Senior Grade) paid by Cancer Research Campaign.

Also, two full-time Higher Clerical Officers.

FIGURE 7.3 Medical Physics Department, Church Hospital

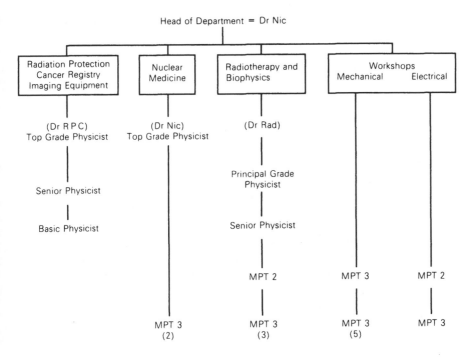

Key events

In considering the situation and the background, a number of key events suggest that action is required in the near future to merge or restructure the two departments. For example, a report of the Working Group of the Regional Sub-Committee for Medical Physics and Bio-Engineering recommended a merger of the two departments and 'a unified management structure to aid efficient rationalisation as a prime objective'. Completed just under 2 years ago, this report gives medical backing to a merger. This is extremely significant given the power of the profession in healthcare.

In the same month, the 'value for money' report by consultants Deloitte Haskins and Sells on the Medical Physics department at Church Hospital was completed. The report pointed to a decline in workload and suggests closure of the mechanical and electrical workshops.

The impending retirement of Dr Nic, Head of Department at Church Hospital, in 6 months' time makes some decisions inevitable.

In addition, there is pressure from the Principal Physicists at St James' for the appointment of a Top Grade Physicist. This pressure is particularly strong from Dr Radphy who considers he has the management experience to fill the post.

Summary of the issues

It is clear that some action will be required to resolve the present situation. The outcome desired is a merger of the two departments, a decision on the new location and a minimum of disruption to the staff and patients affected.

In considering the issues, your attention is drawn to the following points:

- The closure of the Church Hospital is still a possibility, but such a proposal would meet with resistance. In this situation, one person who would be expected to resist actively would be Dr R P C, who was a leader in the first anti-closure campaign.
- There are clearly problems at present at St James' in the management of Medical Physics. These are evidenced in a lack of coordination, no longer-term strategy, poor capital planning, etc. However, each section separately is doing excellent work and the department has a good reputation and an increasing workload.
- Partly as a result of this, the Nuclear Medicine section at St James' has developed into a 'mini-empire' and operates fairly autonomously. Dr N M would like it to be a separate department. Foreseeing Dr Nic's retirement, he expects to take over his work and on this basis has asked for a Senior Registrar post within his section.
- It is absolutely vital within the present cost restrictions that some action is taken during the next financial year and that this action should aim to result in cost savings, either on premises or staffing or both.
- There are increasing demands from consultants in terms of the volume and complexity of work. This often places demands on the use of 'high-tech' equipment and on the technicians and paramedical staff who operate and use it.
- At the technician level, there is a shift of work from mould making and equipment repair to electronics maintenance and service, as well as development work.
- Radiotherapy equipment has to be housed in specially designed buildings. These currently exist in both Church Hospital and St James' Hospital. There is space at both sites for expansion.

Issues to consider

- Consider the case and begin your analysis by highlighting the main management problems to be addressed. You may wish to consider what strategic problems exist and what operational problems exist.
- From the information contained in the case, what aspects of the organisation culture, and professional and individual employee attitudes will act as a hindrance to change?[4]
- Consider the key individual players and their positions in the power hierarchy in the organisation.

Case resolution

- Adopt the role of District Director of Personnel. From your analysis of the three issues outlined in the previous section, consider the available options for action against relevant time-scales.
- Formulate a set of proposals to the District General Manager as to how this matter should be dealt with. These proposals should include an action plan identifying the key proposed changes including the new location and the new structure.
- You should also draw up a process plan on how to implement the changes. Your plan should include time-scales, communication and sequence.

Notes

1. This is a true case but all names have been changed to preserve anonymity.
2. Louise Fitzgerald is senior lecturer in organisational development at Warwick Business School, University of Warwick, Coventry CV4 7AL.
3. As of 1990.
4. For a general consideration of the causes and consequences of resistance to organisational change, see, for example, Beckhard and Harris (1987), Carnall (1990), Johnson (1987), Lippitt *et al.* (1985), Mirvis and Berg (1977), Pettigrew (1990), Tichy (1983) and Wilson (1992a). Consult Hickson *et al.* (1971) and Hinings *et al.* (1974) for an examination of intra-organisational power.
   More specifically, for an analysis of problems of change management within the NHS, see Coombs and Green (1989), Cox (1991) and Strong and Robinson (1990). Also see Case 30 (this volume).

Case 38   Handy Snack (Distributing) Company[1]

Handy Snack (Distributing) Co is a food and drink distribution company with more than 1500 employees and gross annual sales in excess of £52 million. The company purchases snack foods (peanuts, crisps, etc.) as well as bottled and tinned drinks (ranging from fruit juices to exotic alcoholic cocktail drinks), and distributes them to independent retailers throughout the UK and Ireland. Competition in the industry is intense and competitors are continually updating product lines in a bid to gain market share.

Handy Snack has nine regional centres (seven in the UK and two in Ireland), each with its own warehouse, sales staff, and finance and purchasing departments. Since the company's inception 12 years ago, the head office in London has always encouraged each region to be autonomous because of well-recognised variations in localised product demand. For example, the demand for cocktail drinks and the more exotic snacks is highest in the South-east region of the UK, while in the South-west consumers prefer cider and lager beers, and more traditional snacks.

5 years ago, the Board of Directors expressed a desire to have more detailed information on the performance of each region. Consequently, head office introduced a centralised financial reporting system which enabled the Board to compare sales, costs and profits across the nine regions. Each region was treated as a profit centre and the system revealed that profit margins varied markedly from region to region. As these differences became more pronounced, Michael Rosen, the company chairman, decided that a degree of standardisation needed to be imposed. He suspected that some regions were sometimes using lower-quality products in a bid to increase regional profitability and was eager to put a stop to such practices before any harm could be done to the company's reputation for high-quality products. Certainly it was true that most regions were facing cut-throat competition from the larger distributing and discounting organisations who were cutting prices and launching innovative new products in a bid to increase market share.

In order to achieve the required degree of standardisation, Michael Rosen decided to create a new managerial post to oversee the company's regional pricing and purchasing policies. The post was filled by Peter Borden, who was previously employed as a senior finance manager by Handy Snack's closest business rival, National Distributing. Borden reported directly to Pauline Pedder, managing director of finance.

In line with the non-bureaucratic ethos of the company, Pedder encouraged Borden to develop whatever procedures he thought necessary to achieve the desired outcome. Each regional director was notified of Borden's appointment by an official memorandum and it was also announced in the company bi-monthly newsletter.

As he analysed the accounts, Borden decided that two problems needed tackling. Over the long term, Handy Snack should make better use of information technology. He believed information technology could provide timely and accurate information to enable head office to make higher-quality decisions. At present, top managers in the regions were connected to head office by an electronic mail system, but no other employees or sales people were connected.

In truth, head office had experienced considerable difficulty in getting any senior managers to use the E-mail system on a regular basis. The head office in London had even started to receive anonymous messages (presumably from the regional offices). Although harmless enough (e.g. 'Big Brother is Watching You!' and 'Contrary to popular belief, London is not the centre of the Universe!') these messages were perhaps symptomatic of the resentment felt by some regions – particularly those in Scotland and Ireland – at what they saw as head office interference in regional affairs.

For his part, Borden put the spate of anonymous messages down to seasonal high spirits (Christmas was only 8 weeks away) and the problems created by a lack of corporate centralisation. Certainly his experience at National Distributing (a highly centralised organisation) had led him to value strong corporate leadership and control.

In the short term, Borden decided that fragmented pricing and purchasing decisions were a problem. To him the solution was obvious – such decisions should be standardised across all the regions. As a first step, he wanted the financial executive in each region to notify him of any changes in local prices. He also decided that all new contracts for local purchasing (approximately 35 per cent of items purchased) should be cleared through his office.

Borden discussed the proposed changes with Pauline Pedder. She agreed and they submitted a formal proposal to Rosen and the board of directors, who approved the plan. These changes represented a significant change in company policy, but Borden was eager to implement the changes as quickly as possible in order to beat the rush of Christmas orders. He decided to send an electronic mail message and a covering fax to all the financial and purchasing executives in each region, notifying them of the new procedures right away.

Borden showed a draft of the message to Pedder and invited her comments. She said that the message was a good idea but wondered if it was appropriate or sufficient. The regions handled hundreds of items and were used to decentralised decision-making.

'It may be helpful if you were to visit our regional offices and discuss these procedural changes with regional management,' Pedder advised. 'The culture here is quite different to National Distributing. We recruit all regional personnel (including senior managers) from the locality – some of them are proud of the fact that they have never visited London head office!'

'I've got far too much to do here without wasting my time travelling, Pauline,' replied Borden.

'Well, why not wait until the annual company meeting?' she suggested. 'Then you could meet all the local managers, and discuss your ideas with them face-to-face.'

'No.' retorted Borden. 'I can't wait that long to bring in these changes. I think it's important that I make my presence felt as soon as possible. I'll send the messages out tomorrow.'

During the next few days, he received electronic mail replies from three of the regions (from managers who said they would be happy to cooperate).

Yet four weeks later, Borden had not received notices from any region about local price or purchase changes. Informal enquiries by Pauline Pedder revealed that the regions were busy as usual following conventional procedures.

Borden decided to telephone one of the regional managers. Much to his chagrin he discovered that she did not know who he was or what his new purchasing procedures were. 'Besides,' she argued, 'we have enough to worry about reaching difficult profit goals seemingly chosen at random by you lot at head office, without additional procedures and "red tape". My region has always been profitable – why not pick on other, less profitable, regions. No-one has ever had cause to change my working practices before. To be honest, I see no logical reason to start doing so now.'

As Christmas approached, Peter Borden came under increasing pressure from the Board to bring all the regions into line with company procedures and standards.

Case resolution

- Outline and analyse the problems confronting Handy Snack (Distributing) Company and offer recommendations for their resolution.[2]

Notes

1. This case study of a fictitious organisation is based on the case studies of the Dashman Company (Lawrence and Seiler, 1965, pp. 16–17) and Sunflower Incorporated (Daft, 1983, pp. 341–2).
2. For a consideration of problems inherent in the management of organisational change, see Beckhard and Harris (1987), Carnall (1990), Guest *et al.* (1980), Lippitt *et al.* (1985), Neumann (1989), Staw (1982), Tichy (1983) and Wilson (1992a). For an analysis of problems associated with the management of decentralised organisa-

tions, see Daft (1983), Duncan (1979), Jamieson (1979), Kondrasuk (1981), Levinson (1970), and Mintzberg (1979).

Case 39   Volorg: an international charity[1]
David C. Wilson[2]

Brian Smith had enjoyed a good day. He had just been appointed as the Director of Volorg, a charity based in London which operated primarily as a third world overseas aid agency. The selection process for the job had been tough. The organisation had recently reorganised its structure and a major part of the new Director's job was to implement the new structure and make it work effectively. At his interview, Brian had expressed sympathy with the ways in which the reorganisation had been described to him. Coming from the Council of Churches, Brian had been used to a rather centralised and bureaucratic organisation structure. The Council was rule-bound, career progress was slow, everything seemed based upon 'serving your time' in the organisation and things had hardly changed in 20 years. Brian's new job with Volorg seemed very different. Volorg had also been a centralised, bureaucratic organisation based largely around functional departments, but today, far from being a centralised bureaucracy, Volorg had just become a decentralised matrix of activities based largely around project teams, each dealing with a different geographical area of the world.

Each team consisted of specialists (e.g. in nutrition, irrigation, language) and these were coordinated at the centre (London HQ) by a slim administrative and executive staff. Volorg was an established charity. It had always been functionally organised until recently. Founded in 1921, Volorg had originally been an extension of church-based organisations, although it had grown rapidly and consistently up to the 1990s. Employing 500 people (of whom 150 were full-time and the remainder were part-time and voluntary) the organisation was a major provider for Third World overseas aid. It had grown to become one of the top charities in the UK and was readily recognised across the world.

The structural change in Volorg had been the final result of a combination of factors, all of which had happened over the last 20 years or so. During this time, the Third World overseas charities (like most areas of charitable activity) had increasingly recognised that they were in competition with one another. Although income to the Third World 'sector' was increasing (by about 10 per cent per annum) competition for this money was fierce. There were new overseas aid charities entering the field. Other concerns (such as Greenpeace or charities dedicated to saving dolphins and whales) began to compete for the attention and the purses of givers (both individual and corporate).

Brian Smith's predecessor (Mary Swanson) had tried to direct Volorg along a particular strategic path. She argued that the long-term survival of charities depended upon long-term public support. Givers would continue to donate funds to established charities which had a good track record of achievement and which were somehow distinctive from other providers of similar services. Volorg had the distinct advantage of being both church based and non-political. Volorg was also not operational overseas. Instead, it worked in partnership with other church-based charities locally. Volorg provided funds and some expertise if this were necessary. Local agencies carried out operational activities on the ground.

This made Volorg quite different from most of the large Third World charities. Certainly, it had precluded the debates which had centred on other major charities that they were becoming too political (by attempting to remedy the causes rather than the symptoms of poverty). Oxfam, for example, had been subject to intense scrutiny by both the press and the Charity Commissioners for such alleged activities. Swanson viewed such publicity as inevitably damaging and argued that Volorg should stay well away from such areas of activity.

Declining income, however, meant that Swanson could not rely on being a niche player in the Third World sector, nor on a growing (or even steady) supply of voluntary donations. Although in the big league of income receivers, Volorg had been losing around 2 per cent per annum of funds to other Third World charities. Mary's solution was to hire a Deputy Director (Grant Weaver) who came with seemingly impeccable credentials. He had an MBA from a top US Business School. He had been a Director of Corporate Planning in the commercial sector and had held several non-executive positions on the Boards of many UK companies. Weaver had particular skills in corporate planning and finance. He brought these to bear on Volorg's management team.

His first job was to create a strategic planning team (SPT) which comprised all functional heads. Weaver acted as Chairman of this team. The plan was to use this team to make the organisation more efficient and effective, whilst Mary Swanson handled the interface with the outside world (and thus hopefully bringing in increased funding).

At first, things went well. Functional heads spoke freely and suggestions to improve operational aspects of internal organisation (budgets, improved accounting procedures, etc.) were numerous. Many heads said that this was the first time they had talked to their counterparts for many years. In general, however, each function head left his or her staff (many of whom were voluntary) to operate freely within general guidelines agreed in the SPT.

After 2 years, Volorg had suffered its first actual decline in income. Swanson and Weaver met. 'The trouble is,' said Weaver, 'We're acting like a bunch of amateurs. Any other organisation would have got the operational procedures in place and then started to plan strategically. We never did this, we just bumbled on in the same old way. The only thing that changed was that our new accounting system uncovered the loss of income earlier than would have happened previously.'

Weaver poured himself another glass of mineral water and turned aggressively to Swanson. 'Any mediocre MBA would tell you that Volorg cannot compete in the market for funds unless it radically alters its structure. It needs to be flexible, responsive, decentralised and ready to go with the market. Haven't you read Paul Lawrence or Tom Peters?' Mary shook her head. She had heard of neither, although she had a sneaking suspicion that Tom Peters had starred in some recent fiction programme on television. He was quite handsome, she thought to herself. Unlike Weaver, she observed, who had a cold, aloof quality topped off with a sneer rather than a smile.

Yet Swanson had respect for Weaver. He had rationalised the organisation and things were working more smoothly. Perhaps the financial setback was temporary. 'It wasn't' assured Weaver. 'The market has changed, we've got to compete to survive. If we don't change radically we'll go under. Look what Oxfam are doing.' Mary knew that Oxfam had adopted a new structure and it did appear to be working better for them. She listened intently to Weaver. 'I suggest we bring in a management consultant to advise and help me in creating a new plan for Volorg,' said Weaver. 'It so happens that I have a contact from my MBA days with a consultant who also has an interest in charities. He's called Fred Useful.'

Swanson agreed. Useful was not cheap but he had a great deal of empathy with charities and had an outstanding reputation as a management thinker and consultant. Over the next few weeks, Weaver and Useful prepared a blueprint for success. It involved structural reorganisation into a decentralised, project-based set of teams, each of which would be responsible for particular areas in the world. Weaver was pleased that Useful had reinforced his earlier beliefs.

When Brian Smith walked in to his first executive meeting (SPT had been retained although it now represented teams rather than functions) the new structure had been in place for just under 1 year. The agenda for the meeting was full. It ranged from a discussion of proposed re-decorating costs for some offices to the consideration of moving premises for HQ. It was going to be a long afternoon. As discussions progressed, Brian Smith began to realise that Weaver was constantly trying to act as Chairman. Often, Weaver would intervene and cut short some of the discussion. After the meeting, Smith remarked on this to Weaver in a friendly way. Weaver, however, responded that the previous Director had always been happy to let him chair the meeting.

Smith argued that since his brief had been to make the new structure work effectively then he would be Chairman at least for the foreseeable future. Weaver returned to his office.

The next meeting came as a shock to Smith. Weaver had produced figures to show that Volorg was still losing out on income to other Third World charities. He argued that the real source of this loss was twofold. First, Volorg did not discriminate amongst those agencies to which it gave money. Second, the line management of staff had been neglected for years, he argued. In Weaver's view, each member of staff needed clear and formalised job descriptions so that the inter-disciplinary teams could more effectively work together. Both suggestions were the first time anyone had voiced such issues. Smith looked around the table and detected a number of angry and concerned faces.

Two of the project teams argued that specifying to whom money was given implied that a rank ordering of perceived need would have to be drawn up and agreed. 'Who was going to do this and on what criteria?' demanded the team leader. Weaver told the leader that was 'her problem'. That's what she was paid for. A further incident worried Smith at the meeting. One of his key staff said that if her job was to be demarcated by job descriptions, she would be unable to work in the flexible way to which she had become accustomed. The description would limit her role and require others to do the jobs she was willingly doing at the moment. The meeting ended angrily.

Two days later, Smith was faced with a deputation from team staff. They wanted to know which projects were going to be cut under the new plan and what was the logic for not funding certain aid programmes whilst supporting others. In addition, the Trade Union representative informed Smith that there would be problems implementing the job description plan and that staff intended to resist it. Smith related these issues to Weaver some hours later. Weaver was unsympathetic. 'Let them try' he said, 'they don't know when they're well off, they're living in the dark ages of amateurism.'

An emergency meeting of SPT was called. The atmosphere was tense and irritable. Weaver put his case firmly and quickly. Smith argued that perhaps some rationalisation was necessary in order to make the new structure a success. The meeting erupted. One of the team leaders offered her resignation on the spot and two others stormed out of the meeting.

The situation developed rapidly over the following days. Smith called on Mary Swanson (now in retirement) and asked her advice. She was unable to be much help. She thought it was terrible to discriminate amongst aid projects, but thought that this was just hotheadedness and that after things had cooled down, everything would go back to normal. She was wrong. Two further resignations later, Smith was left with virtually no team to cover the Asia and South Pacific regions. Quickly he moved two individuals from another team to fill the gap. 2 days later there was a virtual riot in the team. According to established team members, the new members had little idea how this region worked and what were its key demands. 'They want to rationalise our aid programme but have no knowledge. They are disruptive and unhelpful' argued one of the team to Smith. 'We want them out.'

Weaver overheard the conversation as it spilled down the corridor. He became angry. 'You are all the bloody same' he shouted down the corridor. 'You'll end up caring and sharing and the organisation will go out of business. It'll cease to exist and your jobs will go too! You're all too frightened to face up to reality and make hard decisions.'

Smith's next meeting with the Trustees (the governing body of Volorg) proved difficult. He informed the Trustees of some of the problems they were encountering, although he missed out Weaver's outburst in the corridor. The Trustees recommended sticking to the structure recommended by Useful, but asked Smith if he would consider appointing another Director to concentrate upon advertising and corporate image. The Trustees felt that this was the area in which Volorg was weak. If more funds could be obtained, then this would preclude difficult decisions having to be made over the selective funding of projects.

An advertisement was duly placed and Frank Leigh-Boring was selected from numerous candidates who applied. Frank had come from the commercial sector where he had been in consumer goods advertising. He soon began talking about distinctive competence and premium branding. Many SPT members seemed to nod their assent to his deliberations, although many privately had no idea what Leigh-Boring was going on about. They were soon to find out. Frank embarked upon a new advertising campaign aimed jointly at individual givers and the commercial sector. Organisations such as Marks and Spencer, BP and British Telecom were targeted for corporate gifts and/or pay-roll deduction schemes for their employees. The major problem arose when Volorg's staff discovered that the advertising Leigh-Boring was promoting made claims for the organisation which at the very least stretched the truth (about financial efficiency, target client groups, services provided). The adverts also deliberately made disparaging remarks about other charities in the Third World overseas aid sector.

The conflict came to a head at the next SPT meeting. Figures were produced by Weaver to show that there had been a slight increase in funding over the last 2 months and thanks were extended to Frank Leigh-Boring. Frank then took the floor and argued the case for a stepped up effort in advertising to maximise impact and returns. Two of the teams said that they would have no part in such a scheme. Making only half-true claims and presenting a 'false' image to the public and to corporations was unethical, they argued. They thought that Leigh-Boring had already damaged Volorg's image amongst its current givers and was likely to do more harm than good. A heated row followed during which the team members stormed out of the meeting, saying that if nothing changed they would look for jobs elsewhere. Weaver and Leigh-Boring turned on Brian Smith and asked him to exercise his Director's authority. He should require the teams to get on with their jobs and leave the rest to the professional managers.

Smith was in a dilemma. If the team members left, he knew he would have difficulty in recruiting replacements. On the other hand, the Trustees seemed to support the actions of Weaver and Leigh-Boring. He was going to have to act quickly before things got completely out of hand. But what should he do?

Case resolution

- Outline and analyse the problems confronting Brian Smith and Volorg, and offer recommendations for their resolution.[3]

Notes

1. A pseudonym for an existing organisation.
2. David Wilson is professor of Organisation Studies at Aston Business School, The Triangle, University of Aston, Birmingham B4 7ET.
3. For a consideration of the management issues peculiar to voluntary organisations, see Batsleer *et al.* (1991), Butler and Wilson (1989), Handy (1988), Pierce (1992) and Wilson (1992b).

Case 40   Argus Home and Garden Design Limited[1]

Argus Home and Garden Design Ltd was established in 1969 in Coventry.

Over the years, Argus moved its office several times to accommodate growth and expansion. However, throughout its brief history the company has remained essentially a suburban organisation. In the 1980s, a branch expansion programme was undertaken. Now seven branches have been opened and four others are contemplated within the next 2 years.

Argus is a small organisation, employing approximately 75 people in the headquarters and seven branches. The main branch, Newgate, is the largest and has 18 employees; the other branches are smaller satellite operations. All branch managers report directly to the company chief executive.

Elaine Edwards, manager of the Newgate branch, opened the confidential memorandum from Adam Crawford, Argus chief executive. The memo explained that the failure to keep expenses in line with income had caused the company to fall far short of its objectives for the first 6 months of the year. Some controls had been imposed previously. 2 months ago a total ban had been imposed on new or temporary hiring and salary increases. Also promotions were not to carry any salary rises for the next 6 months.

As a result of these difficulties Crawford's memo stated that it would be necessary to impose more stringent controls on expenditure, especially on personnel, during the second half of the year. By next Friday, all department heads in headquarters and all seven branch managers were to reduce by 10 per cent the number of staff they had at the end of the first half of the year. A list of those to be laid off must be on the chief executive's desk by next Friday morning at 10 o'clock.

The memorandum was written in the style typical of Adam Crawford: short, terse and dictatorial. Crawford liked to keep tight control over the running of the company and rarely consulted management on issues of policy and planning. Indeed, no one could remember the last time he had visited a branch office. In his 15 years as chief executive, all of Crawford's decisions had been based solely on detailed examination of the financial balance sheets. Also, whilst other garden businesses had diversified into areas such as greenhouse and conservatory erection, as well as solar heating panel installation, Crawford steadfastly maintained that Argus should 'stick to the knitting' and focus all its energy on its traditional areas of garden design and maintenance, and plant sales and hire.

Before she had completed reading the memo, Elaine Edwards was on her way to Adam Crawford's office. 'You surely don't expect me to apply this ruling to my branch,' she asked, as she was ushered into his office.

'I most certainly do, Elaine,' Crawford replied calmly. 'If I make an exception in your case, every branch will want to make out a special case. That was the problem 2 months ago when I told everyone to bring spending into line with revenues. It simply didn't work. That is why I have decided on this rather drastic course of action.'

Elaine could not agree. 'I have built the Newgate branch to be the largest and most profitable unit in the organisation. We had countless problems before I took over from Mike Sharrock. Now all our records and reports are up to date and we have established long-range plans. I have spent a great deal of time building my team into the most efficient and profitable unit in the entire organisation. We shouldn't be penalised for carrying some of the less efficient branches.'

'It's true that you've done a good job at Newgate,' Crawford conceded. 'But you have the advantage of being in a relatively wealthy suburban area and therefore have a better market than the other branches. They are in poorer and more competitive areas and have had a much tougher time these last few years as the economic recession has continued. You must remember that our branches operate within different kinds of environments. We have to face this difficulty together and do our share – that's the Argus culture.'

'But as long as we meet and exceed our sales targets and keep our spending down we shouldn't have to face cutbacks,' Elaine persisted. 'I can see the logic of making cuts in the less profitable branches, but surely it's madness to penalise Newgate in order to subsidise money-losing branches elsewhere? That's the economics of decline. And don't forget that our main competitor is planning to open a branch in Newgate next year. Now is not a good time to weaken my branch. We should be expanding it, not cutting it!'

'But if your branch were left untouched, even more drastic cuts would have to be made in other units,' Crawford retorted. 'You accuse me of talking about the economics of decline, yet you seem to be advocating sending some of our branches to oblivion in order to save your own! That's the economics of myopic self-centredness! It is the smaller branches who most need more money to survive. After all, we are all part of the same organisation. I have to consider the best interests of the entire organisation and not just the Newgate branch. It's my job to take the strategic business view. Your job is to run the Newgate branch in line with that strategy to the best of your ability.'

Elaine Edwards stood up. 'That's as may be, but how can I run Newgate to the best of my ability if you intend to wreck staff morale through compulsory redundancies? I have worked really hard to make the Newgate branch profitable and my staff have a genuine commitment to Argus. In return I have an obligation to them, so don't expect a list from me on your desk on Friday. If there are to be any redundancies at Newgate you can start with me.' She stormed out of Crawford's office.

Case resolution

- Outline and analyse the problems confronting Argus Home and Garden Design and offer recommendations for their resolution.[2]

Notes

1. This case study of a fictitious company was inspired by the case of the Sentry Federal Savings and Loan Association prepared by Kast and Rosenzweig (1985, pp. 271–4).
2. This case illustrates the difficulties inherent in maintaining a balance between organisational integration and differentiation. For a general analysis of these difficulties, see Galbraith (1977), Goold (1991), Lawrence and Lorsch (1967), Mintzberg (1979) and Ouchi (1977).

Case 41 The Simkin Cafe Chain[1]

Angela Simkin's first café sold light snacks, exotic salads, cooked pies, ice cream desserts, beverages and sandwiches and had the decor of an old-fashioned Parisian café-bar.

Following Angela Simkin's death, her husband Samuel was eager to expand the business. His wife had never wanted to open more than one outlet despite his constant encouragement. Samuel decided to use his wife's café as a model for a whole chain of outlets throughout the country. He believed that the key to business success was to replicate the original café in every detail. He used standard layout and equipment, and formally outlined detailed instructions for food preparation and for service, specific standards for cleanliness and maintenance and strict methods of record keeping. There was a right way of doing everything in Samuel Simkin's view. He would often cite Ray Kroc and Frederick Taylor as his business gurus.

It was the responsibility of each café manager to train workers and supervisors to follow standard procedures and methods. At least once a month, at irregular intervals, someone from head office would make out a quality audit of each café. This audit included an 8 page check-list covering how work was being done, the condition of food inventories and of equipment, the accuracy with which standard operating procedures were being followed, the friendliness of the café's atmosphere, even the attractiveness of employees' physical appearance. On many occasions, Samuel Simkin would carry out the audit himself. Indeed, all 17 cafés in the Simkin chain could expect to see Samuel at least three times a year. His policy was to visit his cafés without any advanced notice. In truth, he quite liked to see the nervousness such visits engendered in his managers and employees.

In addition to quality audit reports, a monthly financial report for each café showed ratios of food items and supplies used per sales unit, labour hours and wages in relation to sales, and the operating profit before fixed capital and overhead costs.

Samuel Simkin was an energetic man who was convinced that his management system – the 'Simkin System' as he called it – would work and he urged all café managers and employees to follow it without deviation. 'Good citizens' were those managers who kept to the system strictly and made it work. These people regularly received bonuses in the form of free cinema tickets, cheap car hire deals, and the like. At the same time, Samuel ensured that managers who failed to make the grade as 'good citizens' either changed their ways rapidly or were fired.

When Samuel Simkin retired, his niece Laura gave up her job as a financial management consultant to become the chief executive officer of the Simkin café chain. As well as being committed to expansion of the business, Laura was a strong advocate of management by objectives (MBO) and she immediately set about establishing this management technique to coordinate the activities of all the company cafés. She relied more heavily on the café managers than her uncle ever had, and allowed them a considerable degree of autonomy in the way they managed their cafés.

Laura Simkin dropped the monthly financial reporting system initiated by her uncle. Instead, at the beginning of each year the district directors meet with their café managers and agreed on target results for the forthcoming financial year. These results are expressed primarily in terms of total sales and operating profits. Head office control now centres on how well a manager is meeting these agreed targets. The quality audits are still made but no-one pays much attention to them at head office so long as profit margins are maintained or widened.

The MBO programme has proved to be very popular with the café managers and has generated good results from older managers who were brought up under Samuel Simkin's stricter regime. Problems are arising mostly from newer managers. These managers have a strong sense of autonomy and independence. They claim to be adapting to new and changing market demands (for example, the young manager of one of the cafés in a central urban location offers a range of less expensive snacks to cater for diners who are unemployed or on low incomes). On the other hand, the longer serving managers complain that the newer managers are undisciplined and are allowing quality standards to fall in order to meet their financial targets.

Whilst the high employee turnover and low levels of work motivation associated with Samuel Simkin's time as head of the café chain have all but disappeared, Laura is now worried about dropping standards in the cafés and is using 'mystery diners' to check what is happening in various outlets. Reports from these diners go both to café managers and to head office management. In general they confirm that occasionally the food is poor, that some managers are allowing their café to fill up with young people who take over an hour to drink a single cup of coffee, or that the service is rather too casual.

The most recent progress reports on the cafés run by new managers suggest that whilst targets are likely to be reached (even exceeded) in the short term, their standards of decor and service vary markedly from those associated with the traditional Angela Simkin café model upon which the company's prosperity has been built.

As a consequence, the company directors are becoming increasingly anxious about the effects of lower quality on the company's prestige, market position and profits and are demanding action from Laura Simkin.

Case resolution

- Outline and analyse the problems confronting the Simkin Café Chain in the short and long term and offer recommendations for their resolution.[2]

Notes

1. This case study of a fictitious company is based on the case example of 'Sue's Sweet Shops' prepared by Newman (1985, p. 534).
2. For an assessment of the advantages and disadvantages of MBO approaches to organisational control and coordination, see Carroll and Tosi (1976), Ford (1980), Raia (1974) and Umstot (1977). For a more critical analysis of the impact of MBO on organisational behaviour, see Jamieson (1979), Kondrasuk (1981), Levinson (1970), Pringle and Longnecker (1982) and Schuster and Kendall (1974).

Case 42   Franchising corporate values at the Body Shop

The Body Shop philosophy

Body Shop International was founded by Anita and Gordon Roddick in 1976 and is now one of the UK's most successful retail store groups, attaining full Stock Exchange listing in 1986. This success owes much to the growth in environmental consciousness during the 1980s in the UK and elsewhere.

The Roddicks' strategy proscribes product testing on animals, eschews advertising, stresses minimal packaging and the use of only natural ingredients. All the company's cosmetic products are biodegradable and the shops offer a refill service for bottles. It uses recycled paper wherever possible and, as part of its mission to help the developing countries, Body Shop has set up local operations in Nepal, India, Bangladesh and a Mexican refugee camp in Texas.

Their strategy is clearly stated in the mission statement printed in the Body Shop 1987 *Annual Report*:

We take a non-exploitative approach to the world in which we all live and work. And that approach is fundamental to our company.

The products generally consist of ingredients that have been tried and tested over many years of human use: many of these are plant based and are also used in food. The ingredients are there for a purpose – not merely to provide an exotic name for the label. They come from all over the world and out of this we aim to extend trade with Third World countries wherever we can.

The Body Shop does not exist in a vacuum. Our products are produced with regard to a natural world and with regard to the needs of real people.

Anita Roddick's evangelical zeal has done much to heighten Body Shop's image in the consumer and shareholding markets. But how does she keep the organisation running smoothly, profitably and in a 'non-exploitative' way?

Franchising the corporate philosophy

The Roddicks have always been keen to avoid becoming bureaucratic and running into internal political problems. Thus, the management structure of the company is very simple. There are a mere 12 managers at Body Shop headquarters in Rustington and the majority of retail outlets are franchises. The functions of marketing services as well as some elements of finance and accounting are retained within the Body Shop franchise operation whilst the local selling and money collection is dealt with by the franchisees.

Generally speaking, the Roddicks try to remain true to the literal meaning of the word 'franchise' which is derived from the French verb *affranchir*, meaning 'freedom from servitude or restraint'. Hence, the Roddicks are adamant that the franchise agreement should not be weighted on the side of the franchisor, but be mutually beneficial. This is almost unique in franchise agreements according to Peter Tyson, Body Shop's franchise manager. In many franchise agreements, every clause starts, 'the franchisee will . . .', but the Body Shop agreement is a reciprocation: more of a philosophy than a detailed contract. Most of Tyson's time is spent taking possible imitators of the Body Shop to court as more and more retailers attempt to emulate its success. He restricts his involvement with individual franchisees, whenever possible, solely to that of consultancy.

The Roddicks feel very strongly that a franchisee who has invested a large sum of money in setting up a shop should not only receive support from head office, but should be given a reasonable degree of latitude in running their business.[1] For example, franchisees are not limited to selling just Body Shop products – they are allowed to sell 'related sundry products' such as combs, brushes, sponge bags, etc.

Another unusual facet of the Body Shop franchise policy is that Anita and Gordon Roddick are keen to encourage franchisees to expand their businesses. As a couple who always wanted the headroom for expansion in their own ventures, and who always try to enable staff to progress and be promoted, they see the importance of always giving scope for further development of a business.[2]

One such franchisee was Pauline Rawle – who had opened up one of the first Body Shop retail outlets. Indeed, true to the spirit of the Body Shop franchise policy, she held the franchises for a total of six Body Shop branches in the south-east of England. After the initial excitement of setting up and opening these shops had died down, Pauline Rawle found the shops almost running themselves. Her staff were highly committed to the company and worked diligently and with obvious enthusiasm.

However, in May 1991, Rawle began to take personal control of her six branches and brought her own somewhat autocratic management control techniques to bear on her employees. She insisted that they all attended 'mystic violence courses' run by a religious sect called the Victory Church with whom she had become involved. Shop assistants began to feel uneasy when she visited their shop, and staff at one of the shops were extremely upset on being told at an impromptu staff meeting that they had all been sexually abused before they were 3 years old and should seek guidance and solace from the Victory Church. Some staff members felt that they were being brainwashed into joining the Victory Church.[3]

Pauline Rawle's behaviour became increasingly erratic and she developed considerable hostility towards Body Shop. She complained:

> When we started 12 years ago it was a family and it was wonderful. I wouldn't join the Body Shop now. They interfere and control everything and don't respect you.[4]

On occasions she even went so far as to compare the company to Satan. She took over complete control of purchasing for the six shops and within 2 months had allowed stocks to deplete to such an extent that the most popular products were unavailable to customers.

At the height of the 1991 Christmas shopping period, Rawle's six shops were dirty, in poor decorative order and extremely understocked. By February 1992, Anita Roddick started to receive an increasing number of complaints from staff and customers and she sensed that all was not well in the south-east. However, she was reticent to interfere directly in the affairs of a franchisee.

However, events took a turn for the worse in June 1992, when Rawle sacked all 50 of her staff on the grounds of personal disloyalty and closed the six Body Shop branches. Roddick now had to act and she took out a High Court writ claiming £340,000 from Rawle for products supplied and an injunction removing Rawle's control over the six branches.

Granting an immediate injunction, the judge stated that: 'the damage done to Body Shop is damage to its goodwill which really cannot be expressed in terms of money.'

Issues to consider

By the early 1990s, the performance of the Body Shop's shares in the stock market began to reflect the City's growing lack of confidence in the Roddicks' ability to maintain their impressive growth record since going public. At 37½ times earnings, Body Shop stock was still trading at more than twice the market average. To justify this, analysts argued that the company required a huge increase in profits. As a consequence, the Body Shop began rapid expansion into the US, Europe and Asia.

But Gordon Roddick became increasingly concerned that the simple management structure at head office was inappropriate for a rapidly expanding business. Yet, how could the company make the evolution from a pure state of ecological values to a multinational business without destroying the autonomy and commitment of its franchisees?

On the one hand, Anita Roddick argues for the maximisation of franchisee autonomy. Indeed, she maintains that 'you have to learn to love the anarchist, as he will be the one to push you and your company further'.[5]

On the other hand, the somewhat anarchic activities of Pauline Rawle had pushed the Body Shop in the wrong direction entirely!

- In the light of this case, how can the right balance between franchisor control and franchisee autonomy be achieved?[6]

Notes

1. In 1989, the average cost of setting up a Body Shop outlet was £38,688, plus an average licence fee of £5,941 (Felstead, 1990).
2. McKay and Corke (1986), p. 36.
3. These and subsequent details are taken from the manuscript of the High Court case *Body Shop* V. *Pauline Rawle*, 9 July 1992.
4. Quoted in *Sunday Times*, 24 May 1992, p. 28.
5. Quoted in Eales (1990), p. 20. See also Anita Roddick's own book on the philosophy and practice of Body Shop management (Roddick, 1991).
6. For a general consideration of the problems inherent in franchise ownership, see Edens *et al.* (1976) and Felstead (1990, 1991). For a particular example of one franchisor's heavier-handed approach to tackling such problems, see Love (1986).

CHAPTER 8

Technology and organisation

Introduction

Debates about the relationship between technology and organisational behaviour have featured strongly in the development of the academic discipline of OB. Only Case 43 directly engages in the technological determinism versus organisational choice question which has dominated this debate for far too long (see Scarbrough and Corbett, 1992). The other cases in this chapter reveal the technology–organisation relationship to be far more complex than conventional OB texts suggest. Analysis at a number of levels seems appropriate. For example, if one views technology not as simply as hardware but as a process in which flows of knowledge and artefacts are generated and diffused through processes of invention, use and exchange, it is clear that an individual organisation itself is but one site for the shaping of the technology that it applies. Indeed, as Scarbrough and Corbett (1992) note:

> Far from containing or controlling the technology process, the formal boundaries and managerial hierarchies of organization may themselves be restructured by it (p. 23).

Similarly, sole recourse to a unilateral deskilling process (at a societal level), in which technology developed under capitalism inevitably leads to the deskilling and control of labour, does little to convey the uncertainties and interactions of the technology process, nor account for the key role played by individuals and groups:

> Indeed, on occasion the transformational power of technological knowledge may escape the intentions of the powerful and undermine, and not simply reproduce, existing social and economic structures (Scarbrough and Corbett, 1992, p. 23).

Finally, at the meso-level of analysis, it is important to note that technology derives from and enlists subjective experience, and to that extent can be influenced by the ideas and meanings which make sense of that experience. It therefore follows that the development and use of technology within organisations are influenced by the perceptions and meanings that are attached to that development and use by people and groups both within and beyond the organisation.

The seven cases in this chapter reflect a number of these issues and encourage the analyst to take a correspondingly broad and eclectic look at the issues involved within the complex relationship between technology and organisation.

Case 43 describes the implementation of an apparently 'neutral' technology into a tightly knit social community. The effects of this process raise doubts about the validity and relevance of the determinism–choice debate. We return to the UK National Health Service in Case 44 and to the true story of a hospital department's experience with new technology. The lack of computer transparency is emphasised in the case (as is the relationship between technical expertise and tacit knowledge).

Case 45 is a more conventional problem-solving case. It focuses on the use and abuse of management information systems (MISs), and raises questions relating to the control of information and the relationship between social structure and technical expertise and access.

Case 46 outlines details of a UK criminal law case in which a self-confessed hacker is found not guilty by a jury on the grounds that he was addicted to his computer. The OB literature on the psychology of computer use is still very much in its infancy. However, it focuses much of its attention on managerially defined outcome variables such as stress and performance. Broader issues relating to the psychological implications of working with smart machines in an organisational environment – obsession, dependency and technophobia – are under-researched and barely theorised at present.

Case 47 explores another under-researched area, namely the multi-disciplinary design of new technology. Whilst many writers argue that users and social scientists need to get involved in technological design, there are few case studies highlighting the problems inherent in such an undertaking. This study outlines the crux of a debate within a multi-disciplinary design team.

Case 48 is case study of the introduction of office automation into a division of the Internal Revenue Service in the US. The case gives a interesting insight into the party political nature of change in public organisations.

Case 49 has a certain ineffable quality!

Case 43   New technology and the Skolt Lapplanders[1]

Introduced in the early 1960s, the snowmobile was adopted by the Skolt Lapp people to replace reindeer sleds as a means of transportation. This technology brought about easier access to trading posts, more sophisticated health care and a more varied diet and recreation. Yet, within a few years the introduction of this technology had made a profound impact on the Skolt Lapp community.

The Skolt Lapp community, like many traditional communities, was organised around a patriarchal power structure, so that the old men held all the positions of status and authority. However, unlike the younger members of the community, these men lacked the muscular strength and dexterity to ride and maintain the heavy snowmobiles. Given that the new technology symbolised progress and the promise of economic prosperity to many Lapps, this resulted in a decline in the status of the elders relative to the younger, stronger men.

Of even greater significance, and as the snowmobile replaced the reindeer sled as the dominant means of transportation, this status shift was accompanied by the decline in the importance of the elders' knowledge and wisdom concerning the care and use of reindeer herds. Such a shift was encouraged all the more by the rapid drop in calf births that resulted from the effects of the frightening noise of the snowmobiles' engines on pregnant reindeer. Indeed, within 3 years, a majority of the domesticated reindeer herd had returned to the wild. The impact of this should not be under-estimated as, for generations, the reindeer had been of great symbolic and cultural significance to the Skolt Lapps.

Most important of all, the Skolt Lapplanders quickly found themselves dependent on outside suppliers of imported petroleum and spare parts for the snowmobiles. Also, many of the physically ill Lapps became psychologically (and sometimes physically) dependent on the constant supply of non-traditional medicines and drugs which had been unavailable before the introduction of the snowmobile.

Thus, an apparently neutral technology brought about significant (and largely irreversible) cultural changes to a community.

Issues to consider[2]

- To what extent do these events mirror the experiences of small-to-medium-sized enterprises implementing new technology?[3]

- To what extent, if at all, can the adoption of appropriate change management techniques reduce or nullify the impact of new technology on organisations?[4]
- Is technology neutral?[5]

Notes

1. Based on the research of Pelto (1973).
2. See Scarbrough and Corbett (1992) for a useful overview of the general issues raised by this case.
3. See Buchanan and Boddy (1983), Piercy (1984), and Willcocks and Mason (1987).
4. See Blackler (1988), Corbett (1992), McLoughlin and Clark (1988), Orlikowski (1992), Wilkinson (1983), and Zuboff (1988).
5. Albury and Schwartz (1982), Cooley (1987), Mumford (1934), Noble (1984), Shaiken (1985), Webster and Robins (1988), and Zerzan and Carnes (1988), amongst others, argue that technology has significant political qualities.

Case 44   Human–computer interface problems at North Staffordshire Royal Infirmary

In 1982 the North Staffordshire Royal Infirmary took delivery of a new radiotherapy machine. The machine, used to check the spread of cancer through irradiation, was highly computerised and enabled carefully controlled doses of radiation to be administered to individual cancer patients.

Having taken delivery of the machine, staff in the department of radiotherapy physics set about programming its software for a particular type of therapy, called isocentric treatment. Under the supervision of the principal radiotherapy physicist, Margaret Grieveson, the programmers built in an allowance for the distance the radiation beam had to travel.

Unfortunately this allowance had already been incorporated in the original design of the computer software (although this was not clear from the machine's manual) and the error remained undetected until December 1991. Hence, of the 989 patients treated since the machine came into service, many received up to 30 per cent less than the radiation dose prescribed for them. Between 1982 and 1991, there were 598 deaths amongst the group, but it is not clear if the under-treatment hastened these deaths.

On numerous occasions between 1982 and 1991, Margaret Grieveson had called for greater integration between radiation physicists, who do the calculations, and radiographers, who carry out the treatment. However, outside of her own department, Grieveson's role was advisory rather than supervisory and no formal steps were taken to improve inter-departmental integration.

In December 1991, Margaret Grieveson discovered and reported the programming error and as head of radiotherapy physics accepted full responsibility for it. The hospital's general manager, Stuart Gray, immediately moved her to other duties and ordered a full inquiry.

The inquiry, chaired by Sir Peter Baldwin, completed its report 9 months later. The report concluded that although Miss Grieveson accepted personal responsibility for the error, she was not solely to blame. Confused lines of management, poor training procedures when new equipment is installed and an absence of supervisory mechanisms were listed as contributory factors.

At the beginning of October 1992, Margaret Grieveson resumed her job as head of radiotherapy physics, with hospital authorities expressing fullest confidence in her abilities.

Issues to consider

- With reference to the literature on the management of technological change, analyse the events outlined in this case example.[1]

Note

1. See, for example, Clegg and Kemp (1986), McLoughlin and Clark (1988), Orlikowski (1992), Piercy (1984), Scarbrough and Corbett (1992) and Zuboff (1988),

Case 45   Egan and Doyle Publishing[1]

Egan and Doyle (E&D) Publishing was established in Royal Leamington Spa in 1936 and has achieved great success (and consistently high profits) from the publishing and distribution of a wide range of college and university textbooks, journals and periodicals.

According to some commentators, the company's continuing success, in the face of fierce competition from E&D's four main publishing rivals, was down to its flexible, divisionalised structure and the company's extensive network of personal contacts in universities and the business world. Immediately below Brian Gray, the Chief Executive, in the E&D hierarchy were five directors, each responsible for their own division, namely: Periodicals, College Textbooks (Sciences), College Textbooks (Arts and Social Sciences), Trade Journals, and Information Services. These directors were allowed a degree of responsible autonomy in the running of their divisions, and, over the years, they had developed their own way of running things.

Coordination between the divisions was based on meetings between divisional directors and Brian Gray at regularly scheduled strategic management team (SMT) meetings, where each division would let Gray and the others know what was going on and plan future strategies. However, the setting up of the Information Services Division in 1985 (to provide financial, industrial and economic data to individual and corporate customers) had alerted Gray to the advantages of employing new technology within the company to ensure further coordination between the divisions. This coordination seemed particularly important given the growing market demand for complete education and training packages which combined traditional textbooks with interactive computer-aided learning facilities. He had heard rumours from a variety of sources to the effect that E&D's competitors were ready to move into this potentially lucrative market.

Brian Gray followed developments in the personal computer industry closely to see what products the company might provide for this expanding market. He recognised that the widespread availability and low cost of personal and laptop computers was having a major effect on education and training. He foresaw a time when electronic textbooks, based on miniature CD-ROM disks, would outsell traditional written texts and he was keen that E&D would be sufficiently flexible and proactive in the computer field to take full advantage of future innovations and developments.

With this in mind, Gray encouraged the development of an extensive internal management information system. He had the systems department develop computerised information files which were directly accessible to him on his office terminal. Also he had a personal computer installed at home with a modem link to the office computer.

The nature of SMT meetings had changed markedly since the emergence of the Information Services Division. In 1985, E&D Publishing had recruited widely to fill the position of director of Information Services and they had succeeded in attracting some high-quality candidates. Jane Morgan was eventually appointed to head the division. She had come from a well-established American-owned organisation which dealt in business information services. Morgan was well liked and respected among her colleagues. She held an MBA from Warwick Business School and had 5 years' experience in heading up an information services division.

Very quickly, Jane was able to develop E&D's Information Services division into a profitable and growing business. Some of her clients had come with her from her previous company. They knew and liked Jane, so they were happy to transfer their business to E&D. Like the other divisional directors, Jane ran her division autonomously. Hers was the most flexible division in many respects. She allowed her staff to keep extremely flexible hours and didn't mind this so long as tasks were completed on time and to the required standard. Indeed, this had the unintended effect of Jane's workforce working much longer hours than in many of the other divisions. Staff would regularly stay late into the evening or would work week-ends.

SMT meetings initially were smooth and trouble-free. Gray was pleased to see the rapid expansion of the Information Services division and the sizeable group of corporate and individual clients they served. The other directors were also pleased, since the clients Jane dealt with were often interested in the services provided by the other divisions (especially Periodicals and Trade Journals). There was a sizeable spin-off effect of business from Information Services to the other divisions.

Just lately, SMT meetings had become a little strained and difficult. Along with the other divisional directors, Jane had begun to sense Gray taking an increasing interest in the strategies of all the divisions. Since the setting up of the internal management information system (in which Jane's division played a central role), Gray began to view the rightful place of Jane's division as concentrating on providing internal information about financial, marketing and personnel data.

However, over the past 6 months, the introduction of the information system had brought about significant changes in the information flow and power relationships within the organisation. Gray had immediate access to a vast quantity of economic, financial, marketing, and personnel data. He seemed to be captivated by the new system and was continually analysing information in a number of ways and challenging existing ideas and assumptions. He had access to information from all of the divisions and functional departments in E&D.

After a session at the computer terminal, he had a habit of summoning subordinates to his office to ask specific questions about divisional operations and to try out new ideas. He had access to so much information that the divisional directors spent a great deal of time trying to anticipate his questions. They thought that the proliferation of questions was keeping them from getting on with their work and undermining the responsible autonomy to which they had become accustomed.

Unfortunately, Gray had changed long-established patterns of work and was creating considerable unease among his subordinates. On the basis of information obtained from his computer terminal, Gray would call in lower-level managers to get explanations of problems and issues, by-passing the divisional directors and the SMT meetings. Divisional directors were often caught in the middle. Maybe the only answer would be for all of them to get computer terminals. But with everyone absorbed at a terminal, who would do the managerial work of the company?

With the introduction of the management information system, Gray had terminated the regular weekly meetings with divisional directors and other key members of staff and a SMT meeting had not been held for over 5 months. Now Gray only called directors in individually, if and when he deemed it necessary. Morgan and her fellow directors felt that this created many problems for them. The weekly meetings had provided them with information about what was happening throughout the company. They had also been the means for testing new ideas and addressing issues that weren't reflected in the computer output.

Events had now developed to the stage where Gray would not consider a proposal from his divisions if it were not generated and presented on the information system. Two conflicting perspectives had now developed. On the one hand, Gray argued that the company must be restructured to reap the benefits of computerised information systems. On the other hand, many of the divisional directors were fond of asking: 'If computers are the solution, what is the problem?'

Gray's use of the internal management information system had brought undoubted benefits to E&D. He was able to analyse the strengths and weaknesses of the company at a glance, and this enabled him to respond rapidly to new market opportunities. However, Morgan wondered how she could help Gray understand some of the disadvantages of this new technology. Although Gray was committed to using computers to gain competitive advantage over E&D's competitors, other directors wondered if all the benefits of divisionalisation would be undermined by his obsession.

Case resolution

- Outline and analyse the problems confronting E&D Publishing in the short and long term and offer recommendations for their resolution.[2]

Notes

1. This case study of a fictitious company was inspired by the short case 'A new computer for president Franklin' prepared by Kast and Rosenzweig (1985, pp. 270–1).

2. For a discussion of the strengths and weaknesses of divisionalised structures, see Child (1977), Duncan (1979), Galbraith and Kazanzian (1986) and Mintzberg (1979). For a consideration of the relative merits of the different strategies available for the design and use of information systems, see Blackler and Brown (1986), Keen (1985), Otway and Peltu (1983) and Piercy (1984). Finally, Markus (1983), Newman and Rosenberg (1985) and Scarbrough and Corbett (1992) offer analyses of the political aspects of information systems.

Case 46   The cyberpunk: villain or victim?

Introduction

In science fiction novels, cyberpunks are high-tech outlaws who live in a dystopian future dominated by technology:[1]

> It is a world defined by infinitely powerful computers and vast computer networks that create alternative universes filled with electronic demons. Interlopers travel through these computer-generated landscapes. Some of them make their living buying, selling and stealing information.[2]

In the present day, harbingers of cyberpunk (popularly known as hackers) have entered the realm of science fact. They are young people for whom computers and computer networks are an obsession and who have carried that obsession beyond what computer professionals consider ethical and lawmakers consider acceptable.

The public seem divided in their views on hackers. On the one hand they represent heroic figures taking on giant corporations and high-tech surveillance systems. On the other hand, they are sinister trouble-makers, dangerous subversives, possibly spies.

But who are these cyberpunks/hackers? What do they do and what motivates them? As we shall see from the case of young Paul Bedworth, the picture is a complex one.[3]

The cyberpunk as villain

Connie Bedworth bought her son Paul a BBC micro-computer for his eleventh birthday. At the age of 13 he constructed a modem out of parts from two broken modems he found in a rubbish skip outside the local post office. At the age of 14, Paul was invading corporate computer systems in the UK and overseas via international telephone networks.

By the time he was 16, Paul (using the codename Wandii) and his friends (codenamed Pad and Gandalf) had infiltrated the computer systems of The White House, Tokyo Zoo, the Swedish telephone system, the Bank of England, the Foreign Office and the *Financial Times*. Following his arrest by police, he boasted he had the access codes to the US Army base at Greenham Common, NASA, SG Warburg and Lloyds Bank.[4]

Paul gained access via a modem link to the computer network at Leeds Metropolitan University. From there, he gained access to other University networks via JANET (the University Joint Academic Network). He accessed his industrial and commercial targets via JANET and the British Telecom's Packet Switching System. Paul avoided paying for the use of the telephone lines he used by routing data transfers through the free national 0800 telephone service or through JANET. Investigators calculated that Paul had made over 80,000 unauthorised telephone calls (computer to computer) during his hacking activities. For example, the *Financial Times* had to pick up a telephone bill for £24,871 following Paul's illicit placement of a scanning program in the company's computer network. This program automatically dialled other computer telephone numbers.

The victims of Paul's infiltration of the international computer networks included the Brussels-based European Organisation for the Research and Treatment of Cancer (whose network broke down because of Paul's activities) and the Swedish telephone system (which crashed because its network became overloaded).

So what motivates cyberpunks like Paul Bedworthy? The National Computer Centre (NCC) surveyed 900 UK businesses in 1992 and discovered that around 40 per cent of all hacking incidents were perpetrated by former employees. In most cases these incidents represent less of a threat than an irritation to the company. As NCC security specialist, Tony Elbra, says:

> Often it's the chap who's been there for 20 years who's more likely to cause trouble, not the computer whizz kid.[5]

Although a small number of cyberpunks are driven by a desire to 'get back at the system' and to inconvenience (sometimes even to blackmail) big business,[6] a majority are young computer buffs, working alone, who are excited by the intellectual challenge of trying to beat the security of corporate computer systems.[7]

However, all hacking activities are illegal in the UK since the 1990 Computers Misuse Act and the NCC estimates that computer crime such as hacking costs UK business at least £350 million each year. Each time someone hacks into a corporate system it costs that corporation an average of £23,000 (either because of stolen money, increased telephone charges and/or through the cost of investigating the source and extent of the damage caused by the hacker).

The cyberpunk as victim

Paul Bedworth was charged with conspiracy to dishonestly obtain communications services, conspiracy to cause unauthorised modification of computer material and conspiracy to secure unauthorised access to computer material. The police investigation which uncovered the activities of Wandii, Pad and Gandalf involved eight UK police forces and others from as far afield as Singapore and Finland. The evidence amassed by the prosecution was impressive. Stored on floppy disks, if printed out on A4 paper it was estimated that the material would stack 126 feet high.

Paul Bedworth (now aged 19) did not deny the evidence presented in court, yet pleaded not guilty. Defending counsel argued that Paul could not have the criminal intent necessary for him to be convicted because of his 'pathological obsession' for computers. At the end of the 15 day trial, the jury of eight men and three women unanimously agreed with him. Paul Bedworth was found not guilty of all three charges. Detective Sergeant Laptew of West Yorkshire police, who led the investigation, said he was 'devastated' by the verdict.

An important influence on the verdict was the evidence given by Connie Bedworth, who told the court: 'computers turned my boy into a robot.' Paul would not let his mother into his bedroom where his computer and modem were kept. When she had a call-barring code placed on the telephone, Paul broke it and continued hacking. When she confiscated the modem, he burgled the home of his grandmother to get it back.

Connie Bedworth told the court:

> I told him I'd switch off all his stuff but he used to get very aggressive. . . It was no good me trying to stop him because he used to shove me out of his room and down the attic stairs. He was always trying to get rid of me so he could get back to his computer. He got so aggressive I used to have to switch the house electricity supply off at the mains to get him to stop. He just couldn't bear not to be on the computer. He couldn't stop what he was doing. He wanted to be on his computer all the time. Sleep was a waste of time to him.

In expert testimony Professor James Griffith-Edwards, from the University of London's National Addiction Centre, stated:

> We are looking at a young man who denied himself any other form of social life, who sat at his computer in a darkened room, hour after hour, night after night. He is a young man of quite unusual and outstanding intelligence, but there is something

very abnormal about him. I would classify him as suffering from a mental disorder. . . He is addicted to computing.

Issues to consider

- The Paul Bedworth case is not the first to evoke the image of the cyberpunk as a victim of computer addiction. Yet few juries sitting on drugs cases look so indulgently on the mixture of youth and addiction. What is it about the relationship between people and computer technology that promotes such public indulgence?[8]
- Do corporations unwittingly encourage cyberpunks?[9] How far can or should organisations go towards making illicit access to corporate information impossible?
- To what extent are cyberpunks 'children of modernity'?[10]

Notes

1. Excellent examples of the cyberpunk genre in science fiction include Egan (1993), Gibson (1984, 1986, 1988), Kadrey (1988) and Sterling (1988a, 1988b). For an overview, see McCaffery (1992).
2. Hafner and Markoff (1993) p. 9.
3. Details of Paul Bedworth's hacking activities are collated from the numerous media reports made during his trial at Southwark Crown Court, 1–18 March 1993.
4. According to the *Independent* newspaper ('Hacker penetrated MOD', 18 March 1993, p. 1) one of the reasons for bringing Paul to trial was concern over his attempts to access secret electronic intelligence gathering at a US military base near Harrogate and US Navy computers. The police raid on his bedroom allegedly unearthed numerous print-outs of confidential US military information. This evidence was not put before the court because the authorities felt issues of national security outweighed public interest.
5. Quoted in *Daily Telegraph*, 18 March 1993, p. 3.
6. Notorious examples being the Computer Chaos Club of Hamburg, the nefarious 'Dark Avenger' who operates from Sofia, and members of HPVC (Hacking Phreaking Viruses Carding) groups. See Hafner and Markoff (1993), Levy (1984) and Stoll (1989) for more details. Also see Sterling (1993) for a critical evaluation of the way the US security services deal with cyberpunks.
7. See Shotton (1989). Also see Turkle (1984) for a fascinating analysis of the ways in which users appropriate personal computers in order to deal with political and personal frustrations at work.
8. For a consideration of the powerful ideological influences on (and ramifications of) this relationship, see Cooley (1987), Scarbrough and Corbett (1992), Mumford (1934) and Zerzan and Carnes (1988). See Joerges (1989) for an interesting analysis of how social scientists have conceptualised the computer.

9. For a view that many organisations unwittingly encourage obsessive and addictive behaviour from employees, see Schaef and Fassel (1988). See Garson (1988), Rosen and Baroudi (1992) and Zuboff (1988) for the view that the new forms of managerial control enabled by information systems technology inevitably create resistance and a desire to 'break the system'.

10. Put another way, consider the extent to which individuals (and organisations) become addicted to, or at least overly dependent on, computer technology. Then ask yourself whether cyberpunks are inevitable products of this process.

According to Bauman (1989) and Christie (1993) 'children of modernity' are the products of modern industrial society – a society in which moral indifference is socially produced and perpetuated. This process is achieved through division of labour, modern bureaucracy, the obsession with efficiency and rationality, technological and scientific mentality and the dehumanisation of organisational behaviour. In this view the cyberpunks' obsession is neither the product of an abnormal mind nor an abnormal social (or technological) system, but is a logical extension of our major type of social organisation.

Case 47 The inter-disciplinary design of technology

Introduction

In 1982, Howard Rosenbrock, Fellow of the Royal Society and Professor of Control Engineering obtained a research grant to finance a 3 year project to design a human-centred CNC (computer numerically controlled) lathe at the University of Manchester Institute of Science and Technology (UMIST).

From about 1968, Rosenbrock had been devising a theory (and a complex computer software package) to allow the computer-aided design of engineering control systems. The package was designated as human-centred as it enabled control system designers to use their existing skill freely whilst giving them computer support. A designer would investigate a tentative design and instruct the computer to calculate its stability and so forth (using Rosenbrock's computer algorithms). If the design proved to be unsatisfactory in any of these regards, the computer would suggest ways to improve it.

By 1974, Rosenbrock noticed that while his system was successful, the dominant trends in computer-aided design were for a more technology-centred approach 'aimed not at accepting the designer's skill and trying to extend it and make it more productive but rather at replacing his skill by a large computer algorithm'.[1]

Within the world of computer-aided manufacturing, a similar technology-centred trend exists, and against such a background the UMIST lathe project was established.[2] Rosenbrock led the project, aided by a steering committee of organisational and engineering experts. The day-to-day design work was carried out by a design team of two engineers and one social scientist (myself).

As the project progressed, an elegant user–machine interface was designed (and a prototype built) which allowed users to graphically define how a metal part should be machined by the CNC lathe. This was done in such a way as to give the craftsperson full control over machine programming by using conventional terminology and procedures. However, less than 1 year into the project a significant disagreement arose between myself and Professor Rosenbrock relating to the design of a key part of this interface software, called the cutting technology.

Cutting technology refers to the calculations necessary to optimise the way in which metal is removed from the original metal blank. If a tool cuts too quickly or too deeply, it may distort the blank or the tool itself may break. If the tool cuts too slowly it may prove too time-consuming and thus uneconomical. In fact there are many calculations which need to be made in order for the finished part to be made quickly and to a high standard of quality. On manual machines, the skilled users would make the calculations. On later numerical control (NC) machines, the office programmer rather than the user would make the calculations. Our argument concerned who should make the initial cutting technology calculations – the computer or the craftsperson?

Rosenbrock favoured using computer algorithms in order to generate near-optimal cutting conditions. The user would then be free to accept or change the computer's suggestions depending on circumstances. I favoured allowing users to make the relevant calculations, with the computer being used to check them against important physical constraints (tool strength, power of machine, quality of surface finish required, and so forth). This became known as the 'blank table option'.

Although at first sight, only a trivial disagreement, this argument resulted in lengthy debates about the nature of human-centred technology and the relationship between human skill and technological progress. It also created a significant division of opinion within both the design team and the steering committee.[3]

When it became clear that consensus would not easily be reached, Rosenbrock decided it would be helpful if the two of us wrote down our respective points of view and then circulated these (in the format of a debate) for comment to a larger sample of experts. Our exchange of ideas is reprinted in full below.

The debate[4]

Martin Corbett

A technical system that does not provide the experience out of which operating skills can develop will be vulnerable in those circumstances where human intervention becomes necessary. This viewpoint has become increasingly widespread amongst designers and industrial psychologists in the field of process control automation (not least because of the Three Mile Island experience).

Research on process control operators reveals that an operator will be able to generate successful new operating strategies for unusual situations only if he (sic) has an adequate knowledge of the process (see Bainbridge, 1981).[5] There are two problems with this for 'machine-minding' operators:

1. Efficient retrieval of knowledge from long-term memory depends on frequency of use.
2. This type of knowledge develops only through use and feedback about its effectiveness. There is some concern that the present generation of automated systems, which are monitored by former manual operators, are riding on their skills, which later generations of operators cannot be expected to have. Operators can learn very little about the feel of control from watching an automatic controller at work (Brigham and Laios, 1975), although skills improve over many years of informal on-the-job experience.

Indeed, Bainbridge (1978) argues that it is important for operators to maintain and develop their feel for process dynamics. As this can only be done by direct involvement in control this suggests that some control functions should be allocated to the human operator in an automated plant even when this is not technically necessary (cf. Jordan, 1963):

One method which has been tried is for the automatic controller (computer) to suggest a control action, the operator assesses it and then presses an 'accept' button. However, when the computer very rarely makes a mistake the operator comes to 'accept' automatically without any check. This method may be good for giving an operator confidence in the computer's control, but it is no help in maintaining his control skill and useless as a way of monitoring automatic control performance. An alternative is for operators to control the process manually for a short period at the beginning of each shift. This is economically worthwhile if the costs of poorer productivity during this period are less than the costs of lost productivity because the operator is not able adequately to take over control or assess failure. The only other alternative is to use special training sessions on high-fidelity simulators, as in aircraft pilot training' (Bainbridge, 1978, p. 260).

I feel that this has direct relevance to the computer control of cutting calculations on our lathe.

Manual control of a centre lathe involves the operator using his knowledge (acquired through *practical* experience) to determine how a workpiece should be set up, which tools should be used, what cutting sequences are best employed, and what speeds, feeds and cuts should be used. On our lathe all this knowledge is still required (whenever a new workpiece is to be turned) except for the latter which will only be required (and therefore used) for approximately 10 per cent of the time it is required on manual and other MDI CNC lathes. Apart from the fragmentation of the operator's mental planning functions that this engenders, the two problems discussed above remain unsolved.

When operator intervention is needed there is likely to be something wrong with the machining process, so that unusual actions will be needed to control it, and one can argue that the operator needs to be more skilled than average. For this skill to develop (especially in future generations of operators) it would seem essential to re-unite all the operator's mental planning functions and allow him to enter his own values for speeds, feeds and cuts periodically. This practice will then place him in a better position to assess computer suggestions against his own practical knowledge. Ephrath (1980) has reported a study in which system performance was worse with computer aiding, because the operator made the decisions anyway, and checking the computer added to his workload. Indeed, in our system it may be better to allow the computer to check the operator's values against physical constraints, thus supplying speedy feedback and eliminating error, when the operator inputs his own data.

Such a modification is easily written into the present software and, aside from the present argument, will give our cutting technology complete flexibility as it allows for fully manual control and fully automatic (computer) control and all possible combinations of these two extremes through our editing facility.

To avoid the addition of further question and answer interactions at the interface the operator could be presented with a blank table with the option to press 'compute' at any time. If he wishes to enter all his own data he may do so – pressing 'compute' on completion. If he wishes the software to calculate values, he will immediately press 'compute' and the table will be filled. All possible combinations of these two extremes are possible using this facility, thus allowing an operator to pace his own learning and fully exploit his knowledge.

I feel that the present generation of operators, who are trained on manual lathes, may not benefit greatly from this modification. However, if we are concerned with future trends (e.g. CAD linkage to the lathe) then such a modification will be of great benefit to the next generation of operators whose feel for the machining process may be increasingly more indirect.

Howard Rosenbrock

I still cannot generate much enthusiasm for the 'blank table'. I will set out my reservations under a number of heads.

1. I doubt whether your analogy to the process industries, or to aircraft, is appropriate. An aircraft, for example, has no 'stop' button. If a fault occurs in the autopilot, the aircraft must immediately be transferred to manual control, and the pilot must be ready at all times to accept this responsibility. He must also react appropriately to a range of emergency conditions – engine failure on take-off, depressurisation at this altitude, etc. For these reasons he needs to retain and practise his skills continually, whether in flight or by simulation. Similar remarks apply with more or less force to chemical plants, oil refineries, power stations, etc.

    A different analogy, more appropriate to my mind, would be to accounting machines. At one time, the entry of items in a ledger, and their totalling, were separate operations. Clerks developed a very great facility in addition, so that they could add up a column of figures as fast as they could read it. When accounting machines came into use, entry of a new item automatically updated the total.

    Now it would be quite possible to provide an option on the accounting machine which said, in effect, 'do you wish to see the total, or do you wish to produce it yourself, with the option of comparing it with the machine's result afterwards?'. This would be a way of encouraging the clerk to retain his skill in addition, but I think it would not have much appeal. It would be like retaining a skill in using the slide rule, after pocket calculators became a cheaper and better alternative.

2. The difference between the two cases lies in the need for the old skill. If it is needed, it should be retained and appropriate means should be provided for its retention. If it is not needed, then it is pointless to attempt to retain it. We do not need to retain the same skill in point duty for policemen now that we have traffic lights, nor the same skill in mental arithmetic now that we have pocket calculators. It is, of course, good to retain the *ability* to do these things: it is only the level of skill that is necessary which I am querying. At university, I spent many long afternoons in the drawing office gaining competence in designing steam-locomotive valve gear. A colleague took an engineering apprenticeship and spent many months acquiring high skill with a file. Neither of us has used these skills, and both of us feel that the time would have been better spent practising the skills that we do use

    One can argue that the job of the clerk was degraded by the introduction of accounting machines, but this is not an argument for the retention of old skills when they are redundant. Rather it is an argument for a development of the clerk's job which ensured that new skills were provided to take the place of the old.

3. The question then turns on the need for the lathe operator to suggest initial values for cutting conditions. It is fully admitted that initial values (whether obtained from the operator or the computer) may not be satisfactory, and one aspect of the operator's skill is his ability to change the initial values incrementally. This skill needs to be maintained and practised

    In simple situations (short, rigid job, firmly clamped, normal material and tool, cut limited by tool rather than machine power, etc.) the operator's estimate and the computer's will probably agree closely, and both will be a good approximation to what is needed. This, however, is not a very interesting situation, because the conditions will be close to those tabulated by tool manufacturers, and require only memory rather than judgement

    If the situation is less simple, say work which is relatively long and slender, then I believe that the operator will usually be unable to make a first estimate which is close to the allowable maximum. He will probably have to proceed tentatively, starting with relatively light cuts and gradually increasing them until he judges that he has reached the best values. Often he may not carry out this experimentation, because for a small batch-size the gain will not repay the time spent experimenting. If programming is done in the planning office, there is even less chance that the best conditions will be reached. Either way, there is an economic loss.

    If our cutting technology program is successful, it should produce on most occasions a first estimate which is close enough to the maximum to make further improvement by experimentation unnecessary. Sometimes the operator may be able to make a significant improvement, sometimes he may have to reduce the severity of cutting, and sometimes he may have to correct for unusual conditions. All of these actions will use his existing skill and allow it to be practised. Sometimes the operator may make the correction before the cut is taken, but often I think the need for correction will become apparent when cutting begins. For this reason it will be important to be able to stop a cut and re-start with different conditions.

4. In summary, the cutting technology program is intended to give, in the more complicated situations, a better starting point than the operator is likely to produce. This is possible because the operator cannot make calculations of work deflection, etc., as the computer can. Further development, from the initial conditions, is entirely the responsibility of the operator

    I see the area where the operator's skill will continue to be needed as the area where the computer model disagrees with the real world. With experience, the operator will find that the computer is wrong in some circumstances (for example, too conservative, or too severe), because it knows less about the real situation than the operator does. When these conditions recur, he can take appropriate action. They will only occur in a small proportion of cases, but the operator will be handling much more work than he did before, so the opportunity to acquire and use skill need not decline sharply

You, it seems to me, see the operator's skill continuing to lie in the same area as the computer's model, so that he should try to be as good as the computer at what the computer does. This looks backward, rather than forward.

5. Do we wish to use the cutting technology program as a teaching aid? I think we have to assume that operators will have reached an appropriate level of skill before they can accept responsibility for such a system, so we are not thinking of beginners. It would still be possible to envisage the skilled operator using the cutting technology package to improve his own skill in estimating cutting conditions (with the blank table option) so that he can become competitive with the computer. But as I have just said, it is pointless for the operator to compete with the computer in what the computer does best. He should collaborate with the computer, and the computer should collaborate with him, so that together they can do better than either alone.

It seems to me to be sensible to accept the assistance which the computer can give, and to concentrate on the new areas in which the operator's skill will need to develop. There will be many of these, and I will list only a few:

(a) With more severe cutting conditions it will be more important than before to have the best sequence of operations. For example, heavy cutting at the end of the work should be done before the diameter is reduced near the chuck. The selection of this sequence is best left to the operator.

(b) Systematic defects in the cutting technology program will become evident and the operator will learn to anticipate these. For example, since deflections of the work are calculated by dividing it into only a few sections, highly irregular shapes will produce cutting conditions which are less severe than they might be.

(c) Faster cutting will reduce the time which the machine spends working, other things being equal. So more attention will be needed from the operator to organising the flow of work, optimising the sequence of components, etc.

Martin Corbett

Rather than prolong this 'thrust-and-parry' exchange I would like to focus on the core of the engineering–social science dialogue. As I understand it, your philosophy of work design is summed up in the opening paragraph of section 2 in your reply. To paraphrase: if a current skill is needed, it should be retained and appropriate means should be provided for its retention. If it is not needed, retention is pointless.

Such a proposition acquires meaning only when one defines 'need'.

The classical technocentric approach defines this 'need' with respect to the technological state-of-the-art – current skills are retained in those areas of work that have, technically, not yet been solved (i.e. reduced to formal description). The extent to which new skills develop is largely dependent upon the thoroughness of the new design.

A human-centred approach must add social criteria to this purely technical evaluation of skill need. Our debate over the blank table option stems directly from our failure to unite social and engineering criteria concerning cut calculations. We followed a path on which the question 'do we need a cutting technology?' preceded the question 'do we need to retain the operator's skill at calculating cuts?'. Our answer to the first was an arbitrary 'yes', our answer to the second was a qualified 'yes' because our technology can never be 100 per cent accurate or reliable (unlike your accounting machine).

Consider an alternative scenario in which the second question precedes the first:

1. *Do we need shop-floor skill for cut calculations?*
   Yes. It is an area of machining prone to unforeseen disturbance requiring a discretionary skill unsuited to formal description.
2. *Do we need a cutting technology?* Yes. The computer's ability to remember large amounts of data and to make rapid calculations will enable shopfloor skill to develop and protect the operator from error by checking entered data against constraints. The computer complements the operator's skill.

Having made this general decision, the specific details can be worked out through reference to a list of principles (such as the list in Corbett, 1985) and with regard to economic criteria.

The essential difference between the two approaches lies in the relationship between the scientific knowledge contained within the cutting technology software and the practical (often tacit) knowledge of the operator. The first approach follows a Taylorist path insofar as scientific knowledge gradually supersedes practical knowledge as the prime instigator of work practices.

The principle of complementarity discussed in Corbett (1985) implies that scientific knowledge and practical knowledge can peacefully coexist and feed off each other (q.v. Polanyi). The first approach only allows skill (i.e. practical knowledge) to develop when the operator disagrees with the computer (i.e. when scientific knowledge alone is inadequate), implying that the two are mutually exclusive. You imply this when you describe the computer and the operator 'competing' against each other.

Finally, to return to our definition of *need*, the technocentric approach implies a philosophy that views a universal *need* for the application of science steadily replacing any *need* for practical knowledge. An alternative path may be taken which attempts to optimise practical knowledge with the help of scientific knowledge, instead of the other way round. Given your writings on the philosophy of science this may be a rewarding path to explore more fully.

Howard Rosenbrock

We differ more than I thought, but we probably made the differences clear. They seem to me to be philosophical differences, not scientific (i.e. empirically based) ones.

We have agreed at a recent meeting to simulate the blank table option, which can be done fairly simply. Having done so, I believe we should accept whatever empirical result we obtain from operators – that is, whether they want it or not.

I am not very happy about the situation for a number of reasons:

1. The decision goes against the weight of existing evidence obtained from our last simulation.
2. We have not established any principles which show why the blank table option is more important than a multitude of others.
3. Having put the option in, we shall in effect have shifted the burden of proof – can we find reasons for taking it out, rather than can we find reasons for putting it in?

Issues to consider

- What are the main issues being debated here?
- To what extent do they reflect different world views of social scientists and engineers? What are the implications of such conflicting perspectives for the management of user participation in technological design?[6]
- How do you account for the fact that the trend towards the incorporation of human skill into machines is far more dominant than an approach based on allowing human skills to develop alongside technology in a more symbiotic way?[7]
- Is 'human-centred technology' a contradiction in terms?

Notes

1. Rosenbrock (1989), p. 1.
2. See Braverman (1974) and Noble (1984) for elaboration of the argument that developments in computer aided manufacturing have directly resulted in increased managerial and technological control of the labour process and to the deskilling of skilled craftworkers.
3. For more information on the 'blank table debate' and on the UMIST project more generally, see Rosenbrock (1989). Cooley (1987) and Rosenbrock (1990) provide excellent analyses of the philosophical background to this work. See Corbett *et al.* (1991) for detailed analysis of the problems of inter-disciplinary design. See Adler and Winograd (1992) for a critical overview of successful interdisciplinary design projects.
4. This debate was previously published as an appendix to Corbett (1989b). It is reprinted here with the kind permission of the publisher, Springer-Verlag London Limited, and the editor, Howard Rosenbrock.
5. I note with embarrassment that at the time of this written debate I wrongly assumed CNC lathe operation to be the sole prerogative of the male craftsperson. I have resisted the strong temptation to alter a published historical record in order to hide my own shortcomings.
6. See Adler and Winograd (1992), Blackler and Brown (1986), McLoughlin and Clark (1988), Mumford and Weir (1979), Pacey (1983) and Willcocks and Mason (1987).
7. See Albury and Schwartz (1982), Cooley (1987), Hill (1988), Mumford (1934), Scarbrough and Corbett (1992) and Zerzan and Carnes (1988).

Case 48   Technological change in the US Internal Revenue Service[1]

Introduction

In the 1960s, the US Internal Revenue Service (IRS) made a strong commitment to computerisation in order to process tax returns more efficiently. At that time the IRS was envied by other federal organisations as an innovative and creative forerunner in the use of data processing technology.

However, throughout the 1970s and 1980s, the US Congress consistently refused to provide additional funding for new technology and, by 1980, many IRS departments were close to collapse owing to outdated technology, increased workloads and reduced staffing levels.

Within the Collections Division of the IRS, throughout the 1970s, much of the initial processing of a delinquent account (i.e. an individual who had yet to pay the required amount of income tax) was done manually. A clerk would mail the initial request for tax payment in batches of around 500 accounts. Over the next 2 weeks, incoming mail would be associated with case files, followed by a full review. Appropriate follow-up letters would be sent if the account issues were not resolved satisfactorily. This process continued until the remaining stubborn cases were transferred to the Field Division, where an official would contact the taxpayer in person (usually by telephone).

By 1980, the IRS in general, and the Collections Division in particular, were in crisis and there was a danger that the entire system would collapse under the weight of the huge backlog of accounts in need of processing. Top management decided that computerisation was the only salvation. But there was little hope that Congress would support such a venture financially.

In 1981, Roscoe Egger was appointed IRS Commissioner. He brought with him a new vision of the future of tax administration and a passionate interest in management. He focused his attention on three inter-related areas, namely: (1) the establishment of a strategic planning process; (2) the complete revamping of the data processing functions within the IRS; and (3) the decentralisation of administrative decision-making.

Assistant Commissioner of Human Resources, James Lantonio noted that the first 18 months of Egger's tenure were frustrating for both the Commissioner and his managers.

Unfortunately, what Egger articulated and what the organization heard were two different things. Egger was preaching a new vision of management, the Service was hearing a minor tinkering with the current way of doing business. When Egger spoke of a strategic planning process, the organization heard modifications to the long-range planning process. When he spoke of a plan that would drive the budget planning system, they heard only a multi-year budget planning approach. When he talked about an Information Resource Management function, they heard further centralization of the tax processing system. And finally, when he spoke of decentralized decision-making, they heard tighter controls at the Regional level.[2]

The automated delinquent accounts collection system

The Regional Commissioner in Chicago had long been concerned with what he perceived to be the dwindling respect for the voluntary payment of taxes by the average US citizen. He was keen to implement a computerised system to automate the collection of delinquent accounts and, having formed a small task group, set about visiting a number of collection service organisations to see what type of computer systems were available. The group became convinced that the technology was both available and essential to the IRS.

The group proposal for the automation of all the regional collection offices was presented at a meeting in Washington. Commissioner Egger was very impressed and directed the somewhat reluctant Deputy Commissioner to put together a group to develop a presentation to the Treasury Department.

The Deputy Commissioner soon found that almost all IRS departments quickly found legitimate reasons why they should be involved. Executives from these departments all claimed ownership of the project. Ultimately a compromise was reached whereby every executive who could even remotely be involved in the project was designated a member of the Automation Implementation Control Board (AICB). Hence, along with the Regional Commissioner from Chicago, membership included Assistant Commissioners from Data Processing, Compliance, Policy and Management, Computer Services, Planning, Examination, Collection, Support Services and Human Resources. This board reported to the smaller Automation Implementation Control Group (chaired by the IRS Deputy Commissioner), which, in turn, reported to the Automation Policy Review Board.

1 year on, the procurement process ended and a contract was awarded to GC Services in Texas. This bid was based on a joint venture combining GC Services' collection expertise, Arthur Anderson's software development, IBM's hardware and Rockwell International's telecommunications capabilities. The goal was a state-of-the-art computer system to support a single functional activity throughout the IRS – the collection of delinquent accounts. The drawback (and the carrot dangled before the Office of the President by Egger) was that President Reagan expected a quick payback before the presidential elections two years hence.

Plans were immediately developed to have pilot sites on-line within 4 months from contract award. The overall, extremely ambitious plan called for 20 operating sites to be operational within 18 months.

The 'people' issues

As the Automation Implementation Control Group advanced its planning, some members expressed concern that the human aspects of the automation project had been pushed aside by technical and financial considerations. The Assistant Commissioner for Human Resources identified two important problems which needed to be solved. First, the new system, if it worked as planned, was likely to make over 2000 Collections and Field Division employees redundant nation-wide. Second, there would be a need for an entirely new way of training and orienting the remaining employees to work in an automated environment. The jobs of clerks in the Collections Division were routine, whereas the jobs with the new automated systems required considerably more skill and discretion – not least because they would combine the job of Collection Division clerk with that of the more highly qualified Field Division officer.

Whilst the first of these problems could be (and was) handled through conventional union–management negotiating procedures, no formal mechanism existed for dealing with the problem of job redesign and training for large-scale technological change. It was left to a group of organisational psychologists and ergonomists within the Human Resources Division, to put the 'people' issues on the agenda of the Automation Implementation Control Group, via their Assistant Commissioner on the AICB.

This *ad hoc* Human Resources group began to develop long-term programmes to deal with the technological change. They were aware of the alienation and high labour turnover rates associated with the implementation of large automated systems, and feared that the automated collection system would never function properly without significant investments of time and money in the social side of the system.

The Automation Implementation Control Group was sympathetic to these concerns but they were loath to allow anything to interfere with adhering to their very rigid time schedule. Ultimately, they agreed to let the Human Resource group collect data at the pilot sites (but only so long as the data gathering did not interfere with the overall implementation plan).

However, the group met resistance at every turn. Only the prospective system users and line managers actively supported the group's efforts. When a questionnaire was proposed, the Automation Implementation Control Group would only allow it to be of a certain length and duration so as not to interfere with the 'real work'. Executives decided that training should be left until the week before the system went 'live' and that this training should focus on classroom lectures on the technical side of the system.

Issues to consider

- Imagine you are the Assistant Commissioner of Human Resources. You fully support the work of the Human Resources group and are convinced that the automated delinquent accounts collection system is doomed to failure unless investment in the 'people' issues is made during the weeks or months before the system is implemented.
- How would you set about identifying and tackling the 'people' issues surrounding the automation project? Your answer should be in the form of comprehensive notes to use as a basis for a verbal presentation to the Automation Implementation Control Group outlining your concerns and strategic recommendations. You should be prepared to support your

recommendations by reference to the relevant research literature on organisational behaviour.[3]

Notes

1. Much of the information for this case comes from Fallik (1988) – especially the insightful chapter on the politics of technological change contributed by ex-Assistant Commissioner of Human Resources, James Lantonio.
2. Fallik (1988), p. 73.
3. Useful sources here include Adler and Winograd (1992), Child *et al.* (1984), Clegg and Kemp (1986), Corbett (1992), Cornfield (1987), Mumford and Weir (1979), Otway and Peltu (1983), Piercy (1984), Scarbrough and Corbett (1992) and Willcocks and Mason (1987).

Case 49   'Living' with new technology: like pigs to the slaughter?[1]

FIGURE 8.1

Issues to consider

- To what extent does Figure 8.1 provide an apt metaphor for the way (a) people, and (b) organisations tend to relate to technological 'progress'?[2]
- Not everyone benefits from developments in new technology. Which groups of people could the pig represent?[3]

Notes

1. The above sketch is my own version of a cartoon I saw in a magazine some 15 or so years ago. Many thanks to Laura and Maia for their help with this recreation. Despite extensive inquiries I have been unable to ascertain the identity of the artist or the magazine in which his or her original cartoon was published. Should anyone be able to enlighten me on this matter could they please get in touch so that due acknowledgement can be made.
2. For consideration of the ideological ramifications of technological progress, see Albury and Schwartz (1982), Cooley (1987), Hill (1988), Mumford (1934), Scarbrough and Corbett (1992), and Webster and Robins (1988). See Daniel and Hogarth (1990), Rolfe (1990) and Zuboff (1988) for an analysis of employee attitudes towards technological change.
3. See Albury and Schwartz (1982), Beirne and Ramsay (1992), Cockburn (1983), Cooley (1987), Duncan (1981), and especially the critical anthology edited by Zerzan and Carnes (1988).

PART 4

ANALYSING ORGANISATIONAL ENVIRONMENTS

CHAPTER 9

Organisation and environment

Introduction

An organisation of people, like individual people, does not exist in a vacuum. In this last chapter, I offer seven cases which raise issues relating to the nature of the relationship between organisations and the political, economic and socio–cultural environment in which they are located.

Mainstream OB texts tend to focus on the environmental determinism versus organisational choice debate. Despite the rise in popularity of the population ecology perspective (e.g. Hannan and Freeman, 1977) which lies firmly in the determinist camp, most OB texts view the choice perspective as the more useful. The cases offered in this chapter encourage the analysis to consider the relationship between organisational choice and environmental constraint in more detail.

An organisations environment comprises other organisations, of course, and Case 50 examines the relationship of business organisations to one another. The study of the manufacture and selling of steel purlins to the construction industry exposes one of countless cartels which operate in markets throughout the world. OB textbooks, in the main, give the impression that organisations must adapt to their environment if they are to survive or flourish. Case 50 shows how organisations also create or enact their *own* environment in a far more proactive way. Case 51 examines this enactment process in more vivid detail and raises issues about the use and abuse of corporate power.

Case 52 briefly alludes to the possible conflict of interests facing investors and corporate shareholders with deeply-felt Christian beliefs. For example, should the Church of England invest in countries with appalling records of suppressing civil rights?

Case 53 utilises research from the meso-level of organisational analysis in order to raise issues of inter-organisational conflict and cooperation. Sometimes the complexities of economic exchange and organisational strategy can be more clearly understood when they are simplified through analogy. If you regard the analogy in the case as false or misleading, perhaps you would like to reflect why.

Case 54 examines the world of Japanese car manufacturing from the viewpoint of the employee and the management of employee commitment at the Nissan factory in Zama, Japan. The case revisits themes explored in numerous cases earlier in the book, but encourages a more macro-level of analysis.

The power of the multinational corporation is examined in Case 55. Such is the formidable power and reputation of these organisations that several drafts of this case had to be abandoned on legal advice. Some multi-nationals literally do get away with murder and yet OB texts spend little time analysing this most potent of organisational forms. Case 55 is all the more telling as it reveals that organisations (including governmental agencies) cannot simply export problems. Even the most powerful organisations exist within an eco-system where free lunches don't exist and within which everything is connected to everything else.

The final case in the book, Case 56, resembles the first and invites you to consider again the social and cultural forces which shape human attitudes and behaviour.

Case 50   Hadley Industries and the UK cartel culture*

Introduction: the UK cartel culture

Many economic and business commentators believe that UK business has long been steeped in a cartel culture. Some even see this as a major contributing factor to the country's poor post-war economic record.

Agreements and cooperation between businesses in order to avoid competition and to maximise market share have an obvious appeal to business shareholders, as such practices help to stabilise markets (including labour markets) and boost and maintain healthy profit margins. Certainly cartels and price-fixing agreements appear to have been central to the power and longevity of the British Empire (and probably instrumental in its downfall).

---

*Cart'el (n): *an industrial combination for regulating volume and price of output.*

It wasn't until Clement Attlee's Labour government came to power after the Second World War that a serious attempt was made to pass anti-trust legislation to destroy cartels and associated restrictive trade practices. Attlee's actions were spurred on by two particular incidents of cartel activity: one in shipbuilding, the other in the chemicals industry.

First, the UK Labour movement in the 1930s had been powerless to stop the actions of a shipbuilding cartel which, fearful of competition during the economic recession, had taken over the remaining shipyards in the UK and then promptly closed over a third of them. The resulting closure of Palmer's Shipyard in Jarrow contributed significantly to the large-scale unemployment and poverty in the town and to the well-publicised Jarrow hunger marches to London.

The second incident involved ICI which, between the two world wars, had formed an international cartel with the large German chemical and pharmaceutical corporation, IG Farben. Between them the two companies divided up the world chemicals market – IG Farben taking Europe and ICI taking the British Commonwealth territories. The companies agreed to stay out of each other's markets and to leave the US market to Du Pont. The outbreak of war in 1939 disrupted the smooth running of this lucrative agreement as trade with Germany was now considered treasonable. But, in 1943, the UK government were shocked to discover that ICI was trading illicitly with the German corporation. No action was taken at that time as ICI was making a huge contribution to the UK war effort and was in the midst of mass-producing an improved, possibly war-winning, air-to-ground missile. The government also feared the effect on public morale if ICI's illicit dealings were made known.

Attlee felt after the war that the time was right to take on the powerful cartels. But intense lobbying by powerful corporations saw to it that no effective anti-trust legislation was passed. Since then, of course, anti-trust legislation, such as the Restrictive Practices Act, has been passed.

Today, in the UK, the penalty for a first offence is a written warning. Subsequent offences are deemed to be in contempt of Court and punishable by a fine. In the US, by contrast, anti-trust offences often lead to custodial sentences for executive officers within the companies involved.

But legislation has not stopped the operation of cartels in the UK. For example, between 1977 and 1987, ICI was fined a total of £22 million for illegal price-fixing. Three such incidents involved ICI conspiring with the Shell Oil Company to fix the price of polypropylene, PVC and plastic film. Indeed, it transpired that Shell and ICI had developed quite sophisticated mechanisms to disguise their illegal activities. For instance, a carefully planned timetable of price information leaks was drawn up to help create the impression that any price-fixing was unplanned and accidental.

Between 1977 and 1987, the UK Office of Fair Trading has also had to deal with formal and informal cartels operating in a variety of businesses:

including car ferries, betting shops, milk, sugar, road-surfacing materials, glass, central heating oil, ready mixed concrete, and steel purlins.

Hadley Industries and the steel purlin cartel

Steel purlins are widely used in the construction of roofs for factories and large buildings. Between them the companies Ayrshire Metal Trim, Metsec and Wards enjoyed a 90 per cent share of the purlin market in 1985. The Office of Fair Trading suspected the operation of a cartel but were unable to amass sufficient proof to obtain a conviction.

In 1988, the Birmingham company Hadley Industries developed a revolutionary type of steel purlin which could be manufactured using almost 30 per cent less steel than conventional purlins without any weakening of the product's structural strength. The company was confident it had a winner.

However, Hadley found it extremely difficult to break into the purlin market despite the very competitive price of their product. To make matters worse, rumours were flying around Hadley's potential customers – the large construction companies – that the Hadley steel purlins were structurally weak and of poor quality.

Philip Hadley, the company head, decided to track down the source of this misinformation and despatched his sales manager, Clifford Hargreaves, to Ayrshire Metal Trim. Posing as a prospective buyer, Hargreaves was dismayed to hear a Ayrshire sales manager sing the praises not only of the purlins manufactured by Ayrshire, but also those made by Ayrshire's 'competitors' – Wards and Metsec. It was suggested to Hargreaves that he should think twice about buying Hadley's purlins because of the unflattering rumours about the product's strength.

Phillip Hadley persevered with his investigations and was dismayed to discover that Metsec, Wards and Ayrshire were working together, illegally, as a cartel. This cartel posed a serious threat to the survival of his own company as the three other companies were undercutting Hadley Industries on every major construction supply contract and tender (even if this meant losing money in the short term).

In 1990, Hadley eventually got the proof he needed when Mike Thompson resigned from the Ayrshire management team to join Hadley Industries. Thompson's evidence led to the uncovering of the cartel by the Office of Fair Trading. It transpired that the cartel had been operating for 7 very profitable years by beating off all competition from 'bitzers' (the phrase used by cartel members to describe competitors).

In 1991 legal representatives from Metsec, Wards and Ayrshire signed a Court order promising to disband the cartel immediately and permanently.

A spokesman for the Office of Fair Trading commented:

> It shouldn't be down to the government and the law courts to break up these kind of cartels. Companies must know that cartels may bring them short term benefits, but collapse and ruin in the longer term. Cartels encourage laziness, lack of innovation and low efficiency within companies; poor product quality, high prices and the major risk of a consumer backlash. Ultimately, business should police itself.

In Brussells, Peter Sutherland, the European Community's Commissioner for Competition, disagrees and believes that the hard line taken by the US Department of Justice is the only way to counteract the widespread adoption of restrictive practices within a free market economy.

But Don Baker, an anti-trust expert in the US Department of Justice, believes that America's tough anti-trust legislation stems from the US public's distrust of big business and hatred of feeling 'ripped off'. 'Remember the Boston Tea Party,' he advises. Baker believes that people in the UK (and especially politicians) are far too deferential towards big business and hence lack the political will to pass tougher laws.

Issues to consider

- Analyse and explain the behaviour of the members of the steel purlin cartel.
- If UK has a cartel culture, what or where were its origins and how is it sustained? Can it be changed?[1]
- Is the situation different in other countries? Why, or why not?[2]

Notes

1. See Freyer (1992).
2. See Breit and Elzinga (1989), Clinard (1990) and Williamson (1976).

Case 51   IBM and the management of market uncertainty

In 1963, IBM enjoyed a huge 80 per cent market share (by value) of installed and on-order data processing equipment in the US. The company's new 1401 computer model range alone accounted for about a fifth of the entire US computer systems market, and its sales helped push IBM's revenue over the $2 billion mark that year.

Competitors such as Honeywell, Burroughs, General Electric and Control Data knew the true cost of computer manufacture and were eager to compete with IBM (who were achieving an estimated 45 per cent profit margin with the 1401). Honeywell, for example, felt sure they could offer a better and more powerful computer for less money.

Certainly, rapid improvements in technology set the stage for IBM's competitors to launch a particularly effective attack on the commercial core of IBM's near-monopoly. With developments in transistor technology in the 1960s, building a better low-cost machine than the 1401 (which was based on late-1950s technology) posed little problem.

Honeywell launched the H-200 computer system in 1963. It ran faster than the 1401, it cost less and, most important of all, it came with a software package, appropriately named *Liberator*, that enabled 1401 programs to run on Honeywell's machine. The H-200 was an immediate success. Freed from being locked-in to IBM software, many of IBM's customers switched to the H-200 system.

Honeywell's success pushed IBM executives into a state of panic. Sales of the H-200 caused IBM's market share to fall over three percentage points. Honeywell's share rose to 2.5 per cent. IBM's chairman Thomas Watson Junior was desperate to maintain the company's bloated market share. If Honeywell were too successful, he feared that other manufacturers would begin building IBM-compatible machines. Hence, he began a 2 year campaign within the company to maintain market share at all costs.

Watson realised that simply dropping the price of the 1401 would not be enough to see off the Honeywell challenge. So, in 1964, IBM hastily unveiled the System/360 – a range of six computer models which would provide 'unparalleled performance and reliability'. Thomas Watson Junior admitted later:

> By the Spring of '64 our hand was forced and we had to, with our eyes wide open, announce a complete line – some of the machines 24 months early, and the total line an average of 12 months early. I guess all of us who were thinking about the matter realised that we should have problems when we did this, but. . .we were so up against the wall saleswise that had we waited another nine months to announce the line we would have lost positions that we could ill afford to lose.[1]

IBM rushed the System/360 computer systems onto the market to stop competitors, and it was the mere promise of that family of computers, as much as their installation, that saved the day for IBM. Despite the fact that several models did not make it to the purchasers for 2 years, within 6 years of the 360's introduction 18,000 of the systems had been sold in the US. The 360 brought IBM $16 billion in revenues and more than $6 billion in profits.

The 360 became the core of IBM's business. The machines' popularity created *de facto* technical standards which became the basis of US federal laws and of the business plans of dozens of new companies. Most important of all, the system/360 helped IBM push several competing suppliers of complete systems right out of the market.

At the time, the success of the System/360 was attributed to its technical superiority. Indeed, IBM argued that the 360 family was 'one of this country's greatest industrial innovations'.[2] But IBM documents from the time show that exactly the opposite view was held, and that the technical brains in the company felt the System/360 to be 'mediocre'.[3]

Among the major problems IBM identified with the new 360 machine were lack of competitiveness against non-IBM computers of all sizes; its lack of time sharing capability; an inability to operate with more than one processor in a system; a reliance on outdated logic circuitry; and a cumbersome bug-ridden operating system, OS/360.[4] Indeed, the final version of OS/360 simply excluded many of the functions IBM had promised and was so large and inefficient that the smaller 360 machines could not use it. IBM's product test department had identified OS/360 problems early on, but its warnings had gone unheeded by higher management in their rush to announce the new 360 family. As the IBM president Vincent Learson, later recalled:

> We did what the late Charles Kettering, an engineering genius and president of General Motors research division, always advised against: we put a delivery date on something not yet invented.[5]

So why did the 360/System sell so well? Essentially because IBM decided to drop entry-level 360 prices to the absolute minimum. This would ensure that any 1401 users thinking of switching to Honeywell would seriously consider an entry-level 360 first. In the longer term, Honeywell would pose a serious threat to IBM only if it could build a large enough customer base. Very low priced entry-level 360 systems would frustrate that mission and ensure IBM's continued dominance.

> To drive the technically troubled 360s to success, IBM once again exploited monopoly power that was wholly unavailable to competitors. It was price discrimination – setting prices high, relative to cost, on equipment that faced no competition, and setting prices low where competition was effective – that made the 360s so successful and so profitable. . . In effect, IBM gave away entire 360 systems to win those few strategically important customers that were otherwise free to take their business elsewhere at any particular point in time.'[6]

This price discrimination operated at three levels: memory configurations for the central processing unit, computer hardware peripherals, and field personnel customer support.

Table 9.1 reveals how memory-based price discrimination operated in 1966. Profit estimates reveal that, with the exception of the 360/50, the entry-level versions were priced to lose money in December 1966. The basic processor with only a minimum amount of memory lost money, but with every additional kilobyte of memory the overall profit margins increased.

Of course, the lowest-memory processors were very competitive in luring customers away from Honeywell and other competitors. However, once the customers had installed the computer they soon realised they needed extra memory in order to run all but the most basic applications. Indeed, the failings of the OS/360 operating system meant that most applications required at least 16 kilobytes of memory (because most of its code had to reside in memory rather than on disk). IBM were pleased to discover that 360/System customers moved up its memory scale rather quickly.

TABLE 9.1 Total revenues and profits for IBM CPUs, by memory size (1966 estimates, in $ millions)

Model Memory size	Revenues	Profits	% profit
360/20			
4K	15.6	−5.8	−37.2
8K	133.2	9.0	6.8
16K	8.1	1.0	11.9
360/30			
8K	44.9	−5.2	−11.6
16K	279.0	33.6	12.0
32K	555.5	160.1	28.8
64K	417.7	134.7	32.2
360/40			
16K	0.6	−0.6	−96.8
32K	30.8	7.0	22.7
64K	167.2	53.9	28.8
128K	194.6	75.9	39.0
360/50			
64K	4.9	0.4	8.4
128K	98.5	28.9	28.9
256K	288.0	88.9	30.9
512K	68.0	28.2	41.5
360/65			
128K	2.9	−1.7	−59.3
256K	79.8	−12.0	−15.1
512K	94.1	4.3	4.6
1 Meg	8.4	1.2	13.9

Source: Plaintiff Exhibit 1962A, *US* v. *IBM* Anti-trust case (1975–82).

TABLE 9.2 **Percentage distribution of income versus cost of IBM field personnel installing 360 systems, 1967**

Size of account ($)	Installed Value (%)	Person Years (%)	Difference (%)
Under 2,500	5.4	17.5	+12.1
2,500–10,000	9.5	14.7	+5.2
10,000–50,000	23.0	22.9	−0.1
50,000–100,000	12.0	9.7	−2.3
Over 100,000	51.0	35.2	−15.8

Source: Plaintiff Exhibit 5310A *US* v. *IBM* anti-trust case (1975–82).

Hence, in 1966, customers would lease their entry-level (16k memory) 360/40 system for an average of only 15½ months, while the 32k, 64k, 128k and 256k memory models remained under lease for 66, 55, 50, and 47 months, respectively.[7] This clever memory-based pricing carefully camouflaged the favours bestowed on first-time users.

Similarly, profits from 360 peripherals were high but only for locked-in customers. The most popular entry-level tape drives were priced to break even at best.

An additional tactic entailed providing valuable field personnel assistance at no extra cost to customers who were installing their first 360 system. Certainly, the early problems with OS/360 meant such assistance was invaluable. Small customer accounts got a very good deal from IBM as they were effectively being subsidised by IBM's larger locked-in customers (see Table 9.2). Even though many of the 1000 or so large account holders doubtless took exception to being milked as a 'cash cow', they had no recourse at that time as there was no other supplier offering IBM-compatible equipment.

Table 9.2 reveals that although small account holders (less than $2500) constituted only 5.4 per cent of the revenue, they received over 17 per cent of the skilled time of IBM field personnel – more than three times what they paid for. This is a significant difference in financial terms. The 12.1 per cent difference between what small account holders paid and the value of the installation service they received represented around $200 million.

The combination of money-losing processor and peripheral prices and additional services not reflected in the profit estimates leads to the conclusion that IBM was in fact losing money on many of the simplest entry-level systems it installed for first-time users of 360 computers. It was in fact buying new 360 users – something its less well-endowed competitors such as Honeywell, even with technically superior and less expensive systems, were in no position to do. And this was all accomplished without arousing anti-trust scrutiny.[8]

Postscript: the *US* v. *IBM* anti-trust case[9]

Despite the subtleties of IBM's price discrimination, the success of the System/360 in killing off competition led to the commencement of a preliminary anti-trust enquiry by the US Department of Justice in 1964. After considerable delays, the trial commenced in May 1975.

On 8 January 1982, after the case for the prosecution had been presented under the supervision of a total of eight Assistant Attorney Generals, the ninth – William Baxter (President Reagan's newly appointed anti-trust chief) – withdrew the case as being 'without merit'.

Despite protests from some of the former Assistant Attorney Generals, there was no review of this decision. Yet evidence surfaced that before he had any official involvement with the trial, Baxter had written to President Carter in 1978 informing him that 'the IBM case should never have been brought'.[10] Evidence also came to light during a hearing in front of the Subcommittee on Monopolies and Commercial Law of the House Committee of the Judiciary in 1982 that Baxter had been retained by IBM as a consultant to review certain aspects of the anti-trust case shortly after the case had been filed. The House Subcommittee made no further inquiries into these allegations.

Later that year, the authors of *In Search of Excellence*[11] quickly found IBM and declared that its success was due to excellence in management. Meanwhile, President Reagan publicly declared IBM a 'national treasure'.

Issues to consider

- While organisations can learn and adapt to their environment, this case shows they can also change and control the environment. To what extent is this the exclusive prerogative of large corporations like IBM? How can small companies exert an influence over their environment?[12]
- Assess the ethical issues raised by this case.[13]

Notes

1. Plaintiff's Exhibit 1630 (*US* v. *IBM* anti-trust suit, 1975–82).
2. Statement made in IBM pre-trial brief in *US* v. *IBM* anti-trust suit.
3. Plaintiff's Exhibit 6671 (*US* v. *IBM* anti-trust suit, 1975–82).
4. DeLamarter (1988) pp. 61–2.
5. DeLamarter (1988), p. 62.
6. DeLamarter (1988) pp. 67–8.

7. Plaintiff's Exhibit 1962A (*US* v. *IBM* anti-trust suit, 1975–82).
8. DeLamarter (1988), p. 85.
9. More details of this eight year case can be found in DeLamarter (1988). DeLamarter's highly critical work stands in complete contrast to the interpretation of the case offered by the economist Frank Fisher in his trial testimony for IBM. Fisher outlined his views in more detail after the trial (Fisher *et al.* 1983a, 1983b).
10. *New York Times*, 10 March 1982, p. 14.
11. Peters and Waterman (1982)
12. For example, see Aldrich (1977, 1979), Bedeian (1987), Daft (1983), Demison (1984), Hannan and Freeman (1977), Harrigan (1986), Miner *et al.* (1990), Pfeffer and Salancik (1979) and Thompson (1972).
13. See Buono and Nichols (1985), Clinard (1990), Freeman (1990), Hoffman and Moore (1990), Saul (1981) and Vaughan (1983) for insightful analyses of corporate morality and social responsibility. Cannon (1993) offers a well documented account of the roots of corporate responsibility (although, somewhat unfortunately in this case, the author cites IBM as a company with a good record of corporate responsibility).

Case 52   The ethics of church investment

In 1948, the Church of England established the Church Commissioners. The role of this organisation was to manage the financial and property assets which the Church has amassed since the reign of Henry VIII. The Commissioners inherited agricultural land, residential property, and equity and gilt-edged investments. The role of the Church Commissioners was to safeguard the livings and pensions of clerics, but by the 1970s this had been shared with the diocese out of contributions from church members.

At the end of 1991, the Commissioners had an investment portfolio worth £2.3 billion. Of this, £950 million was invested in property, £320 million was held in cash, and £1.03 billion was invested on the Stock Exchange.

A number of clergymen had become increasingly concerned about the nature of these Stock Market investments and particularly about the socially irresponsible behaviour and poor ecological record of many of the large companies Church investments were supporting. Consequently, in the Spring of 1992, three of these men – Richard Harries, Bishop of Oxford; Michael Bourke, Archdeacon of Bedford, and the Reverend William Whiffen – brought a legal action against the Church Commissioners who manage these investment funds.

In High Court, the men argued that Christian morality should outweigh monetary advantages in the way church money is invested. Also they opined that the Commissioners should give precedence to Christian ethics in investment even though there might be a risk of financial loss.

In court, the counsel for the Church Commissioners, Robert Walker, read extracts from the Sermon on the Mount in the Gospel of Saint Matthew which urges Christians to take a moral stance on financial investments. The extracts he quoted included: "do not store up for yourselves treasures on earth;" "you cannot serve God and money;" and "do not be anxious about tomorrow; tomorrow will look after itself."

Mr Walker argued that the Commissioners would be acting fecklessly if they followed Christ's cautionary words. He told the court:

> It might be a sign of outstanding sanctity in an individual but it is neither permissible nor admirable in those in the position of stewards responsible for the stipends, pensions, and housing of present and future generations of Church of England clergy.

In his role as protector of charity, the Attorney-General, Sir Patrick Mayhew, supported the Commissioners and stated, through his counsel, that an important part of a charity's work was raising money and thus its interests and purposes were served by raising as much money as possible.

The court hearing lasted 3 days and, at the close, the judge announced that he was reserving judgement.

Issue to consider

- What would your judgement be?[1]

Note

1. See Lloyd (1990) for an assessment of the relative merits of ethical and 'conventional' investment portfolios. See Bowie and Freeman (1992) and Mann (1992) for analyses of the broader ethical issues raised by the case.

Case 53   To boldly go from prisoners' dilemma to executive decision[1]

'The way Federation Enterprises runs its business is illogical, Captain,' argued Ms Leach.

'It's true that the company is fairly aggressive in its strategy,' the Captain conceded. 'But when Galactica Products Limited threatened our market share, it was logical to launch a takeover bid. Unfortunately, Galactica Products were able to fend us off this time around.'

'But it is the hostile nature of Federation Enterprises' strategy that is illogical,' Leach insisted. 'That failed bid cost both corporations a lot of money and a lot of goodwill.'

The Captain smiled back at his friend and colleague. 'I can't agree with you there, Leach. Cooperation is not the nature of the beast known as business. "Dog eat dog" is probably a more apt way to describe the way businesses behave when conducting business with each other. It would be illogical for a business to do otherwise.'

'With respect, Captain, that is where you are guilty of faulty logic,' Leach replied calmly. 'I fail to see how consuming members of your own species contributes to species survival. Obviously you concur with Gore Vidal's view that it is not enough to succeed – others must fail.'

The Captain made no comment.

'But to return to the world of business,' Leach continued. 'Let us consider the nature of the "beast" (as you insist on calling it). First, it seems self-evident that business dealings are not zero-sum. It is possible for one organisation to succeed without another failing as a direct consequence. Neither the creation of wealth nor economic growth could occur if each accretion of wealth had to be paid for by an equal destruction elsewhere. If you view the success of a company solely in terms of market share (rather than profitability) then perhaps business is zero-sum. But as far as I understand the 'beast', survival and profit are the ultimate interdependent goals. Market share, at best, must be seen as but one means to attaining these goals.'

'What are you getting at?' asked the Captain, with a hint of irritation in his voice.

'Just this, Captain.' replied Leach, unruffled. 'If one accepts that business is a positive-sum game involving a series of iterations (rather than a one-off), then inter-corporate cooperation rather than hostility is the most logical management strategy for long-term profitability and survival.[2] I'm not referring to illegal cartels here you understand, but about a management strategy that communicates cooperative as opposed to hostile intent.'

'Explain it to me,' asked the Captain, sceptically.

'By all means. Doubtless you have heard of the 'Prisoners' Dilemma' – a strategy game popularised in 1960s social psychology research.[3] It owes its name to an imaginary situation in which two accomplices are awaiting trial in a criminal court, and each has the option of informing on the other with the hope of receiving a lighter prison sentence for him or herself. They are being held in separate rooms and cannot communicate with each other. If neither of them informs on the other, both their sentences are likely to be moderate; if one informs but the other doesn't, the informer receives only a light sentence, but the other receives a severe one. If both inform they will both receive moderate sentences and so be worse off than if they both kept quiet. Since the two players make their decisions independently, the dilemma for each of them is whether they can trust the other not to inform.'

'The game is usually represented as a matrix of possible outcomes. There are two score-maximising players and two strategies; cooperation (remaining quiet) and defection (informing). Player A knows if he or she chooses defection and player B cooperates, A will score a maximum five points whilst B will score zero. Each also knows that if they both cooperate, they will score three points and that if they both defect, both will score one point. The matrix of possible outcomes looks like this [see Figure 9.1].'[4]

'You will notice, Captain, that there is a presumption about the nature of the game embedded in this scoring arrangement. If two players are playing only one game, the best strategy is to defect. This is true even though each player knows the other will see things in the same way. The player goes for a score of five knowing that he or she will probably only get a score of one. But if the game is iterated indefinitely, cooperation is the best strategy insofar as it maximises the combined scores of the two players. After all, a series of scores of three is three times as profitable as a series of scores of one. Now, imagine the players are corporations and that the game is iterated for an undisclosed number of plays. What is the best strategy for, say, player A?'

'Let me see,' mused the Captain. 'In theory, mutual cooperation is the best strategy. Unfortunately, there is no way A should or could trust B not to defect, so it's too risky to cooperate on every play as you could end up with zero every time. I would defect every play. That way I would never score zero, although player B might.'

FIGURE 9.1   The prisoners' dilemma

Player B

		COOPERATE (keep silent)	DEFECT (inform)
Player A	COOPERATE (keep silent)	A = 3 B = 3	A = 0 B = 5
	DEFECT (inform)	A = 5 B = 0	A = 1 B = 1

Source: Based on Axelrod (1984).

'Fascinating. But, mutual defection is bound to result and that is three times worse (in points scoring terms) than mutual cooperation,' Leach corrected. 'If the players are corporations, profits will be permanently lower than they could be and the resultant lack of mutual trust may ultimately put you both out of business.'

'Okay, Leach. Let's hear your point,' said the Captain, with mounting irritation.

'The best long-term strategy is to play tit-for-tat (TFT),' Leach explained. 'This involves player A, for example, always cooperating on the first move and thereafter always repeating what player B did on the previous move. The researcher Robert Axelrod carried out a large number of tournaments between hundreds of players employing a range of strategies and TFT was never beaten.[5] Although the player employing TFT never wins an individual game, that player wins the tournament by achieving the highest overall score. Axelrod coined TFT the "nice strategy" because it never involved being the first to defect.'

'So, Captain,' concluded Leach. 'I contend that cooperation rather than hostility is the logical strategy for Federation Enterprises. More precisely, the corporation whose strategy communicates cooperative intent soonest, and so elicits cooperation, has a good chance of emerging the overall winner. Surely, now that you are conversant with the relevant facts, even you cannot dispute this.'

Issues to consider

- Critically assess Leach's argument.[6] If her logic is sound, why is corporate profit-making such a 'cut-throat' business?

Notes

1. This fictitious exchange of ideas was inspired by Lloyd's (1990) analysis of reciprocity theory in relation to the evolution of the 'nice' organisation.
2. There are some interesting parallels between this argument and research findings on interpersonal cooperation and prosocial behaviour. For example, see the work of Argyle (1991), Clark (1991), Hinde and Groebel (1991) and Nielsen (1988).
3. See Eiser (1978) for a concise description and analysis of this research. Oskamp (1970) details more strategic aspects of the game.
4. This matrix and scoring system is based on Axelrod's (1984) iterative version of the Prisoner's Dilemma.
5. Described in Axelrod (1984).

6. Dissenting views include those of Chen and MacMillan (1992), Porter (1980, 1985) and Schelling (1960). Finally, see Knights (1992) for a post-modernist critique of the whole concept of strategy.

Case 54   Employee commitment to the Nissan Motor Company[1]

The delegation from the Commission of European Communities' FAST (Forecasting and Assessment in Science and Technology) programme were ushered into the executive board room. There they were formally greeted by Mr Ichimura, general manager of the Nissan car plant at Zama (located 35 kilometres southwest of Tokyo).

Speaking through an interpreter, Mr Ichimura described the facilities at the Zama plant to an attentive audience: 'Covering a land area of approximately 210 acres, the factory produces 35,000 cars per month. Since the factory was opened in 1965, over 10 million cars have been produced here at Zama. Zama is one of Nissan's key car assembly facilities and was one of the world's first automobile plants to employ body assembly robots.'

Mr Masine (production director) then described the 5 levels of hierarchy employed at Zama (directors, general managers, section managers, supervisors and workers) and stressed the important contribution made by the plant's 5200 skilled employees in maintaining the extremely high standards of quality.

Next came the eagerly awaited guided tour of the factory. The facilities were impressive and the delegates were especially appreciative of the Intelligent Body Assembly System (IBAS) in Assembly Plant 2. This flexible assembly cell comprised advanced robotic handling and welding, coupled with laser scanning and monitoring. In a series of elegant dance-like motions, various body panels were positioned on the car chassis and spot welded into place by a variety of robots. What particularly impressed the engineers among the FAST delegation was the fact that a small mixed batch of different Sunny and Prestea car and models were being assembled during the 10 minutes they were watching.

For my part, I noticed a complete absence of workers around the IBAS. My initial thought was that a group of workers were hiding in the wings waiting for the delegation to leave. However, I realised that the layout of the technology meant that any kind of human manual intervention (in the event of a breakdown, for example) would be extremely difficult. Via our guide-interpreter, I asked the section supervisor about the provision for manual back-up. I was informed that none had been made by the in-house engineers who had designed and built the system. I must have looked surprised at this answer, as he gently assured me that this was neither an oversight nor a problem. It transpired that the IBAS was designed to operate without error and without any manual intervention (except routine maintenance). If the laser scanner detected any misalignment, appropriate adjustments were made automatically. 'The system has been running for 2 years and has never malfunctioned. We expect the next 2 years to be the same,' the supervisor said proudly.

It was towards the end of the tour that the question of the exportability of Japanese management techniques (as exemplified by Nissan) was raised. My conversation with one of the section managers about human resource management techniques proved surprisingly enlightening.[2]

'Here at the Zama plant, as with many Japanese manufacturing plants, we use many methods to make sure our workers are happy and productive,' he began. At first I though he was talking about the incessant *musak* being piped through the factory tannoy system (every few minutes a tune annoyingly reminiscent of 'Greensleeves' would reverberate around the huge building). I was mistaken.

'In the West you think employee suggestion schemes can lead to direct improvements in working practices and labour productivity, do you not?' he inquired. I nodded. 'Our engineers designed and built the production process here at Zama. There is very little scope for improvement. I can only recall about three suggestions ever being made here which made any significant change to the way the work is carried out. That is not because our employees make poor suggestions, but because our engineers are so good! Here at Zama the only real function of quality suggestion schemes is to help workers concentrate on the work they are doing,' he continued.

'Once workers start daydreaming, performance deteriorates. We have found that the best way to help workers keep their minds on their work is to demand suggestions for improving the quality and efficiency of the work carried out by each of them. Every month, we expect each worker to suggest ways to improve the work they carry out. You will appreciate that a worker who has been here for, let us say, 5 years will have great difficulty in fulfilling this obligation. So workers help each other to work out ideas and suggestions for quality improvements. Often I have heard workers discussing such matters during lunch breaks. I am sure they do so after work also. In this way even long-serving workers remain committed to their work and to quality.'

As we continued the tour of the factory, I saw a large noticeboard in the main assembly plant. The names of all the section workers are displayed on it, and a mark is put against each name once that person's suggestion has been forwarded to the supervisor.[3]

In establishing this highly visible record of workers' suggestions, Nissan management seem keen to harness the workers' sense of duty. The writer

Ruth Benedict describes the Japanese as possessed of a 'shame culture' in which every worker has a fundamental duty (*giri*) not only to do good work, but also to match exactly the contribution made by other members of the work group.[4] Hence failure to make the requisite number of suggestions (and the subsequent danger of failing to repay *giri*) is likely to induce profound feelings of shame in letting one's colleagues down.

As we neared the end of our tour, the candid section manager argued that any attempts by Western businesses to import Japanese management techniques based on group working were doomed to failure unless these techniques are geared towards fostering *giri* and *gaman* (a resigned acceptance and endurance of hardship without complaint) in the work group members. Workers freely identity with colleagues in work groups, but unless management develop the means to ensure that group's commitment is to the goals of the organisation and not to norms counter-productive to the meeting of those goals, productivity levels will not rise. Group identity is a 'double edged sword'.

Our tour guide-interpreter told us later that Japanese people are very proud of their uniqueness: 'But you have to work hard at being Japanese. Managers who have spent more than 6 months abroad at first find it difficult to re-adapt to being Japanese again. I think some of their more conventional colleagues never really trust them again once they have been over to the West.'

I inquired how individual workers and managers cope with the drive towards consensus in all decisions (it is not as if conflict is unusual in Japan[5]). Our guide explained that Japanese people can be unhappy with the company they work for and yet not complain or dissent. This is partly to do with *giri* and *gaman* and partly to do with the fact that Japanese culture demands less consistency between an individual's attitudes and behaviour. In the UK, for example, if a person who knows you are a vegetarian sees you eating beef in a restaurant, they are likely to regard you as inconsistent, weak-willed, or even untrustworthy.

In Japanese culture such inconsistency of thought and deed is far less problematic. The notions of *omote* (meaning 'front') and *ura* (meaning 'back') help explain this. *Omote* is presented to the public as a socially acceptable aspect of the self, whereas *ura* is an aspect of the self hidden from public view. Both are recognised socially and the appropriate use of them is highly valued.[6]

Issues to consider

- To what extent are suggestion schemes and quality circles more a means to manufacture employee consent and commitment than to manufacture higher-quality products?[7]

- How far can cultural differences explain the problems experienced by many Western companies in applying Japanese management techniques?[8]
- What are the implications of cultural relativism for the study and management of organisational behaviour?

Notes

1. The events outlined in this case took place on 13 November 1991, during the author's visit to Japan as a member of the CEC-FAST delegation.
2. This section manager asked not to be named. The views expressed are his own and hence do not necessarily reflect company policy or the views of Nissan senior management. All delegation members had been requested to leave cameras and tape recorders on the courtesy coach which had brought us to the plant before the tour began. Hence, what follows is not verbatim but is based on a combination of memory and shorthand notes taken at the time of the conversation. The reconstructed account given here is an 'accurate approximation'!
3. This is very similar to the weekly postings of each employee's suggestion rate carried out by Toyota management at the car plant described by Kamata (1983).
4. See Benedict (1946).
5. For example, there is an on-going protest over proposals to extend Narita airport (Tokyo's major international airport), with local farmers (armed with barrels of human faeces and with considerable local support) going into battle with thousands of riot police.
6. See Doi (1986) and Kashima *et al.* (1992). For a more general analysis of Japanese culture, see Hendry (1992), Mita (1993) and Rosenberger (1992).
7. For a critical evaluation of the relationship between Japanese management practices and employee attitudes and behaviour, see Kondo (1990), Lincoln and Kalleberg (1992) and Odaka (1975). For a more general analysis of the manufacture of consent, see Burawoy (1979), Grenier (1988), Keenoy (1992), Knights (1990), and Wells (1987).
8. See, for example, Briggs (1988), Graham (1988), Kenney and Florida (1992), Oliver and Davies (1990), Oliver and Wilkinson (1992), Sethi *et al.* (1984), Thompson and McHugh (1990, Chapter 5), and Wilkinson and Oliver (1990). See Cole (1979) and Luthens *et al.* (1985) for a comparison of the organisational commitment of US and Japanese employees.

Case 55   Multi-national corporations and the circles of pesticide poisoning

In 1982 the Oxford Committee on Famine Relief (Oxfam) estimated that in the Third World there are 375,000 pesticide poisonings with a resultant 10,000 deaths every year.[1] One of the major reasons for this is that many multi-national chemical corporations export pesticides which have been banned in the US and elsewhere. Indeed, US law allows US manufacturers to export even the most deadly pesticides (e.g. DDT, paraquat, dioxin and parathion) as long as they are marked 'FOR EXPORT ONLY'. As a result, US corporations like Union Carbide, Du Pont, Dow, American Cyanamid, and Monsanto annually ship overseas at least 68 million kilograms of pesticides that are totally prohibited, severely restricted or never registered for use in the US.[2]

Another way of legally exporting banned pesticides is by shipping the separate chemical ingredients to a Third World country where the corporations manufacture the product in what they call their 'formulation plants'. The product is then sold locally or exported to other developing countries.

These formulation plants are often operated with far lower equipment and worker safety standards than those employed by the same corporation in the US. As a direct consequence of these double safety standards, an estimated 8000 people were killed[3] and another 200,000 injured when a gas cloud of methyl isocyanate, a deadly chemical used to make the pesticide Sevin Carbaryl, leaked out of a storage tank at the Union Carbide plant in Bhopal, India.

Investigations carried out before this disaster in 1984 revealed that, despite the highly dangerous nature of the manufacturing process, safety standards were so low that the Bhopal plant presented 'serious potentials for sizeable releases of toxic materials'.[4] Investigations after the disaster revealed that the tank storing the deadly methyl isocyanate had not been working properly for 5 months, and that the workers who were operating the faulty equipment were inadequately trained.[5]

> As the Bhopal tragedy exemplified, the health and safety of workers throughout the world is threatened when multinationals shift hazardous work processes abroad in an effort to avoid strict US worker protection laws. . . In Third World countries, safety standards are generally quite low and government plant inspections poor, due either to understaffing or underfunding. US transnationals frequently set up manufacturing operations in the very foreign countries where there is little regard for worker safety.[6]

An important factor in the increasing number of pesticide-related deaths and injuries is the failure of pesticide producers to include warnings in Third World countries about the possible dangers of using the deadly compounds. Details of appropriate clothing and respirator use are rarely printed on the packaging.[7]

Worse yet:

> In countries where most people cannot read, what use are warning labels on pesticide packages? In countries that outlaw unions that could protect farm workers, what chance do peasants have against crop duster's rain of poison? In countries with

neither enough scientists to investigate pesticide dangers, nor enough trained government officials to enforce regulations, should foreign pesticide makers be given a free hand to push products so dangerous they are banned at home?[8]

Thus, Third World people suffer the double risk of producing highly dangerous pesticides and then using them in the fields.

But consumers in the so-called 'developed' world of the US and Europe are now increasingly under threat from the growing use of dangerous pesticides overseas. Most of the pesticides manufactured in, or exported to, the Third World by multinationals are used to increase large-scale export crops such as coffee, tomatoes, bananas and pineapples. Hence, banned pesticides have created what Weir and Schapiro call a 'circle of poison' as agricultural products containing residues of banned US pesticides are imported into the US for consumption.[9]

For example, a 1978 report by the Food and Drug Administration calculated that approximately 10 per cent of the food imported into the US contained significant residues of illegal pesticides. Findings in another FDA report at that time revealed that just under 50 per cent of imported green coffee beans contained traces of pesticides banned in the US.[10] Large amounts of beef imported from Central America have also been contaminated by illegal pesticides:

> Thus, when an American eats a hamburger or drinks a cup of coffee in a fast-food restaurant, there is always the possibility that he or she may be poisoned because of a US corporation's unethical behaviour in exporting a banned pesticide overseas.[11]

Issues to consider

- 'If one country bans your product, move to where sales are still legal'. Is this a good corporate strategy?
- What are the implications of the 'circles of poison' for the regulation of multi-national corporate behaviour?[12]

Notes

1. Mokhiber (1988), p. 108.
2. Weir and Schapiro (1981) pp. 77–8.
3. According to official Indian government figures, 3415 people died as a direct result of the gas leak at the Union Carbide plant. Kurzman (1987) argues that a figure of over 8000 is probably more accurate given that thousands of bodies were cremated

by Hindus or buried by Muslims without notifying the authorities. Neither figure includes the fourfold increase in still births women in Bhopal suffered over the ensuing years.

4. See Mokhiber (1988), pp. 86–96, and Weir (1987).
5. See Kurzman (1987) and Shrivastava *et al.* (1988).
6. Clinard (1990), pp. 140-1.
7. Similarly, in the multi-national pharmaceutical industry, safety labelling varies from country to country in a very cynical manner. For example, on packets of their oral contraceptive drug, Ovulen, destined for domestic US sales, the Searle Company list the following 'side effects' (sic): 'Nausea, loss of hair, nervousness, jaundice, high blood pressure, weight change and headaches.' The farther south the product is sold, however, the safer the drug appears to be! In Mexico, only nausea and weight change are listed. In Brazil and Argentina, according to Searle, Ovulen has no 'side effects' at all – or at least none worth mentioning (cited in Coleman, 1985, p. 108). For further consideration of the unethical behaviour of pharmaceutical multinationals, see Braithwaite (1984) and Silverman *et al.* (1982).
8. Weir and Schapiro (1981), p. 17.
9. Weir and Schapiro (1981), p. 1.
10. Weir and Schapiro (1981), p. 29.
11. Clinard (1990), p. 148. There is also a circle of ecological destruction involved here. Ehrlich and Ehrlich (1981) note that the rainforests are being sacrificed to maintain the flow of meat destined almost exclusively to be hamburgers served by fast-food chains. Over a quarter of all Central American forests have been destroyed in the past 20 years to produce grazing land for the production of beef for US consumption alone.
12. Useful sources here include the works cited above. Also see Andrews (1989), Bradshaw and Vogel (1981), Harris (1986), Nader *et al.* (1976), Stone (1975) and Vaughan (1983).

Case 56   A cross-cultural comparison of work values

Introduction

Numerous motivation theorists outline the importance of certain character-istics of work and the work environment in promoting job satisfaction. But to what extent do the motivation theories of Maslow, Herzberg, McClelland, Hackman and Oldham, etc. reflect what motivates a particular, possibly unique, sample of the working population, namely the average American employee?

Can we really generalise such theories to the global working population? Mainstream OB textbooks certainly imply as much. But if we cannot generalise from the US experience there are obvious implications for the human resources management policies of multi-national corporations and for international post-merger management.

In 1989, Don Elizur and colleagues carried out a study to examine the importance and structure of work values for respondents from different countries.[1] These data provide an excellent basis for assessing the cultural specificity of work values and motivation. Additional data are supplied by the author's own survey findings.

A cross-cultural study of motivation

The method employed by Elizur and his colleagues was to collect data by questionnaire from samples of managers and employees from a variety of countries. The average sample size was 285. The authors' own UK sample comprised 148 respondents. The age range and gender mix of the samples were similar.

The questionnaire was designed to represent the major perspectives outlined by basic theories of motivation. 24 items were selected and respondents were asked to indicate for each item the extent to which it is important. (using response categories ranging from 'very unimportant' to 'very important'). The items included the following:

- Job interest, to do work which is interesting to you
- Achievement in work
- Advancement, opportunities for promotion
- Self-esteem, that you are valued as a person
- Use of ability and knowledge in your work
- Autonomy, independence in work
- Job security, permanent job
- Supervisor, a fair and considerate boss
- Pay, the amount of money you receive
- Co-workers, fellow workers who are pleasant and agreeable

This selection of items are listed in Table 9.3. Table 9.3 also indicates the survey results from the US, the UK, Germany, the Netherlands, Taiwan, Korea, Hungary and China. The major similarities and differences between these work population samples can be more clearly comprehended by considering the rank order of the items based on the marginal distributions as represented in Table 9.3.

So we see, for example, that interesting work was considered to be the most important work value by respondents from the US, Germany, and the Netherlands. Yet the same item was considered to be much less important

TABLE 9.3   Rank ordering of work values for a sample of eight countries

	USA	UK	Germany	Netherlands	Taiwan	Korea	Hungary	China
Interesting work	1	2	1	1	2	3	6	5
Achievement	2	6	7	2	1	1	2	1
Advancement	3	7	10	5	4	7	10	6
Self-esteem	4	5	9	9	3	9	7	3
Use abilities	5	4	6	6	8	4	5	2
Autonomy	6	9	5	4	7	10	9	4
Job security	7	8	4	8	5	2	8	10
Good boss	8	10	3	7	6	6	1	7
Good pay	9	3	8	10	10	8	4	9
Co-workers	10	1	2	3	9	5	3	8

from the viewpoint of the Hungarian and Chinese respondents. Also, interesting cross-cultural disparities are in evidence for the last three items; good boss, good pay, and friendly co-workers.

Issues to consider

- What are the implications of these findings for universalistic motivation theories, such as those espoused by Maslow, Herzberg and Aldefer?
- How far is mainstream OB culture-bound?[2]
- What are the implications, if any, of these results for the practice of effective international human resource management?[3]

Notes

1. The results were finally published in Elizur *et al.* (1991).
2. See Deregowski *et al.* (1983), Hofstede (1980), Laurent (1983) and Tayeb (1989).
3. See Prasad and Shety (1976), Ronen (1986) and Stopford and Wells (1972).

Bibliography

Abrams, D. and Hogg, M. A. (eds) (1990) *Social Identity Theory: Constructive and Critical Advances.* London: Harvester Wheatsheaf.

Abse, D. (1973) *The Dogs of Pavlov.* London: Vallentine, Mitchell & Company.

Acar, W. and Aupperle, K. E. (1984) 'Bureaucracy as organizational pathology.' *Systems Research, 1,* 157–166.

Ackroyd, S. and Crowdy, P. (1989) 'Can culture be managed? Working with "raw" material: The case of the English slaughtermen.' *Personnel Review, 19,* 3–13.

Adler, P. S. and Winograd, T. A. (eds) (1992) *Usability: Turning Technologies Into Tools.* New York: Oxford University Press.

Adorno, T. W., Frenkel-Brunswik, E., Levinson, D. J. and Sanford, R. N. (1950) *The Authoritarian Personality.* New York: Harper.

Albrecht, G. L. (1979) 'Defusing technological change in juvenile courts: The probation officers struggle for professional autonomy.' *Sociology of Work and Occupations, 6,* 259–282.

Albury, D. and Schwartz, J. (1982) *Partial Progress: The Politics of Science and Technology.* London: Pluto Press.

Aldrich, H. (1977) 'Visionaries and villains: The politics of designing interorganizational relations', in E. Burack and A. Negandhi (eds), *Organization Design: Theoretical Perspectives and Empirical Findings.* Kent, Ohio: Kent State University Press.

———— (1979) *Organizations and Environment.* Englewood Cliffs: Prentice Hall.

Allinson, C. W. (1984) *Bureaucratic Personality and Organization Structure.* Aldershot: Gower.

Amnesty International (1973) *Amnesty International Report on Torture.* New York: Author Press.

Anderson, N. R. and King, N. (1993) 'Innovation in organizations', in C. L. Cooper and I. T. Robertson (eds), *International Review of Industrial and Organizational Psychology 1993.* Chichester: Wiley.

Anderson, N. R. and Shackleton, V. (1993) *Successful Selection Interviewing.* Oxford: Blackwell.

Andrews, K. R. (1989) *Ethics in Practice: Managing the Moral Corporation.* Boston: Harvard Business School Press.

Angle, H. L. and Perry, J. L. (1986) 'An empirical assessment of organizational commitment and organizational effectiveness.' *Administrative Science Quarterly, 26,* 1–14.

Anthony, P. D. (1989) 'The paradox of the management of culture or "He who leads is lost."' *Personnel Review, 19,* 3–8.

Argyle, M. (1991) *Cooperation: The Basis of Sociability.* London: Routledge.

261

Armstrong, P. (1984) 'Competition between the organizational professions and the evolution of management control strategies', in K. Thompson (ed.), *Work, Employment and Unemployment*. Milton Keynes: Open University Press.

———— (1986) 'Management control strategies and inter-professional competition: The cases of accountancy and personnel management', in D. Knights and H. Willmott (eds), *Managing the Labour Process*. Aldershot: Gower.

———— (1987) 'The rise of accounting controls in British capitalist enterprises.' *Accounting, Organizations and Society, 12*, 121–137.

Arnold, J., Robertson, I. T. and Cooper, C. L. (1991) *Work Psychology*. London: Pitman Press.

Aronson, E. and Mills, J, (1959) 'The effect of severity of initiation on liking for a group.' *Journal of Abnormal and Social Psychology, 59*, 177–81.

Ashworth, B. E. and Humphrey, R. H. (1993) 'Emotional labor in service roles: The influence of identity.' *Academy of Management Review, 18*, 88–115.

Ashworth, B. E. and Lee, R. T. (1990) 'Defensive behavior in organizations: A preliminary model.' *Human Relations, 43*, 621–648.

Axelrod, R. (1984) *The Evolution of Cooperation*. New York: Basic Books.

Bainbridge, L. (1978) 'The process controller', in W. T. Singleton (ed.), *The Analysis of Practical Skills*. Lancaster: MTP Press.

———— (1981) 'Mathematical equations or processing routines?', in J. Rasmussen and W. B. Rouse (eds), *Human Detection and Diagnosis of Systems Failures*. New York: Plenum Press.

Barber, N. (1968) *Sinister Twilight*. London: Collins.

Baritz, L. (1960) *Servants of Power*. Middletown: Wesleyan University Press.

Barrett, M. and Sutcliffe, P. (1993) 'Leadership theories: A critique and its implications for management education.' *Strategic Management Working Paper, 24*, Faculty of Business, Queensland University of Technology.

Bartunek, J. M. and Moch, M. K. (1991) 'Multiple constituencies and the quality of working life: Intervention at FoodCom', in P. J. Frost, L. F. Moore, M. R. Louis, C. C. Lundberg and J. Martin (eds), *Reframing Organizational Culture*. London: Sage.

Bass, B. M. (1985) *Leadership and Performance Beyond Expectations*. New York: Free Press.

Batsleer, J., Cornforth, C. and Paton, R. (eds) (1991) *Issues in Voluntary and Non-Profit Management*. London: Addison-Wesley.

Baucus, M. S. and Near, J. P. (1991) 'Can illegal corporate behavior be predicted? An event history analysis.' *Academy of Management Journal, 34*, 9–36.

Bauer, R. A., Collar, E., Tang, V., Wind, J. and Houston, P. R. (1992) *The Silverlake Project: Transformation at IBM*. New York: Oxford University Press.

Bauman, Z. (1989) *Modernity and the Holocaust*. London: Polity Press.

Baumrind, D. (1964) 'Some thoughts on ethics of research after reading Milgram's "Behavioral Study of Obedience".' *American Psychologist, 19*, 421–423.

Bazerman, M. H., Giuliano, T. and Appelman, A. (1984) 'Escalation of commitment in individual and group decision making.' *Organizational Behaviour and Human Performance, 33*, 141–152.

Becker, H. S. (1963) *Outsiders*. New York: Free Press.

Beckhard, R. and Harris, R. (1987) *Organization Transitions: Managing Complex Change*, 2nd edn. New York: Addison Wesley.

Bedeian, A. G. (1987) 'Organization theory: Current controversies, issues, and directions', in C. L. Cooper and I. T. Robertson (eds), *International Review of Industrial and Organizational Psychology 1987*. Chichester: Wiley.

Beirne, M. and Ramsay, H. (eds) (1992) *Information Technology and Workplace Democracy*. London: Routledge.

Belden, T. and Belden, M. (1962) *The Lengthening Shadow*. Boston: Little, Brown & Company.

Bem, D. J. (1972) 'Self-perception theory', in L. Berkowitz (ed.), *Advances in Experimental Social Psychology*, vol. 6. New York: Academic Press.

Bem, S. L. and Bem, D. J. (1989) 'Training the woman to know her place: The power of unconscious ideology', in H. J. Leavitt, L. R. Pondy, and D. M. Boje (eds), *Readings in Managerial Psychology*, 4th edn. Chicago: Chicago University Press.

Bendfeldt-Zachrisson, F. (1985) 'State (political) torture: Some general, psychological and particular aspects.' *International Journal of the Health Services*, 15, 339–349.

Benedict, R. (1946) *The Chrysanthemum and the Sword*. Tokyo: Charles Tuttle.

Bennett, G. H. (1944) *Why Singapore Fell*. London: Angus & Robertson.

Bennis, W. (1959) 'Leadership theory and administrative behaviour.' *Administrative Science Quarterly*, 22, 259–301.

———— (1990) *Why Leaders Can't Lead: The Unconscious Conspiracy Continues*. San Francisco: Jossey-Bass.

Bennis, W. and Nanus, B. (1985) *Leaders*. New York: Harper & Row.

Berger, P. L. and Luckmann, T. (1967) *The Social Construction of Reality*. New York: Doubleday.

Berman, D. J. (1978) *Death on the Job: Occupational Health and Safety Struggles in the United States*. New York: Monthly Review Press.

Beynon, H. (1973) *Working For Ford*. London: Allen Lane.

Bhagat, R. S., Kedia, B. L., Crawford, S. E. and Kaplan, M. R. (1990) 'Cross-cultural issues in organizational psychology: Emergent trends and directions for research in the 1990s', in C. L. Cooper and I. T. Robertson (eds), *International Review of Industrial and Organizational Psychology 1990*. Chichester: Wiley.

Biggart, N. W. (1989) *Charismatic Capitalism*. Chicago: Chicago University Press.

Biggart, N. W. and Hamilton, G. G. (1984) 'The power of obedience.' *Administrative Science Quarterly*, 29, 540–549.

Blackler, F. (1988) 'Information technologies and organizations: Lessons from the 1980s and issues for the 1990s.' *Journal of Occupational Psychology*, 61, 113–128.

Blackler, F. and Brown C. A. (1978) *Job Design and Management Control*. Farnborough: Saxon House.

———— (1980) *Whatever Happened to Shell's New Philosophy of Management?* Farnborough: Saxon House.

———— (1986) 'Alternative models to guide the design and implementation of the new information technologies into work organizations.' *Journal of Occupational Psychology*, 59, 287–313.

Blass, T. (1991) 'Understanding behavior in the Milgram obedience experiment: The role of personality, situations, and their interactions.' *Journal of Personality and Social Psychology*, 60, 398–413.

Blau, J. R. (1979) 'Expertise and power in professional organizations.' *Sociology of Work and Occupations*, 6, 103–123.

Blocklyn, P. L. (1988) 'Making magic: The Disney approach to people management.' *Personnel*, 14, December, 28–35.

Boisjoly, R. P., Curtis, E. F. and Mellican, E. (1989) 'Roger Boisjoly and the Challenger disaster: The ethical dimensions.' *Journal of Business Ethics*, 8, 217–230.

Bowditch, J. L. and Buono, A. F. (1990) *A Primer on Organizational Behaviour*, 2nd edn. Chichester: Wiley.

Bowen, M. G. (1987) 'The escalation phenomenon reconsidered: Decision dilemmas or decision errors?' *Academy of Management Review*, 12, 52–66.

Bowie, N. E. and Freeman, R. E. (eds) (1992) *Ethics and Agency Theory: An Introduction*. New York: Oxford University Press.

Box, S. (1971) *Deviance, Reality and Society*. London: Holt, Rinehart and Winston.

Bradshaw, T. and Vogel, D. (eds) (1981) *Corporations and Their Critics: Issues and Answers to the Problems of Corporate Social Responsibility*. New York: McGraw-Hill.

Braithwaite, J. (1984) *Corporate Crime in the Pharmaceutical Industry*. London: Routledge & Kegan Paul.

Braverman, H. (1974) *Labor and Monopoly Capital*. New York: Monthly Review Press.

Breakwell, G. N. (1986) *Coping With Threatened Identities*. London: Methuen.

Brehmer, B. (1980) 'In one word: Not from experience.' *Acta Psychologica*, 45, 223–241.

Breit, W. and Elzinga, K. G. (1989) *Antitrust Casebook*. London: Holt, Rinehart & Winston.

Brett, J. M. and Rognes, J. K. (1986) 'Intergroup relations in organizations', in P. S. Goodman and associates (eds), *Designing Effective Work Groups*. San Francisco: Jossey-Bass.

Brewin, C. R. (1988) *Cognitive Foundations of Clinical Psychology*. London: Lawrence Erlbaum Associates.

Brief, A. P. and Nord, W. R. (1988) *Meanings of Occupational Work: A Collection of Essays*. New York: Lexington Books.

Briggs, P. (1988) 'The Japanese at work: Illusions of the ideal.' *Industrial Relations Journal*, 19, 24–30.

Brigham, F. R. and Laios, L. (1975) 'Operator control in the control of a laboratory process plant.' *Ergonomics*, 18, 49–54.

Brittan, A. (1989) *Masculinity and Power*. Oxford: Basil Blackwell.

Brown, M. H. and Hosking, D.-M. (1984) 'Distributed leadership and skilled performance as successful organization in social movements.' *Human Relations*, 39, 65–79.

Brown, R. H. (1978) 'Bureaucracy as praxis: Towards a political phenomenology of formal organizations.' *Administrative Science Quarterly*, 23, 365–382.

Bruckberger, R. L. (1959) *Images of America*. New York: Viking Press.

Bryman, A. (1992) *Charisma and Leadership in Organizations*. London: Sage.

Buchanan, D. A. and Boddy, D. (1983) *Organizations in the Computer Age*. Aldershot: Gower.

Buffo (undated) *Amazing Tales of Political Pranks and Anarchist Buffoonery*. London: Spectacular Times.

Buono, A. F. and Nichols, L. T. (eds) (1985) *Corporate Policy, Values and Social Responsibility*. New York: Praeger Books.

Burawoy, M. (1979) *Manufacturing Consent*. Chicago: University of Chicago Press.

Burger, J. M. and Petty, R. E. (1981) 'The low-ball compliance technique: Task or person commitment?' *Journal of Personality and Social Psychology*, 40, 492–500.

Burnes, B. and Fitter, M. (1987) 'Control of advanced manufacturing technology: Supervision without supervisors?', in T. D. Wall, C. W. Clegg and N. J. Kemp (eds), *The Human Side of Advanced Manufacturing Technology*. Chichester: Wiley.

Burns, T. and Stalker, G. M. (1961) *The Management of Innovation*. London: Tavistock.

Butler, R. J. and Wilson, D. C. (1989) *Managing Voluntary and Non-Profit Organizations: Strategy and Structure*. London: Routledge.

Cannon, T. (1993) *Corporate Responsibility*. London: Financial Times/Pitman Press.

Carnall, C. A. (1990) *Managing Change in Organizations*. London: Prentice Hall.

Carroll, S. J. and Tosi, H. L. (1976) *Management By Objectives: Applications and Research*. New York: Macmillan.

Catt, I. (1973) *Computer Worship*. London: Pitman Press.

Chen, M.-J. and MacMillan, I. C. (1992) 'Nonresponse and delayed response to competitive moves: The roles of competitor dependence and action irreversibility.' *Academy of Management Journal*, 35, 539–570.

Cherns, A. B. (1976) 'The principles of sociotechnical design.' *Human Relations*, 29, 783–792.

——— (1987) 'Principles of sociotechnical design revisited.' *Human Relations*, 40, 153–162.

Child, J. (1977) *Organization: A Guide to Problems and Practice*. London: Harper & Row.

Child, J., Fores, J., Glover, I. and Lawrence, P. (1983) 'A price to pay? Professionalism and work organization in Britain and West Germany.' *Sociology*, 17, 24–43.

Child, J., Loveridge, R., Harvey, J. and Spencer, A. (1984) 'Microelectronics and the quality of employment in services', in P. Marstand (ed.), *New Technology and the Future of Work and Skills*. London: Frances Pinter.

Christie, N. (1993) *Crime Control as Industry*. London: Routledge.

Christie, R. and Jahoda, M. (eds) (1954) *Studies in the Scope and Method of 'The Authoritarian Personality'*. Glencoe, Illinois: Free Press.

Cialdini, R. B. (1985) *Influence: Science and Practice*. New York: Scott, Foresman & Company.

——— (1989) 'Commitment and consistency: Hobgoblins of the mind', in H. J. Leavitt, L. R. Pondy, and D. M. Boje (eds), *Readings in Managerial Psychology*, 4th edn. Chicago: Chicago University Press.

Clark, M. S. (ed.) (1991) *Prosocial Behaviour*. London: Sage.

Claybrook, J. (1984) *Retreat From Safety: Reagan's Attack on America's Health*. New York: Pantheon Books.

Clegg, C. W. and Kemp, N. J. (1986) 'Information Technology: Personnel where are you?' *Personnel Review*, 15, 8–15.

Clegg, C. W., Kemp, N. J. and Legge, K. (eds) (1985) *Case Studies in Organizational Behaviour*. London: Harper & Row.

Clinard, M. B. (1983) *Corporate Ethics and Crime: The Role of Middle Management*. Beverly Hills: Sage.

——— (1990) *Corporate Corruption: The Abuse of Power*. New York: Greenwood Press.

Clinard, M. B. and Yeager, P. C. (1980) *Corporate Crime*. New York: Free Press.

Cockburn, C. (1983) *Brothers: Male Dominance and Technological Change*. London: Pluto Press.

——— (1991) *In The Way of Women*. London: Macmillan.

Cohen, A. (1992) 'Antecedents of organizational commitment across occupational groups: A meta-analysis.' *Journal of Organizational Behavior*, 13, 539–558.

Cohen, M. D., March, J. G. and Olsen, J. P. (1972) 'A garbage can model of organizational choice.' *Administrative Science Quarterly*, 17, 1–25.

Cohen, S. and Taylor, L. (1992) *Escape Attempts*, 2nd edn. London: Routledge.

Cole, R. E. (1979) *Work, Mobility and Participation: A Comparative Study of Japanese and American Industry*. Los Angeles: University of California Press.

Coleman, J. E. (1985) *The Criminal Elite: The Sociology of White Collar Crime*. New York: St Martin's Press.

Colesman, J. S. (1982) *The Asymmetric Society*. New York: Syracuse University Press.

Collins, E. (1983) 'Managers and lovers.' *Harvard Business Review*, 61, 141–153.

Collinson, D. L. (1992) *Managing the Shopfloor*. Berlin: Walter de Gruyter.

Collinson, D. and Knights, D. (1986) 'Men only: Theories and practices of job segregation in insurance', in D. Knights and H. Willmott (eds), *Gender and the Labour Process*. Aldershot: Gower.

Collinson, D., Knights, D. and Collinson, M. (1990) *Managing to Discriminate*. London: Routledge.

Conger, J. A. and Kanungo, R. N. (1987) 'Toward a behavioral theory of charismatic leadership in organizational settings.' *Academy of Management Review*, 12, 637–647.

Cook, M. (1988) *Personnel Selection and Productivity*. Chichester: Wiley.

Cooley, M. J. E. (1987) *Architect or Bee? The Human Price of Technology.* London: Hogarth Press.

Coombs, R. and Green, K. (1989) 'Work organization and product change in the service sector: The case of the UK National Health Service', in S. Wood (ed.), *The Transformation of Work: Skill, Flexibility and the Labour Process.* London: Unwin Hyman.

Coopey, J. and Hartley, J. (1991) 'Reconsidering the case for organizational commitment.' *Human Resource Management Journal, 1*(3), 18–34.

Corbett, J. M. (1985) 'Prospective work design of a human centred CNC lathe.' *Behaviour and Information Technology, 4,* 201–214.

———— (1987) 'A psychological study of advanced manufacturing technology: The concept of coupling.' *Behaviour and Information Technology, 6,* 441–453.

———— (1989a) 'Automate or innervate? The role of knowledge in advanced manufacturing systems.' *AI and Society, 3,* 198–208.

———— (1989b) 'Towards a design methodology: A psychologist's view', in H. H. Rosenbrock (ed.), *Designing Human Centred Technology: A Cross Disciplinary Project in Computer-aided Manufacturing.* London: Springer-Verlag.

———— (1992) 'Work at the interface: Advanced manufacturing technology and job design', in P. Adler and T. Winograd (eds), *Usability: Turning Technologies into Tools.* New York: Oxford University Press.

Corbett, J. M., Rasmussen, L. B. and Rauner, F. (1991) *Crossing the Border: The Social and Engineering Design of Computer Integrated Manufacturing Systems.* London: Springer-Verlag.

Corbett, J. M., Martin, R., Wall, T. D., and Clegg, C. W. (1989) 'Technological coupling as a predictor of intrinsic job satisfaction: A replication study.' *Journal of Organisational Behavior, 10,* 91–95.

Cornfield, D. B. (ed.) (1987) *Workers, Managers, and Technological Change: Emerging Patterns of Labor Relations.* New York: Plenum Press.

Coser, L. A. (1974) *Greedy Institutions: Patterns of Undivided Commitment.* New York: Free Press.

Cousins, N. (1987) *The Pathology of Power.* New York: W. W. Norton & Co.

Cox, D. (1991) 'Health service management: A sociological view', in J. Gabe, M. Bury and M. Calman (eds), *The Sociology of the Health Service.* London: Routledge.

Crawley, B., Pinder, R. and Herriot, P. (1990) 'Assessment centre dimensions, personality and aptitudes.' *Journal of Occupational Psychology, 63,* 211–216.

Cray, E. (1980) *Chrome Colossus: General Motors and Its Times.* New York: McGraw-Hill.

Crozier, M. (1964) *The Bureaucratic Phenomenon.* Chicago: University of Chicago Press.

Cullen, F. T., Maakestad, W. J. and Cavender, G. (1987) *Corporate Crime Under Attack: The Ford Pinto Case and Beyond.* Cincinnati: Anderson.

Cyert, R. and March, J. G. (1963) *A Behavioral Theory of the Firm.* Englewood Cliffs: Prentice Hall.

Daft, R. L. (1983) *Organization Theory and Design.* St Paul, MN: West Publishing.

Daft, R. L. and Sharfman, M. P. (eds) (1990) *Organization Theory: Case and Applications,* 3rd edn. St Paul, MN: West Publishing.

Daneke, G. A. (1985) 'Regulation and the sociopathic firm.' *Academy of Management Review, 10,* 15–20.

Daniel, W. W. (1987) *Workplace Industrial Relations and Technical Change.* London: Pinter.

Daniel, W. W. and Hogarth, T. (1990) 'Worker support for technical change.' *New Technology, Work and Employment, 5,* 85–93.

Danziger, J. N. (1979) 'The skill bureaucracy and intraorganizational control: The case of the data processing unit.' *Sociology of Work and Occupations, 6,* 204–226.

Deal, T. and Kennedy, A. (1988) *Corporate Cultures: The Rites and Rituals of Corporate Life.* Harmondsworth: Penguin.

Dean, W. and Morgenthaler, J. (1991) *Smart Drugs and Nutrients: How To Improve Your Memory and Increase Your Intelligence Using The Latest Discoveries in Neuroscience*. New York: B & J Publishing.

DeJong, W. (1979) ' An examination of self-perception mediation of the foot-in-the-door effect.' *Journal of Personality and Social Psychology, 34*, 195–202.

De Keyser, V., Ovale, T., Wilpert, B. and Quintanilla, S. (1988) *The Meaning of Work and Technological Options*. Chichester: Wiley.

DeLamarter, R. T. (1988) *Big Blue: IBM's Use and Abuse of Power*. London: Pan/ Macmillan.

Demison, D. B. (1984) 'The importance of boundary scanning roles in strategic decision-making.' *Journal of Management Studies, 21*, 131–152.

Dent, J. F. (1991) 'Accounting and organizational cultures: A field study of the emergence of a new organizational reality.' *Accounting, Organizations & Society, 16*, 705–732.

Deregowski, J., Dziurawiec, S. and Annis, R. C. (eds) (1983) *Explorations in Cross-Cultural Psychology*. Lisse, Netherlands: Swets & Zeitlinger.

Dixon, N. F. (1979) *On the Psychology of Military Incompetence*. London: Futura Publications.

Doi, T. (1986) *The Anatomy of Self*. Tokyo: Kodansha International.

Dorfman, P. W. and Stephan, W. G. (1984) 'The effects of group performance on cognitions, satisfaction and behaviour: A process model.' *Journal of Management, 10*, 173–192.

Dornbusch, N. (1953) *The Military Academy as an Assimilating Institution*. Greensboro: University of North Carolina Press.

Drazin, R. (1990) 'Professionals and innovation: Structural-functional versus radical-structural perspectives.' *Journal of Management Studies, 27*, 245–263.

Drucker, P. (1988) 'The coming of the new organization.' *Harvard Business Review, 66*, 45–53.

Duncan, M. (1981) 'Microelectronics: Five areas of subordination', in L. Levidow and B. Young (eds), *Science, Technology and the Labour Process: Marxist Studies*, vol. 1. London: CSE Books.

Duncan, R. (1979) 'What is the right organization structure?' *Organizational Dynamics*, Winter, 59–80.

Dussauge, P., Hart, S. and Ramanantsoa, B. (1987) *Strategic Technology Management*. Oxford: Wiley.

Eales, R. (1990) 'In praise of chaos.' *Eurobusiness, 2*, January, 18–20.

Eastman, J. W. (1984) *Safety versus Styling: The American Automobile Industry and the Development of Automobile Safety, 1900–1966*. Lanham: University Press of America.

Easton, G . (1982) *Learning From Case Studies*. London: Prentice Hall International.

Edens, F. N., Self, D. R. and Douglas, T. D. (1976) 'Franchisors describe the ideal franchisee.' *Journal of Small Business Management, 14*, 39–47.

Egan, G. (1993) *Quarantine*. London: Legend Books.

Ehrlich, P. and Ehrlich, A. (1981) *Extinction: The Causes and Consequences of the Disappearance of Species*. New York: Random House.

Eiser, J. R. (1978) 'Cooperation and competition between individuals', in H. Tajfel and C. Fraser (eds), *Introducing Social Psychology*. Harmondsworth: Penguin.

———— (1986) *Social Psychology: Attitudes, Cognition and Social Behaviour*. Cambridge: Cambridge University Press.

Elbing, A. (1978) 'Dilemma . . . and decision', in A. Elbing *Behavioral Decisions in Organizations*, 2nd edn. Glenview, IL: Scott, Foresman & Company.

Elizur, D., Borg, I., Hunt, R. and Beck, I. K. (1991) 'The structure of work values: A cross cultural comparison.' *Journal of Organizational Behavior, 12*, 21–30.

Elliott, M. W. and Beauchamp, T. L. (1989) 'Du Pont's policy of exclusion from the workplace', in T. L. Beauchamp, *Case Studies in Business, Society, and Ethics.* Englewood Cliffs: Prentice Hall.

Elsbach, K. D. and Sutton, R. I. (1992) 'Acquiring organizational legitimacy through illegimate actions: A marriage of institutional and impression management.' *Academy of Management Journal*, 35, 699–738.

Ephrath, A. R. (1980) 'Verbal presentation', *NATO Symposium on Human Detection and Diagnosis of Systems Failures.* Roskilde, Denmark. Reported in Bainbridge (1981).

Ermann, M. D. and Lundman, R. J. (1982) *Corporate Deviance.* New York: Holt, Reinhart & Winston.

Etzioni, A. (1961) *A Comparative Analysis of Complex Organizations.* Glencoe, Illinois: Free Press.

Ewing, D. W. (1983) *Do It My Way or You're Fired!* New York: Wiley.

Ezzamel, M. and Bourn, M. (1990) 'The roles of accounting information systems in an organization experiencing financial crisis'. *Accounting, Organizations & Society*, 15, 399–424.

Fallik, F. (1988) *Managing Organizational Change: Human Factors and Automation.* London: Taylor & Francis.

Farberman, H. A. (1975) 'A crimogenic market structure: The automobile industry.' *Sociological Quarterly*, 16, 438–457.

Faulkner, R. R. (1973) 'Orchestra interaction: Some features of communication and authority in an artistic organization.' *Sociological Quarterly*, 14. 147–157.

Feldman, S. P. (1989) 'The broken wheel: The inseparability of autonomy and control in innovation within the organization.' *Journal of Management Studies*, 26, 83–102.

Felstead, A. (1990) 'A chance to be your own boss: The myth or reality of franchise ownership?' In: M. Poole and G. Jenkins (eds), *New Forms of Ownership.* London: Routledge.

———— (1991) 'The social organization of the franchise: A case of controlled self-employment' *Work, Employment and Society*, 5, 37–57.

Festinger, L. (1964) *Conflict, Decision and Dissonance.* London: Tavistock.

Feynman, R. P. (1988) *What Do You Care What Other People Think?* London: Unwin Hyman.

Fiedler, F. E. and House, R. J. (1988) 'Leadership theory and research: A report of progress', in C. L. Cooper and I. T. Robertson (eds), *International Review of Industrial and Organizational Psychology 1988.* Chichester: Wiley.

Fine, G. A. (1988) 'Letting off steam? Redefining a restaurant's work environment', in M. D. Jones, M. D. Moore and R. C. Snyder (eds), *Inside Organizations: Understanding the Human Dimension.* London: Sage.

Fischer, P., Stratmann, W., Lundsgaarde, H. and Steele, D. (1980) 'User reaction to PROMIS.' *Computer Applications in Medical Care*, 3, 1722–1730.

Fisher, F., Mancke, R. B. and McKie, J. W. (1983a) *IBM and the US Data Processing Industry: An Economic Analysis.* New York: Praeger.

Fisher, F., McGovan, J. J. and Greenwood, J. E. (1983b) *Folded, Spindled, and Mutilated: Economic Analysis and US v. IBM.* Cambridge, MA: MIT Press.

Fletcher, C. A. (1982) 'Assessment centres', in D. MacKenzie-Davey and M. Harris (eds), *Judging People: A Guide to Orthodox and Unorthodox Methods of Assessment.* London: McGraw-Hill.

Ford, C. H. (1980) 'MBO: An idea whose time has gone?'. *Business Horizons*, December 1980, 45–51.

Ford, H. (1923) *My Life and Work.* London: William Heinemann.

Foreman, D. (1990) *Confessions of an Eco-Warrior.* New York: Harmony Books.

Foucault, M. (1979) *Discipline and Punish: The Birth of the Prison*. Harmondsworth: Penguin.

Fox, A. (1980) 'The meaning of work', in G. Esland and G. Salaman (eds), *The Politics of Work and Occupations*. Milton Keynes: Open University Press.

Francis, A. and Winstanley, D. (1988) 'Managing new product development: Some alternative ways to organize the work of technical specialists.' *Journal of Marketing Management*, 4, 249–260.

Frank, N. (1985) *Crimes Against Health and Safety*. New York: Harrow & Heston.

Franke, R. (1979) 'The Hawthorne experiments: A review.' *American Sociological Review*, 47, 858–866.

Freeman, J. L. and Fraser, S. C. (1966) 'Compliance without pressure: The foot-in-the-door technique.' *Journal of Personality and Social Psychology*, 4, 195–203.

Freeman, R. E. (1990) 'Ethics in the workplace: Recent scholarship', in C. L. Cooper and I. T. Robertson (eds), *International Review of Industrial and Organizational Psychology 1990*. Chichester: Wiley.

French, J. and Raven, B. (1958) 'The bases of social power', in D. Cartwright (ed.), *Studies in Social Power*. Ann Arbor, Michigan: Institute for Social Research Publications.

Frese, M. (1982) 'Occupational socialisation and psychological development: An underdeveloped research perspective in industrial psychology.' *Journal of Occupational Psychology*, 55, 209–224.

Freyer, T. A. (1992) *Regulating Big Business: Antitrust in Great Britain and the United States, 1880–1990*. Cambridge: Cambridge University Press.

Fukami, C. V. and Larson, E. W. (1984) 'Commitment to company and union: Parallel models.' *Journal of Applied Psychology*, 69, 367–371.

Gal, R. and Mangelsdorff, A. D. (eds) (1991) *Handbook of Military Psychology*. Chichester: Wiley.

Galbraith, J. R. (1977) *Organization Design*. Reading, MA: Addison-Wesley.

Galbraith, J. R. and Kazanzian, R. K. (1986) *Strategy Implementation; Structure, Systems and Process*. New York: West Publishing.

Garson, B. (1988) *The Electronic Sweatshop*. New York: Simon & Schuster.

Geary, J. (1992) 'Pay, control and commitment: Linking appraisal and reward.' *Human Resource Management Journal*, 2(4), 34–54.

Gemmill, G. (1986) 'The mythology of the leader role in small groups.' *Small Group Behavior*, 17, 41–50.

Gemmill, G. and Oakley, J. (1992) 'Leadership: An alienating social myth?' *Human Relations*, 45, 113–130.

Gerard, G. and Mathewson, G. (1966) 'The effect of severity of initiation on liking for a group.' *Journal of Abnormal and Social Psychology*, 10, 370–376.

Gibb, C. A. (1958) 'An interactional view of the emergence of leadership', in C. A. Gibb (ed.), *Leadership*. Harmondsworth: Penguin.

———— (1969) 'Leadership', in G. Lindzey and E. Aronson (eds), *Handbook of Social Psychology*, vol. 4, 2nd edn. Reading, MA: Addison-Wesley.

Gibson, J. (1990) 'Factors contributing to the creation of a torturer', in P. Suedfeld (ed.), *Psychology and Torture*. New York: Hemisphere Books.

Gibson, J. and Haritos-Faroutos, M. (1986) 'The education of a torturer.' *Psychology Today*, 20, 50–58.

Gibson, W. (1984) *Neuromancer*. London: Victor Gollancz.

———— (1986) *Count Zero*. London: Victor Gollancz.

———— (1988) *Mona Lisa Overdrive*. London: Victor Gollancz.

Glad, B. (ed.) (1990) *Psychological Dimensions of War*. Beverly Hills: Sage.

Glazer, P. M. and Glazer, M. P. (1989) *The Whistle Blowers: Exposing Corruption in Government and Industry*. New York: Basic Books.

Glick, W. H., Jenkins, G. D. and Gupta, N. (1985) 'Method versus substance: How strong are underlying relationships between job characteristics and attitudinal outcomes?', *Academy of Management Journal, 29*, 441–464.

Goffman, E. (1959) *The Presentation of Self in Everyday Life*. New York: Doubleday.

Goldstein, J. H., Davis, R. W. and Herman, D. (1975) 'Escalation of aggression: Experimental studies.' *Journal of Personality and Social Psychology, 31*, 162–170.

Goodman, P. S., Ravlin, E. and Bateman, T. (1987) 'Understanding groups in organizations', in B. Staw and L. L. Cummings (eds), *Research in Organizational Behavior*, vol. 9. Greenwich, Conn.: JAI Press.

Goold, M. (1991) 'Strategic control in the decentralised firm.' *Sloan Management Review*, Winter 1991, 69–81.

Gordon Bennett, H. (1944) *Why Singapore Fell*. London: Angus & Robertson.

Gouldner, A. W. (1957) 'Cosmopolitans and locals: Toward an analysis of latent social roles.' *Administrative Science Quarterly, 2*, 281–306.

———— (1958) 'Cosmopolitans and locals: Toward an analysis of latent social identity.' *Administrative Science Quarterly, 3*, 444–480.

———— (1964) *Patterns of Industrial Bureaucracy*. New York: Free Press.

Gowler, D. and Legge, K. (1983) 'The meaning of management and the management of meaning: A view from social anthropology', in M. J. Earl (ed.), *Perspectives on Management: A Multidisciplinary Analysis*. Oxford: Oxford University Press.

Gowler, D., Legge, K. and Clegg, C. (eds) (1993) *Case Studies in Organizational Behaviour and Human Resource Management*. London: Paul Chapman.

Graham, I. (1988) 'Japanisation as mythology.' *Industrial Relations Journal, 19*, 69–75.

Gray, J. L. (1979) 'The myths of the myths about behaviour mod in organizations: A reply to Locke's criticisms of behaviour modification.' *Academy of Management Review, 4*, 121–129.

Greenhalgh, L. (1987) 'Interpersonal conflicts in organizations', in C. L. Cooper and I. T. Robertson (eds), *International Review of Industrial and Organizational Psychology 1987*. Chichester: Wiley.

Greiner, L. E. (1972) 'Evolution and revolution as organizations grow.' *Harvard Business Review, 50*, 37–46.

Grenier, G. (1988) *Inhuman Relations: Quality Circles and Anti-Unionism in American Industry*. Philadelphia: Temple University Press.

Grindley, K. (1992) *Managing IT at Board Level: The Hidden Agenda Exposed*. London: Pitman Press.

Guest, D. E. (1992) 'Employee commitment and control', in J. F. Hartley and G. M. Stephenson (eds), *Employment Relations: The Psychology of Influence and Control at Work*. Oxford: Blackwell.

Guest, D. E., Williams, R. and Dewe, P. (1980) 'Workers' perceptions of changes affecting the quality of working life', in K. D. Duncan, M. M. Gruneberg and D. Wallis (eds), *Changes in Working Life*. Chichester: Wiley.

Gutek, B. (1985) *Sex and the Workplace*. San Francisco: Jossey-Bass.

Hackman, J. R. and Oldham, G. R. (1980) *Work Redesign*. Reading, MA: Addison-Wesley.

Hafner, K. and Markoff, J. (1993) *Cyberpunk: Outlaws and Hackers on the Computer Frontier*. London: Corgi Books.

Handy, C. (1988) *Understanding Voluntary Organizations*. Harmondsworth: Penguin.

———— (1992) *Understanding Organizations*, 4th edn. Harmondsworth: Penguin.

Hannan, M. T. and Freeman, J. H. (1977) 'The population ecology of organizations.' *American Journal of Sociology, 82*, 929–964.

———— (1984) 'Structural inertia and organizational change.' *American Sociological Review, 49*, 189–202.

Haritos-Faroutos, M. (1988) 'The official torturer: A learning model for obedience to authority of violence.' *Journal of Applied Social Psychology, 18*, 1107–1120.

Harpaz, I. (1989) 'Non-financial employment commitment: A cross-national comparison.' *Journal of Occupational Psychology, 62*, 147–150.

Harré, R. (1979) *Social Being.* Oxford: Blackwell.

Harrigan, K.R. (1986) *Managing For Joint Venture Success.* New York: Lexington Books.

Harris, N. (1986) *The End of the Third World.* Harmondsworth: Penguin.

Harrison, R. (1970) 'Choosing the depth of organizational intervention.' *Journal of Applied Behavioural Science, 6*, 181–202.

Hassenfeld, Y. (ed.) (1992) *Human Services as Complex Organisations.* London: Sage.

Hater, J. and Bass, B.M. (1988) 'Superiors' evaluations and subordinates' perceptions of transformational and transactional leadership.' *Journal of Applied Psychology, 73*, 695–702.

Haug, M. (1977) 'Computer technology and the obsolescence of the concept of profession', in R. Haug and J. Dofny (eds), *Work and Technology.* Beverly Hills: Sage.

Hearn, J. and Parkin, W. (1987) *'Sex' at Work.* Brighton: Wheatsheaf.

Hearn, J., Sheppard, D.L., Tancred-Sherriff, P. and Burrell, G. (eds) (1989) *The Sexuality of Organization.* London: Sage.

Heilbroner, R.L. (ed.) (1972) *In The Name of Profit.* New York: Doubleday.

Heller, F. (1991) 'The underutilisation of applied psychology.' *The European Work and Organizational Psychologist, 1*, 9–25.

Hendry, J. (1992) *Wrapping Culture: Politeness, Presentation, and Power in Japan and Other Societies.* Oxford: Oxford University Press.

Herbst, P.G. (1976) 'Non-hierarchical organisations', in F.E. Emery (ed.), *Systems Thinking*, vol. 2. Harmondsworth: Penguin.

Herriot, P. (ed.) (1989) *Assessment and Selection in Organizations.* Chichester: Wiley.

Hewstone, M. (1991) *Causal Attribution: From Cognitive Processes to Collective Beliefs.* Oxford: Blackwell.

Hickson, D.J., Butler, R.J., Cray, D., Mallory, G.R. and Wislon, D.C. (1986) *Top Decisions: Strategic Decision-Making in Organizations.* Oxford: Blackwell.

Hickson, D.J., Hinings, C.R., Lee, C.A., Schneck, R.E. and Pennings, J.M. (1971) 'A strategic contingencies theory of intra-organizational power.' *Administrative Science Quarterly, 16*, 216–229.

Hill, C.W.L., Kelley, P.C., Bradley R.A., Hitt, M.A. and Hoskisson, R.E. (1992) 'An empirical examination of the causes of corporate wrongdoing in the United States.' *Human Relations, 45*, 1055–76.

Hill, S. (1988) *The Tragedy of Technology.* London: Pluto Press.

Hills, S.L. (1987) (ed.) *Corporate Violence: Injury and Death for Profit.* Totowa, NJ: Rowan & Littlefield.

Hinde, R.A, and Groebel, J. (eds) (1991) *Cooperation and Prosocial Behaviour.* Cambridge: Cambridge University Press.

Hines, R. (1988) 'Financial accounting: In communicating reality, we construct reality.' *Accounting, Organizations and Society, 13*, 79–94.

Hinings, C.R., Hickson, D.J., Pennings. J.M. and Schneck, R.E. (1974) 'Structural conditions of intraorganizational power'. *Administrative Science Quarterly, 19*, 22–44.

Hirschhorn, L. (1988) *The Workplace Within: Psychodynamics of Organization Life.* Cambridge, MA: MIT Press.

Hochschild, A.R. (1983) *The Managed Heart: The Commercialization of Human Feeling.* Berkeley: University of California Press.

———— (1990) 'Ideology and emotion management: A perspective and path for future research', in T. D. Kemper (ed.), *Research Agendas in the Sociology of Emotions*. Albany: State University Press.

Hoffman, W. M. and Moore, J. M. (eds) (1990) *Business Ethics: Problems in Corporate Morality*. New York: McGraw-Hill.

Hofstede, G. (1980) *Culture's Consequences: International Differences in Work-Related Values*. London: Sage.

Hogg, M. A. and Abrams, D. (1991) *Social Identifications: A Social Psychology of Intergroup Relations and Group Processes*. London: Routledge.

Hollander, E. P. (1964) *Leaders, Groups and Influence*. New York: Oxford University Press.

———— (1974) 'Processes of leadership emergence.' *Journal of Contemporary Business*, 3, 19–33.

Hollway, W. (1991) *Work Psychology and Organizational Behaviour*. London: Sage.

Holmes, H. and Holmes, R. (1988) 'Walt Disney – 1987', in F. R. David, *Strategic Management*. Columbus, Ohio: Merrill.

Hopper, T. and Armstrong, P. (1991) 'Cost accounting, Controlling labour and the rise of conglomerates.' *Accounting, Organizations & Society*, 16, 405–438.

Hopper, T., Storey, J. and Willmott, H. (1987) 'Accounting for accounting: Towards the development of a dialectical view', *Accounting, Organizations & Society*, 12, 437–456.

Hosking, D.-M. and Morley, I. E. (1992) *The Social Psychology of Organizing*. London: Harvester-Wheatsheaf.

House, R. J. and Baetz, M. L. (1979) 'Leadership: Some empirical generalizations and new research directions', in B. Staw and L. L. Cummings (eds), *Research in Organizational Behavior*, vol. 1. Greenwich, Conn.: JAI Press.

Hunt, V. (1979) *Work and the Health of Women*. Boca Raton: CRC Press.

Huws, U., Korte, W. B. and Robinson, S. (1990) *Telework: Towards the Elusive Office*. Chichester: Wiley.

Jacques, E. (1955) 'Social systems as a defense against persecutory and depressive anxiety', in M. Klein, P. Heiman and R. Mohey-Kyrle (eds), *New Directions in Psychoanalysis*. London: Tavistock.

James, N. (1989) 'Emotional labor: Skill and work in the social regulation of feelings.' *Sociological Review*, 37, 15–42.

Jamieson, B. D. (1979) 'Behavioural problems with management by objectives', in B. D. Huseman and A. B. Carroll (eds), *Readings in Organizational Behaviour*. New York: Allyn & Bacon.

Janis, I. L. (1972) *Victims of Groupthink*. Boston: Houghton Mifflin.

———— (1982) *Groupthink*. Boston: Houghton Mifflin.

Janis, I. L. and Mann, L. (1977) *Decision Making: A Psychological Analysis of Conflict, Choice and Commitment*. New York: Free Press.

Jardin, A. (1970) *The First Henry Ford: A Study of Personality and Business Leadership*. Cambridge, MA: MIT Press.

Joerges, B. (1989) 'Romancing the machine – Reflections on the social scientific construction of computer reality.' *International Studies of Management and Organization*, 19, 24–50.

Johnson, B. S. (ed.) (1973) *All Bull: The National Serviceman*. London: Quarter Books.

Johnson, G. (1987) *Strategic Change and the Management Process*. Oxford: Blackwell.

Johnson, P. and Gill, J. (1993) *Management Control and Organizational Behaviour*. London: Paul Chapman Publishing.

Jones, G. R. (1983) 'Psychological orientation and the process of organizational socialisation: An interactionist perspective.' *Academy of Management Review*, 8, 464–474.

Jordan, N. (1963) 'Allocation of functions between man and machines in automated systems.' *Journal of Applied Psychology, 47,* 161–165.

Josephson, E. (1952) 'Irrational leadership in formal organizations.' *Social Forces, 31,* 109–117.

Kadrey, R. (1988) *Metrophage.* London: Victor Gollancz.

Kamata, S. (1983) *Japan in the Fast Lane: An Insider's Account of Life in a Japanese Auto Factory.* London: Allen & Unwin.

Kanter, R. M. (1977) *Men and Women of the Corporation.* New York: Basic Books.

———— (1989) *When Giants Learn to Dance.* New York: Irwin.

Kaplan, M. F. (1987) 'The influence process in group decision-making', in C. Hendrick (ed.), *Group Processes.* London: Sage.

Kashima, Y., Siegal, M., Tanaka, K. and Kashima, E. S. (1992) 'Do people believe behaviours are consistent with attitudes? Towards a cultural psychology of attribution processes.' *British Journal of Social Psychology, 31,* 111–124.

Kast, F. E. and Rosenzweig, J. E. (1985) *Organization and Management: A Systems and Contingency Approach.* New York: McGraw-Hill.

Katz, J. A. (1987) 'Playing at innovation in the computer revolution', in M. Frese, E. Ulich and W. Dzida (eds), *Psychological Issues of Human Computer Interaction in the Workplace.* Amsterdam: North-Holland.

Katz, R. L. (1978) 'The Crown Fastener company case', in A. Elbing, *Behavioral Decisions in Organizations,* 2nd edn. Glenview, Illinois: Scott, Foresman & Company.

Kaufmann, H. (1967) 'The price of obedience and the price of knowledge.' *American Psychologist, 22,* 321–322.

Keen, P. (1985) 'Information systems and organizational design', in E. Rhodes and D. Wield (eds), *Implementing New Technologies: Choice, Decision and Change in Manufacturing.* Oxford: Blackwell.

Keenoy, T. (1992) 'Constructing control', in J. F.. Hartley and G. M. Stephenson (eds), *Employment Relations: The Psychology of Influence and Control at Work.* Oxford: Blackwell.

Keller, M. (1989) *Rude Awakening: The Rise, Fall, and Struggle for Recovery of General Motors.* New York: William Morrow.

Kelley, H. H. (1971) *Attribution in Social Interaction.* Morristown, NJ: General Learning Press.

Kelly, J. E. (1982) *Scientific Management, Job Design and Work Performance.* London: Academic Press.

———— (1985) 'Management's redesign of work', in D. Knights, H. Willmott, and D.Collinson (eds), *Job Redesign: Critical Perspectives on the Labour Process.* Aldershot: Gower.

———— (1992) 'Does job re-design theory explain job re-design outcomes?' *Human Relations, 45,* 753–774.

Kelman, H. C. (1967) 'Human use of human subjects: The problem of deception in social psychological experiments.' *Psychological Bulletin, 67,* 1–11.

Kelman, H. C. and Hamilton, V. L. (1989) *Crimes of Obedience: Toward a Social Psychology of Authority and Obedience.* New Haven, CT: Yale University Press.

Kenney, M. and Florida, R. (1992) *Beyond Mass Production: The Japanese System and Its Transfer to the US.* New York: Oxford University Press.

Kerr, S. (1975) 'On the folly of rewarding A, while hoping for B.' *Academy of Management Journal, 18,* 769–783.

Kets de Vries, M. F.R. (1989) 'Alexithymia in organizational life: Organization man revisited.' *Human Relations, 42,* 1079–1093.

Kets de Vries, M. F.R. and Miller, D. (1984a) 'Neurotic style and organizational pathology.' *Strategic Management Journal, 5,* 35–55.

——————— (1984b) *The Neurotic Organization*. San Francisco: Jossey-Bass.

Kiesler, C. A. (1971) *The Psychology of Commitment*. London: Academic Press.

Kinnersly, P. (1974) *The Hazards of Work: How to Fight Them*. London: Pluto Press.

Klein, L. (1962) 'Some implications of rationalised production,' *Occupational Psychology, 36*, 18–27.

Knights, D. (1990) 'Subjectivity, power and the labour process', in D. Knights and H. Willmott (eds), *Labour Process Theory*. London: Macmillan.

——————— (1992) 'Changing spaces: The disruptive impact of a new epistemological location for the study of management.' *Academy of Management Review, 17*, 514–536.

Knights, D. and Willmott, H. (eds) (1986) *Gender and the Labour Process*. Aldershot: Gower.

Knights, D., Willmott, H. and Collinson, D. (eds) (1985) *Job Redesign: Critical Perspectives on the Labour Process*. Aldershot: Gower.

Kohn, M. L. and Schooler, C. (1983) *Work and Personality: An Inquiry into the Impact of Social Stratification*. New York: Ablex Publishing.

Kondo, D. (1990) *Crafting Selves: Power, Gender and Discourse of Identity in a Japanese Workplace*. Chicago: Chicago University Press.

Kondrasuk, J. N. (1981) 'Studies in MBO effectiveness.' *Academy of Management Review, 6*, 419–430.

Koslowsky, M. (1990) 'Staff/line distinctions in job and organizational commitment.' *Journal of Occupational Psychology, 63*, 167–173.

Kotter, J. P. (1990) *A Force For Change: How Leadership Differs From Management*. New York: Free Press.

Kruglanski, A. W. and Mackie, D. M. (1990) 'Majority and minority influence: A judgemental process analysis', in W. Stroebe and M. Hewstone (eds), *European Review of Social Psychology*, vol. 1. Chichester: Wiley.

Kunda, G. (1992) *Engineering Culture: Control and Commitment in a High-Tech Corporation*. Philadelphia: Temple University Press.

Kurzman, D. (1987) *The Killing Wind*. London: McGraw-Hill.

Laffin, J. (1973) *Americans in Battle*. New York: Crown Publishers.

Lane, R. E. (1991) *The Market Experience*. Cambridge: Cambridge University Press.

Larson, J. R. and Christensen, C. (1993) 'Groups as problem-solving units: Towards a new meaning of social cognition.' *British Journal of social Psychology, 32*, 5–30.

Laurent, A. (1983) 'The cultural diversity of Western conceptions of management.' *International Studies of Management and Organizations, 13*, 75–89.

Lawrence, P. R. and Dyer, D. (1983) *Renewing American Industry*. New York: Free Press.

Lawrence, P. R. and Lorsch, J. W. (1967) *Organization and Environment*. Harvard: Harvard Business School Press.

Lawrence, P. R. and Seiler, J. A. (1965) *Organizational Behavior and Administration: Cases, Concepts and Research Findings*. Homewood, IL: Irwin & Dorsey.

Leonard, J. N. (1932) *The Tragedy of Henry Ford*. New York: Putnam Press.

L'Etang, H. (1969) *Pathology of Leadership*. London: Heinemann.

Levin, D. P. (1989) *Irreconcilable Differences: Ross Perot Versus General Motors*. Boston: Little, Brown & Company.

Levinson, H. (1970) 'Management by whose objectives?', *Harvard Business Review, 48*, 125–134.

Levy, S. (1984) *Hackers: Heroes of the Computer Revolution*. New York: Doubleday.

Levy-Leboyer, C. (1986) 'Applying psychology or applied psychology?' In: F. Heller (ed.), *The Use and Abuse of Social Science*. London: Sage.

Lewis, C. (1985) *Employee Selection*. London: Hutchinson.

Lincoln, J. R. and Kalleberg, A. L. (1992) *Culture, Control and Commitment: A Study of Work Organization and Work Attitudes in the United States and Japan*. Cambridge: Cambridge University Press.

Lindon, E. (1972) 'The demoralisation of an army.' *New York Saturday Review*, 8 January 12–15.

Lippitt, G. L., Langseth, P. and Mossop, J. (1985) *Implementing Organizational Change. A Practical Guide to Managing Change Efforts*. San Francisco: Jossey-Bass.

Lloyd, T. (1990) *The Nice Company*. London: Bloomsbury Press.

Locke, E. A. (1977) 'The myth of behaviour modification in organizations.' *Academy of Management Review*, 2, 543–553.

———— (1979) 'Myths in the myths of the myths of behaviour mod on organizations.' *Academy of Management Review*, 4, 131–136.

Love, J. F. (1986) *McDonald's: Behind the Arches*. London: Bantam Press.

Love, R. L. (1989) 'The absorption of protest', in H. J. Leavitt, L. R. Pondy and D. M. Boje (eds), *Readings in Managerial Psychology*, 4th edn. Chicago: University of Chicago Press.

Lukes, S. (1974) *Power: A Radical View*. London: Macmillan.

Luthens, F., McCaul, H. S. and Dodd, N. G. (1985) 'Organisational commitment: A comparison of American, Japanese and Korean employees.' *Academy of Management Journal*, 28, 213–219.

Maas, A. and Schaller, M. (1991) 'Intergroup biases and the cognitive dynamics of stereotype formation', in W. Stroebe and M. Hewstone (eds), *European Review of Social Psychology*, vol. 2. Chichester: Wiley.

MacGregor-Burns, J. (1978) *Leadership*. New York: Harper & Row.

Mallik, R. (1975) *And Tomorrow . . . the World: Inside IBM*. London: Millington.

Manes, C. (1990) *Green Rage: Radical Environmentalism and the Unmaking of Civilisation*. Boston: Little, Brown & Company.

Manley, W. W. (1992) *Handbook of Good Business Practice: Corporate Codes of Conduct*. London: Routledge.

Mann, A. (1992) *No Small Change: Money, Christians and the Church*. Norwich: Canterbury Press.

March, J. G. (1987) 'Ambiguity and accounting: The elusive link between information and decision making.' *Accounting, Organizations & Society*, 12, 153–168.

Markus, L. M. (1983) 'Power, politics and MIS implementation.' *Communications of the ACM*, 26, 6–37.

Markus, L. M. and Bjorn-Andersen, N. (1987) 'Power over users: Its exercise by system professionals.' *Communications of the ACM*, 26, 430–444.

Markus, L. M. and Pfeffer, J. (1983) 'Power and the design and implementation of accounting and control systems.' *Accounting, Organizations and Society*, 8, 205–18.

Marquis, S. S. (1923) *Henry Ford: An Interpretation*. Boston: Little, Brown & Company.

Martin, J. and Siehl, C. (1983) 'Organizational culture and counterculture: An uneasy symbiosis.' *Organizational Dynamics*, 12, 52–64.

Martin, R. and Wall, T. D. (1989) 'Attentional demand and cost responsibility as stressors in shopfloor jobs.' *Academy of Management Journal*, 32, 69–86.

Maslow, A. (1971) *The Further Reaches of Human Nature*. New York: Viking Press.

Matza, D. (1969) *Becoming Deviant*. London: Prentice Hall.

McCaffery, L. (ed.) (1992) *Storming the Reality Studio: A Casebook of Cyberpunk and Postmodern Science Fiction*. Durham, NC: Duke University Press.

McCann, J. and Galbraith, J. R. (1981) 'Interdepartmental relationships', in P. C. Nystrom and W. H. Starbuck (eds), *Handbook of Organizational Design*, vol. 2. New York: Oxford University Press.

McCarten, J. (1940) 'The little man in Henry Ford's basement.' *American Mercury*, June, 2–10.

McClure, J. (1991) *Explanations, Accounts, and Illusions: A Critical Analysis.* Cambridge: Cambridge University Press.

McConnell, M. (1987) *Challenger: A Major Malfunction.* New York: Doubleday.

McKay, G. and Corke, A. (1986) *The Body Shop: Franchising a Philosophy.* London: Pan Books.

McKenna, R. (1989) *Who's Afraid of Big Blue? How Computer Companies Are Challenging IBM and Winning.* London: Addison-Wesley.

McLoughlin, I. and Clark, J. (1988) *Technological Change at Work.* Milton Keynes: Open University Press.

McSweeney, B. (1989) 'The roles of accounting in organizational maintenance and change: Insights from a case study', in R. Mansfield (ed.), *Frontiers of Management: Research & Practice.* London: Routledge.

Meaning of Work International Research Team (1987) *The Meaning of Work: An International View.* London: Academic Press.

Mechanic, D. (1962) 'Sources of power of lower participants in complex organizations.' *Administrative Science Quarterly, 7,* 349–364.

Meindl, J.R., Ehrlich, S.B. and Dukerich, J.M. (1985) 'The romance of leadership.' *Administrative Science Quarterly, 30,* 78–102.

Merton, R.A. (1938) 'Social structure and anomie.' *American Sociological Review, 3,* 672–682.

———— (1940) 'Bureaucratic structure and personality.' *Social Forces, 18,* 560–568.

Miceli, M.P. and Near, J.P. (1985) 'Characteristics of organizational climate and perceived wrongdoing associated with whistle-blowing decisions.' *Personnel Psychology, 38,* 525–543.

Michels, R. (1949) *Political Parties.* New York: Free Press.

Milgram, S. (1963) 'Behavioral study of obedience.' *Journal of Abnormal and Social Psychology, 67,* 371–378.

———— (1964) 'Issues in the study of obedience: A reply to Baumrind.' *American Psychologist, 19,* 848–852.

———— (1967) 'Some conditions for obedience and disobedience to authority.' *Human Relations, 18,* 57–76.

———— (1974) *Obedience to Authority: An Experimental View.* New York: Harper & Row.

———— (1977) *The Individual in a Social World: Essays and Experiments.* Reading, MA: Addison-Wesley.

Miller, A.G. (1986) *The Obedience Experiments: A Case Study of Controversy in Social Science.* New York: Praeger.

Mills, C.W. (1951) *White Collar.* Oxford: Oxford University Press.

Miner, A., Amburgey, T. and Stearns, T. (1990) 'Interorganizational linkages and population dynamics: Buffering and transformational shields.' *Administrative Science Quarterly, 35,* 689–713.

Mintzberg, H. (1979) *The Structuring of Organizations: A Synthesis of the Research.* New York: Prentice Hall.

Mirvis, P.H. and Berg, D.N. (1977) *Failures in Organizational Development and Change.* Chichester: Wiley.

Mita, M. (1993) *The Social Psychology of Modern Japan.* New York: Kegan Paul International.

Mitchel, J.O. (1975) 'Assessment center validity: A longitudinal study.' *Journal of Applied Psychology, 60,* 573–579.

Mixon, D. (1974) 'If you won't deceive, what can you do?', in N. Armistead (ed.), *Reconstructing Social Psychology.* Harmondsworth: Penguin.

Mokhiber, R. (1988) *Corporate Crime and Violence: Big Business Power and the Abuse of Public Trust.* San Francisco: Sierra Club Books.

Molander, E. A. (1980) 'Regulating reproductive risks in the workplace', in E. A. Molander (ed.), *Responsive Capitalism: Case Studies in Corporate Social Conduct.* New York: McGraw-Hill.

Moore, R. I. (1985) 'Preface', in E. Peters (ed.), *Torture.* New York: Basil Blackwell.

Moorhead, G. and Griffiths, R. W. (1992) *Organizational Behavior,* 3rd edn. Barton: Houghton Mifflin.

Morgan, D. H.J. (1975) 'Autonomy and negotiation in an industrial setting.' *Sociology of Work and Occupations,* 2, 203–226.

Morgan, G. (1985) *Images Of Organization.* London: Sage.

Morley, I. (1992) 'Intra-organizational bargaining', in J. F. Hartley and G. M. Stephenson (eds), *Employment Relations: The Psychology of Influence and Control at Work.* Oxford: Blackwell.

Morris, C. W. (1949) *Signs, Language and Behaviour.* London: Prentice Hall.

Morrow, P. C. (1983) 'Concept redundancy in organizational research: The case of work commitment.' *Academy of Management Review,* 8, 486–500.

Morse, N. C. and Weiss, R. (1955) 'The function and meaning of work and the job.' *American Sociological Review,* 20, 191–198.

Moscovici, S. (1985) 'Social influence and conformity', in G. Lindzey and E. Aronson (eds), *The Handbook of Social Psychology,* 3rd edn. New York: Random House.

Moscovici, S. and Mugny, G. (1983) 'Minority influence', in P. B. Paulus (ed.), *Basic Group Processes.* New York: Springer-Verlag.

Mowday, R., Steers, R. and Porter, L. (1982) *Employee–Organization Linkages: The Psychology of Commitment, Absenteeism and Turnover.* New York: Academic Press.

Muchinsky, P. M. (1986) 'Personnel selection methods', in C. L. Cooper and I. T. Robertson (eds), *International Review of Industrial and Organizational Psychology 1986.* Chichester: Wiley.

Mugny, G. and Perez, J. A. (1991) *The Social Psychology of Minority Influence.* Cambridge: Cambridge University Press.

Muktananada, S. (1980) *The Perfect Relationship.* Geneshpuri, India: Gurudeu Siddha Peeth.

Mumford, E. and Weir, D. (1979) *Computer Systems in Work Design: The ETHICS Method.* London: Associated Business Press.

Mumford, L. (1934) *Technics and Civilisation.* New York: Harcourt Brace Jovanovich.

Myers, C. S. (1920) *Mind and Work: The Psychological Factors in Industry and Commerce.* London: University of London Press.

Nader, R. (1972) *Unsafe At Any Price.* New York: Grossman Press.

Nader, R., Green, M. J. and Seligman, J. (1976) *Taming the Giant Corporations.* New York: Norton & Company.

Neilsen, E. H. (1972) 'Understanding and managing intergroup conflict', in J. W. Lorsch and P. R. Lawrence, *Managing Group and Intergroup Relations.* Homewood, Illinois: Irwin & Dorsey.

Nellmann, D. O. and Smith, L. F. (1981) 'Just-in-time versus just-in-case production/inventory systems.' *Production and Inventory Management,* 23, 12–21.

Neumann, J. E. (1989) 'Why people don't participate in organizational change', in R. W. Woodman and W. A. Pasmore (eds), *Research in Organizational Change and Development,* vol. 3. Greenwich, Conn.: JAI Press.

Nevins, A. (1954) *Ford: The Times, The Man, The Company.* New York: Scribner Press.

Newman, M. and Rosenberg, D. (1985) 'Systems analysts and the politics of organizational control.' *International Journal of Management Science,* 13, 393–406.

Newman, W. H. (1985) 'Case: Sue's Sweet Shops', in F. E. Kast and J. E. Rosenzweig, *Organization and Management: A Systems and Contingency Approach*. New York: McGraw-Hill.

Nichols, T. (1975) 'The "socialism" of management: some comments on the new "human relations".' *Sociological Review*, 23, 245–265.

Nielsen, R. (1988) 'Cooperative strategy.' *Strategic Management Journal*, 9, 475–492.

Noble, D. (1984) *Forces of Production: A Social History of Industrial Automation*. New York: Alfred Knopf.

Norris, D. R. and Niebuhr, R. H. (1983) 'Professionalism, organizational commitment and job satisfaction in an accounting organization.' *Accounting, Organization and Society*, 9, 49–59.

O'Brien, G. E. (1992) 'Changing meanings of work', in J. F. Hartley and G. M. Stephenson (eds), *Employment Relations: The Psychology of Influence and Control at Work*. Oxford: Blackwell.

Odaka, K. (1975) *Towards Industrial Democracy: Management and Workers in Modern Japan*. Cambridge, MA: Harvard University Press.

Oldham, J. (1979) 'Social control of voluntary work activity.' *Sociology of Work and Occupations*, 6, 379–403.

Olins, W. (1978) *The Corporate Personality: An Inquiry Into the Nature of Corporate Identity*. London: Design Council Publications.

Oliver, N. (1991) 'The dynamics of just-in-time.' *New Technology, Work and Employment*, 6, 19–27.

Oliver, N. and Davies, A. (1990) 'Adopting Japanese-style manufacturing methods: A tale of two (UK) factories.' *Journal of Management Studies*, 27, 555–570.

Oliver, N. and Wilkinson, B. (1992) *The Japanisation of British Industry*. Oxford: Blackwell.

Olson, M. (1983) *The Rise and Decline of Nations*. New Haven: Yale University Press.

Organ, D. W. and Greene, C. N. (1981) 'The effect of formalisation on professional involvement: A compensatory process approach.' *Administrative Science Quarterly*, 26, 237–252.

Orlikowski, W. J. (1992) 'The duality of technology: Rethinking the concept of technology in organizations.' *Organization Science*, 3, 398–407.

Oskamp, S. (1970) 'Effects of programmed strategies on cooperation in the Prisoner's Dilemma and other mixed-motive games.' *Journal of Conflict Resolution*, 15, 225–259.

Otway, H. and Peltu, M. (1983) *New Office Technology: Human and Organizational Aspects*. London: Frances Pinter.

Ouchi, W. G. (1977) 'The relationship between organizational structure and organizational control.' *Administrative Science Quarterly*, 22, 95–113.

Pacey, A. (1983) *The Culture of Technology*. Oxford: Blackwell.

Padsakoff, P. M., Williams, L. J. and Todor, W. D. (1986) 'Effects of organizational formalization on alienation among professionals and non-professionals.' *Academy of Management Journal*, 33, 725–755.

Page, M. R.H. (1981) 'Management of military organization', in W. T. Singleton (ed.), *Management Skills*. Lancaster: MTP Press.

Parker, I. and Shotter, J. (eds) (1990) *Deconstructing Social Psychology*. London: Routledge.

Parmalee, M. A., Near, J. P. and Jensen, T. C. (1982) 'Correlates of whistle-blowers' perceptions of organizational retaliation.' *Administrative Science Quarterly*, 27, 17–34.

Parsons. H. M. (1974) 'What happened at Hawthorne?' *Science*, 183, 922–932.

Pascale, R. (1985) 'The paradox of corporate culture: Reconciling ourselves to socialization'. *California Management Review*, 27, 26–41.

————— (1989) 'Fitting new employees into the company culture', in H. J. Leavitt, L. R. Pondy and D. M. Boje (eds), *Readings in Managerial Psychology*, 4th edn. Chicago: University of Chicago Press.

Paton, R. (1978) 'Some problems of co-operative organisation.' *Co-operatives Research Monographs 3*. Milton Keynes: Open University Press.

————— (1983) 'Powers visible and invisible', in R. Paton, S. Brown, R. Spear, J. Chapman, M. Floyd and J. Mamwee (eds), *Organizations: Cases, Issues, Concepts*. London: Harper & Row.

Pedigo, J. and Singer, B. (1982) 'Group process development: A psychoanalytic view.' *Small Group Behavior, 13*, 496–517.

Pelto, P. J. (1973) *The Snowmobile Revolution: Technology and Social Change in the Artic*. Menlo Park, CA: Cummings.

Pelton, R. (1988) *Mind Foods and Smart Pills*. San Francisco: Newton Books.

Peltz, D. (1967) 'Creative tensions in a research and development climate.' *Science, 57*, 160–171.

Perrolle, J. A. (1986) 'Intellectual assembly lines: The rationalisation of managerial, professional and technical work.' *Computers and Social Sciences, 2*, 111–121.

Peters, C. and Branch, T. (1972) *Blowing the Whistle: Dissent in the Public Interest*. New York: Praeger.

Peters, T. J. and Waterman, R. H. Jr. (1982) *In Search of Excellence: Lessons from America's Best-Run Companies*. New York: Harper & Row.

Pettigrew, A. (1973) *The Politics of Organizational Decision-Making*. London: Tavistock.

————— (1990) 'Is corporate culture manageable?' In: D. C. Wilson and R. Rosenfeld, *Managing Organizations: Text, Readings and Cases*. London: McGraw-Hill.

Pfeffer, J. (1981) *Power in Organizations*. Boston: Pitman Press.

Pfeffer, J. and Salancik, G. (1979) *The External Control of Organizations*. New York: Harper & Row.

Pierce, J. L. (1992) *Volunteers: The Organizational Behaviour of Unpaid Workers*. London: Routledge.

Piercy, N. (ed.) (1984) *The Management Implications of New Information Technology*. London: Croom-Helm.

Pitsiladis, P. E. (1983) 'Case: Ward Metal Products Ltd. (Quebec)', in R. L. Daft, *Organization Theory and Design*. St Paul, MN: West Publishing.

Plant, S. (1992) *The Most Radical Gesture: The Situationist International in a Postmodern Age*. London: Routledge.

Pollert, A. (1981) *Girls, Wives, Factory Lives*. London: Macmillan.

Pondy, L. R. (1967) 'Organizational conflict: Concepts and models.' *Administrative Science Quarterly, 12*, 296–320.

Pondy, L. R., Frost, P., Morgan, G. and Dandridge, T. (eds) (1983) *Organizational Symbolism*. Greenwich, Conn.: JAI Press.

Porter, M. E. (1980) *Competitive Strategy: Techniques for Analyzing Industries and Competitors*. New York: Free Press.

————— (1985) *Competitive Advantage: Creating and Sustaining Superior Performance*. New York: Free Press.

Prasad, S. B. and Shety, Y. K. (1976) *An Introduction to Multinational Management*. Englewood Cliffs: Prentice Hall.

Prince, L. (1988) *Leadership and the Negotiation of Order in Small Groups*, Unpublished PhD thesis. Birmingham: University of Aston.

Pringle, C. D. and Longnecker, J. G. (1982) 'The ethics of MBO.' *Academy of Management Review, 7*, 177–186.

Pryor, J. B. and Ostrom, T. M. (1987) 'Social cognition theory of group process', in B. Mullen and G. R. Goethels (eds), *Theories of Group Behaviour*. New York: Springer-Verlag.

Pugh, D. (1979) 'Effective coordination in organizations.' *Advanced Management Journal*, Winter 1979, 31–45.

Quarstein, V. A., McAfee, R. B. and Glassman, M. (1992) 'The situational occurrences theory of job satisfaction.' *Human Relations*, *45*, 859–873.

Quinn, R. E. (1977) 'Coping with cupid: The formation, impact and management of romantic relationships in organizations.' *Administrative Science Quarterly*, *22*, 30–45.

Quinn, R. E. and Cameron, K. (1983) 'Organizational life cycles and shifting criteria of effectiveness.' *Management Science*, *29*, 33–51.

Rae, J. B. (ed.) (1969) *Henry Ford*. Englewood Cliffs: Prentice Hall.

Raelin, J. (1986) *The Clash of Cultures: Managers and Professionals*. Chicago: University of Chicago Press.

Raff, D. M.G. (1989) 'Looking back at the Five-Dollar Day.' *Harvard Business Review*, *67*, 180–182.

Raia, A. P. (1974) *Managing By Objectives*. Glenview, Illinois: Scott, Foresman.

Randall, D. M. (1987) 'Commitment and the organization: The organization man revisited.' *Academy of Management Review*, *12*, 460–471.

———— (1990) 'The consequences of organizational commitment: Methodological investigation.' *Journal of Organizational Behavior*, *11*, 361–378.

Ray, C. A. (1986) 'Corporate culture: The last frontier of control.' *Journal of Management Studies*, *23*, 287–297.

Reich, W. (ed.) (1990) *Origins of Terrorism: Psychologies, Ideologies, Theologies, States of Mind*. Cambridge: Cambridge University Press.

Reichers, A. E. (1986) 'Conflict and organizational commitment.' *Journal of Applied Psychology*, *71*, 508–514.

Reilly, R. R. and Chao, G. T. (1982) 'Validity and fairness of some alternative employee selection procedures.' *Personnel Psychology*, *35*, 1–62.

Reppy, J. (1979) 'The automobile air bag', in D. Nelkin (ed.), *Controversy: Politics of Technical Decisions*. Beverly Hills: Sage.

Reynolds, J. I. (1980) *Case Method in Management Development*. Geneva: International Labour Office.

Robertson, I. T., Gratton, L. and Sharpley, D. (1987) 'The psychometric properties and design of managerial assessment centres: Dimensions into exercises won't go.' *Journal of Occupational Psychology*, *60*, 187–195.

Roddick, A. (1991) *Body and Soul*. London: Ebury Press.

Rodgers, W. (1969) *THINK: A Biography of the Watsons and IBM*. New York: Stein & Day.

Roethlisberger, F. J. and Dickson, W. J. (1964) *Management and the Worker*. New York: Wiley (first published in 1938).

Rokeach, M. (1960) *The Open and Closed Mind*. New York: Basic Books.

Rolfe, H. (1990) 'In the name of progress? Skill and attitudes towards technological change.' *New Technology, Work and Employment*, *5*, 107–121.

Ronen, S. (1986) *Comparative and International Management*. New York: Wiley.

Rooum, D. (1993) *What is Anarchism?* London: Freedom Press.

Rose. M. J. (1988) *Industrial Behaviour*, 2nd edn Harmondsworth: Penguin.

Rosen, M. and Baroudi, J. (1992) 'Computer-based technology and the emergence of new forms of managerial control', in A. Sturdy, D. Knights and H. Willmott (eds), *Skill and Consent: Contemporary Studies in the Labour Process*. London: Routledge.

Rosen, M. and Widgery, D. (eds) (1991) *The Chatto Book of Dissent*. London: Chatto & Windus.

Rosenberger, N. R. (1992) *Japanese Sense of Self*. Cambridge: Cambridge University Press.

Rosenbrock, H. H. (ed.) (1989) *Designing Human Centred Technology: A Cross Disciplinary Project in Computer-Aided Manufacturing*. London: Springer-Verlag.

———— (1990) *Machines With a Purpose*. Cambridge: Cambridge University Press.

Rotondi, T. (1976) 'Identification, personality needs and managerial position.' *Human Relations, 29*, 507–515.

Runcie, J. F. (1988) '"Deviant behaviour": Achieving autonomy in a machine-paced environment', in M. D. Jones, M. D. Moore and R. C. Snyder (eds), *Inside Organizations: Understanding the Human Dimension*. London: Sage.

Sackett, P. R. and Dreher, G. F. (1982) 'Constructs and assessment centre dimensions: Some troubling empirical findings.' *Journal of Applied Psychology, 67*, 401–410.

Salaman, G. (1981) *Class and the Corporation*. London: Fontana.

Salancik, G. R. (1977) 'Commitment and the control of organizational behaviour and belief', in B. M. Staw and G. R. Salancik (eds), *New Directions in Organizational Behaviour*. Chicago: St Clair Press.

———— (1982) 'Commitment is too easy!', in M. L. Tushman and W. L. Moore (eds), *Readings in the Management of Innovation*. London: Pitman Press.

Salancik, G. R. and Pfeffer, J. (1978) 'A social information processing approach to job attitudes and task design.' *Administrative Science Quarterly, 23*, 224–253.

Sanger, D. E. (1986) 'Engineers tell of punishment for shuttle testimony.' *New York Times*, 11 May p. 7.

Saul, G. K. (1981) 'Business ethics: Where are we going?' *Academy of Management Review, 6*, 269–276.

Sayer, A. (1986) 'New developments in manufacturing: the Just-In-Time system'. *Capital and Class, 30*, 43–72.

Scarbrough, H. and Corbett, J. M. (1992) *Technology and Organization: Power, Meaning and Design*. London: Routledge.

Scarce, R. (1990) *Eco-Warriors: Understanding the Radical Environmental Movement*. Chicago: Noble Press.

Schaef, A. W. and Fassel, D. (1988) *The Addictive Organization*. New York: Harper & Row.

Schein, E. H. (1961) 'Management development as a process of influence.' *Sloan Management Review, 2*, 41–50.

———— (1980) *Organizational Psychology*, 2nd edn. Englewood Cliffs: Prentice Hall.

———— (1985) *Organizational Culture and Leadership*. San Francisco: Jossey-Bass.

———— (1989) 'The role of the founder in creating organizational culture', in H. J. Leavitt, L. R. Pondy, and D. M. Boje (eds), *Readings in Managerial Psychology*, 4th edn. Chicago: Chicago University Press.

Schelling, T. C. (1960) *The Strategy of Conflict*. Cambridge, MA: Harvard University Press.

Schneer, J. A. and Chanin, M. N. (1987) 'Manifest needs as personality predispositions to conflict-handling behaviour.' *Human Relations, 40*, 575–590.

Schneider, S. C. and Dunbar, R. L.M. (1992) 'A psychoanalytic reading of hostile takeover bids.' *Academy of Management Review, 17*, 537–567.

Schnelle, K. E. (1967) *Case Analysis and Business Problem Solving*. New York: McGraw-Hill.

Schofield, J. (1990) 'Father, son and holy terrors'. *Manchester Guardian*, 6 September, p. 24.

Schuler, R. S. (ed.) (1991) *Case Problems in Management and Organizational Behaviour*. St Paul, MN: West Publishing.

Schuster, F. and Kendall, A. F. (1974) 'Management by objectives – where we stand: A survey of the Fortune 500.' *Human Resource Management*, Spring 1974, 8–11.

Scott, J. (1985) *Weapons of the Weak: Everyday Forms of Resistance.* New Haven: Yale University Press.

Scott, R. (1972) 'Job expectancy – an important factor in labor turnover.' *Personnel Journal*, 55, 360–363.

Sehlinger, B. (1987) *The Unofficial Guide to Disneyland.* New York: Prentice Hall.

Sethi, S. P., Namiki, N. and Swanson, C. L. (1984) *The False Promise of the Japanese Miracle: Illusions and Realities of the Japanese Management System.* Boston: Pitman Press.

Shabecoff, P. (1981) 'Industry and women clash over hazards in the workplace.' *New York Times*, 3 January p. 12.

Shaiken, H. (1985) *Work Transformed: Automation and Labor in the Computer Age.* New York: Holt, Rinehart & Winston.

Shapiro, B. S. (1977) 'Can marketing and manufacturing coexist?' *Harvard Business Review*, 55, 104–114.

Sheridan, J. E. (1992) 'Organizational culture and employee retention.' *Academy of Management Journal*, 35, 1036–1056.

Shotton, M. (1989) *Computer Addiction: A Study of Computer Dependency.* London: Taylor & Francis.

Shrivastava, P., Mitroff, I. I., Miller, D. and Miglani, A. (1988) 'Understanding industrial crises.' *Journal of Management Studies*, 25, 283–304.

Silver, J. (1987) 'The ideology of excellence: Management and neo-conservatism.' *Studies in Political Economy*, 24, 105–129.

Silverman, D. (1970) *The Theory of Organisations.* London: Heinemann.

Silverman, M., Lee, P. R. and Lydecker, M. (1982) *Prescriptions for Death: The Drugging of the Third World.* Berkeley: University of California Press.

Simon, H. A. (1960) *The New Science of Management Decision.* New York: Harper & Row.

Smircich, L. and Morgan, G. (1982) 'Leadership: The management of meaning.' *Journal of Applied Behavioural Science*, 18, 257–273.

Smith, K. K. and Berg, D. N. (1987) *Paradoxes of Group Life: Understanding Conflict, Paralysis, and Movement in Group Dynamics.* San Francisco: Jossey-Bass.

Smith, P. B. and Peterson, M. F. (1988) *Leadership, Organizations and Culture.* London: Sage.

Smith, M. and Robertson, I. T. (1986) *The Theory and Practice of Systematic Staff Selection.* London: Macmillan.

Smyth, J. (1961) *Sandhurst.* London: Weidenfeld.

——— (1971) *Percival and the Tragedy of Singapore.* London: MacDonald.

Sobel, R. (1981) *IBM: Colossus in Transition.* New York: Time Books.

Staub, E. (1992) *The Roots of Evil: The Origins of Genocide and Other Group Violence.* Cambridge: Cambridge University Press.

Staw, B. M. (1976a) *Intrinsic and Extrinsic Motivation.* Morristown, NJ: General Learning Press.

——— (1976b) 'Knee deep in the big muddy: A study of escalating commitment to a chosen course of action.' *Organizational Behaviour and Human Performance*, 16, 27–44.

——— (1982) 'Counterforces to change', in P. S. Goodman and Associates (eds), *Change in Organizations: New Perspectives on Theory, Research and Practice.* San Francisco: Jossey-Bass.

Staw, B. M. and Fox, F. V. (1977) 'Escalation: The determinants of commitment to a chosen course of action.' *Human Relations*, 30, 431–450.

Sterling, B. (ed.) (1988a) *Mirrorshades: The Cyberpunk Anthology.* London: Paladin.

——— (1988b) *Islands in the Net.* New York: Ace Books.

——— (1993) *The Hacker Crackdown.* New York: Viking Press.

Stodgill, R. M. (1974) *Handbook of Leadership: A Survey of Theory and Research.* New York: Free Press.

Stoll, C. (1989) *The Cuckoo's Egg.* New York: Doubleday.

Stone, C. (1975) *Where the Law Ends: The Social Control of Corporate Behaviour.* New York: Harper & Row.

Stopford, J. and Wells, L. T. (1972) *Managing the Multinational Enterprise.* New York: Basic Books.

Storr, A. (1992) *Human Destructiveness: The Roots of Genocide and Human Cruelty.* London: Routledge.

Strong, P. and Robinson, J. (1990) *The NHS Under New Management.* Milton Keynes: Open University Press.

Stumpf, S. A. and Hartmann, K. (1984) 'Individual exploration to organizational commitment or withdrawal.' *Academy of Management Journal, 27,* 308–329.

Sward, K. (1948) *The Legend of Henry Ford.* New York: Russell & Russell.

Sykes, A. and Bates, J. (1962) 'A study of conflict between formal company policy and the interests of informal groups.' *Sociological Review, 10,* 175–193.

Tajfel, H. and Turner, J. C. (1985) 'The social identity theory of intergroup behavior', in S. Worchel and W. G. Austin (eds), *Psychology of Intergroup Relations.* Chicago: Nelson-Hall.

Tayeb, M. H. (1989) *Organizations and National Culture: A Comparative Analysis.* London: Sage.

Taylor, L. and Walton, P. (1971) 'Industrial sabotage: Motives and meanings', in S. Cohen (ed.), *Images of Deviance.* Harmondsworth: Penguin.

Thompson, J. D. (1972) *Organizations In Action.* New York: McGraw-Hill.

Thompson, P. and Bannon, E. (1985) *Working the System.* London: Pluto Press.

Thompson, P. and McHugh, D. (1990) *Work Organisations: A Critical Introduction.* London: Macmillan.

Tichy, N. (1983) *Managing Strategic Change.* Chichester: Wiley.

Tichy, N. and Devanna, M. (1987) *The Transformational Leader.* New York: Wiley.

Trice, H. M. and Beyer, J. M. (1985) 'Using six organizational rites to change culture', in R. H. Kilmann, S. Saxton and R. Sherpa (eds), *Gaining Control of the Corporate Culture.* San Francisco: Jossey-Bass.

Turkle, S. (1984) *The Second Self: Computers and the Human Spirit.* New York: Simon & Schuster.

Ulman, R. and Abse, D. (1983) 'The group psychology of mass madness: Jonestown.' *Political Psychology, 4,* 637–661.

Umstot, D. (1977) 'MBO + job enrichment: How to have your cake and eat it too.' *Management Review, 17,* February, 21–26.

Utley, M. E., Richardson, D. R. and Pilkington, C. J. (1989) 'Personality and interpersonal conflict.' *Personality and Individual Differences, 10,* 287–293.

Van Knippenberg, A. and Ellemers, N. (1990) 'Social identity and intergroup differentiation processes', in W. Stroebe and M. Hewstone (eds), *European Review of Social Psychology,* vol. 1. Chichester: Wiley.

Van Maanen, J. (1976) 'Breaking-in: socialisation to work', in R. Dubin (ed.), *Handbook of Work, Organization and Society.* Chicago: Rand McNally.

——— (1991) 'The smile factory: Work at Disneyland', in P. J. Frost, L. F. Moore, M. R. Louis, C. C. Lundberg and J. Martin (eds), *Reframing Organizational Culture.* London: Sage.

Van Maanen, J. and Kunda, G. (1989) 'Real feelings: Emotional expressions and organization culture', in B. Staw and L. L. Cummings (eds), *Research in Organizational Behavior,* vol. 11. Greenwich, Conn.: JAI Press.

Van Maanen, J. and Schein, E. H. (1979) 'Toward a theory of organizational socialisation', in B. Staw and L. L. Cummings (eds), *Research in Organizational Behavior*, vol. 1. Greenwich, Conn.: JAI Press.

Vandiver, K. (1972) 'Why should my conscience bother me?' In: R. L. Heilbroner and associates, *In The Name of Profit*. New York: Doubleday.

———— (1978) 'The aircraft brake scandal', in A. Elbing (ed.), *Behavioural Decisions in Organizations*, 2nd edn. Glenview, Illinois: Scott, Foresman & Company.

Vaneigem, R. (1983) *The Revolution of Everyday Life*. London: Left Bank Books and Rebel Press.

Vaughan, D. (1983) *Controlling Unlawful Organizational Behaviour: Social Structure and Corporate Misconduct*. Chicago: University of Chicago Press.

Vernon, H. M. (1924) *On the Extent and Effects of Variety in Repetitive Work*. London: HMSO.

Veroff, J. (1982) 'Assertive motivations: Achievement versus power', in A. J. Stewart (ed.), *Motivation and Society*. San Francisco: Jossey-Bass.

Vieira, J. (1992) 'How to bridge the gap between the long-term thinking marketing department and the short-term thinking sales force.' *Business Marketing*, January, 15–21.

Vroom, V. H. and Jago, A. G. (1988) *The New Leadership: Managing Participation in Organizations*. Pittsburgh: Pittsburgh Press.

Wainwright, J. and Francis, A. (1984) *Office Automation, Organization and the Nature of Work*. Aldershot: Gower.

Walby, S. (1986) *Patriarchy at Work*. Cambridge: Polity Press.

Wall, T. D., Corbett, J. M., Martin, R., Clegg, C. W. and Jackson, P. R. (1990) 'Advanced manufacturing technology, work design and performance: A change study.' *Journal of Applied Psychology, 75*, 691–697.

Walter, N. (1984) *About Anarchism*. London: Freedom Press.

Walton, R. E. and Dutton, J. M. (1969) 'The management of interdepartmental conflict: A model and review.' *Administrative Science Quarterly, 14*, 73–84.

Wanous, J. P. (1980) *Organizational Entry: Recruitment, Selection and Socialization of Newcomers*. Reading, MA: Addison-Wesley.

Ward, C. (1988) *Anarchy in Action*. London: Freedom Press.

Warr, P. B., Cook, J. D. and Wall, T. D. (1979) 'Scales for the measurement of some work attitudes and aspects of well-being.' *Journal of Occupational Psychology, 52*, 129–148.

Watson, P. (1980) *War on the Mind: Military Uses and Abuses of Psychology*. Harmondsworth: Penguin.

Watson, T. J. and Petre, P. (1990) *Father, Son and Co: My Life at IBM*. New York: Bantam Books.

Webb, J. and Cleary, D. (1994) *New Technology and the Management of Expertise*. London: Routledge.

Webster, F. and Robins, F. (1988) *Information Technology: A Luddite Analysis*. New York: Ablex Publishing.

Weir, D. (1987) *The Bhopal Syndrome*. San Francisco: Sierra Club Books.

Weir, D. and Schapiro, M. (1981) *Circles of Poison: Pesticides and People in a Hungry World*. San Francisco: Institute for Food Development and Policy.

Wells, D. (1987) *Empty Promises: Quality of Working Life Programs and the Labor Movement*. New York: Monthly Review Press.

West, M. A. and Farr, J. L. (eds) (1990) *Innovation and Creativity at Work: Psychological and Organizational Strategies*. Chichester: Wiley.

Wetherbe, J. C., Dock, V. T., and Mandell, S. L. (eds) (1988) *Readings in Information Systems: A Managerial Perspective*. St Paul, MN: West Publishing.

Whorton, M. D. (1985) 'Considerations about reproductive hazards', in J. S. Lee and W. N. Rom (eds), *Legal and Ethical Dilemmas in Occupational Health*. Ann Arbor: Butterworth.

Whyte, G. (1986) 'Escalating commitment to a course of action: A reinterpretation.' *Academy of Management Review, 11,* 311–321.

———— (1989) 'Groupthink reconsidered.' *Academy of Management Review, 14,* 40–56.

Whyte, W. (1956) *The Organization Man*. New York: Doubleday.

Wiener, Y. and Vardi, Y. (1980) 'Relationships between job, organization and career commitments and work outcomes – an integrative approach.' *Organizational Behavior and Human Performance, 26,* 81–96.

Wilkinson, B. (1983) *The Shopfloor Politics of New Technology*. Harmondsworth: Penguin.

Wilkinson, B. and Oliver, N. (1990) 'Obstacles to Japanization: The case of Ford UK.' *Employee Relations, 12,* 17–21.

Willcocks, L. and Mason, D. (1987) *Computerising Work: People, Systems Design and Workplace Relations*. London: Paradigm Books.

Williams, L. (1992) 'Torture and the torturer.' *The Psychologist, 5,* 305–308.

Williamson, O. E. (1976) *Markets and Hierarchies: Analysis and Antitrust Implications*. New York: Free Press.

Willmott, H. (1993) 'Strength is ignorance; slavery is freedom: Managing culture in modern organizations.' *Journal of Management Studies, 30,* 463–477.

Wilson, D. C. (1992a) *A Strategy of Change: Concepts and Controversies in the Management of Change*. London: Routledge.

———— (1992b) 'The strategic challenges of cooperation and competition in British voluntary organizations: Toward the next century.' *Non-Profit Management and Leadership, 2,* 239–254.

Wolpe, H. (1968) 'A critical analysis of some aspects of charisma.' *Sociological Review, 16,* 305–318.

Woodcock, G. (1977) *The Anarchist Reader*. London: Fontana Collins.

Wright, J. P. (1979) *On a Clear Day You Can See General Motors: John Delorean's Look Inside the Automobile Giant*. New York: Avon Books.

Wyatt, S. and Frazer, J. A. (1928) *The Comparative Effects of Variety and Uniformity in Work*. London: HMSO.

Yetton, P. W. (1984) 'Leadership and supervision', in M. Gruneberg and T. D. Wall (eds), *Social Psychology and Organizational Behaviour*. Chichester: Wiley.

Zaleznik, A. (1977) 'Managers and leaders: Are they different?' *Harvard Business Review, 55,* 67–78.

Zaleznik, A. and Kets de Vries, M. F. R. (1975) *Power and the Corporate Mind*. Boston: Houghton Mifflin.

Zerzan, J. and Carnes, A. (eds) (1988) *Questioning Technology: A Critical Anthology*. London: Freedom Press.

Zimbardo, P. G. and Leippe, M. R. (1991) *The Psychology of Attitude Change and Social Influence*. New York: McGraw-Hill.

Zuboff, S. (1988) *In the Age of the Smart Machine*. London: Heinemann.

Index